The Co

# Report on the Effects of Artificial Respiration, Intravenous

# Injection of Ammonia

The Co

**Report on the Effects of Artificial Respiration, Intravenous Injection of Ammonia**

ISBN/EAN: 9783742854490

Manufactured in Europe, USA, Canada, Australia, Japa

Cover: Foto ©Thomas Meinert / pixelio.de

Manufactured and distributed by brebook publishing software
(www.brebook.com)

The Co

# Report on the Effects of Artificial Respiration, Intravenous

# Injection of Ammonia

# REPORT

ON THE

## ECTS OF ARTIFICIAL RESPIRATION, INTRAVENOUS INJECTION OF AMMONIA,

AND ADMINISTRATION OF VARIOUS DRUGS, &c.

IN

## INDIAN AND AUSTRALIAN SNAKE-POISONING;

AND

## the Physiological, Chemical, and Microscopical Nature of Snake-Poisons.

BY

## THE COMMISSION APPOINTED TO INVESTIGATE THE SUBJECT.

Calcutta:
PRINTED AT THE BENGAL SECRETARIAT PRESS.

1874.

# THE INFLUENCE OF ARTIFICIAL RESPIRATION, INTRAVENOUS INJECTION OF AMMONIA, ETC.,

IN

## Indian and Australian Snake-Poisoning.

FROM experiments made in London with the dried poison of the *Naja Tripudians*, Drs. Fayrer and Lauder Brunton were led to infer that artificial respiration, applied to animals or human beings, poisoned by any of the *Thanatophidia of India*, might prove successful in prolonging or saving life. Dr. Fayrer states, in a letter[*] dated 29th November, 1872, to Her Majesty's Secretary of State for India, that "since my return to London, I have, in conjunction with Dr. Lauder Brunton, been making further investigations into the subject of snake-poisoning, especially with a view of ascertaining if there be any means of saving life; and, though I cannot say that that desirable object of research has been attained, I am satisfied that the results of certain experiments are interesting and important, as they point in that direction. I have recorded an opinion, derived from a long and elaborate series of experiments, that none of the so-called antidotes possess the virtues or powers attributed to them; but in the experiments recently made, it is ascertained, beyond a doubt, that the life of an animal poisoned by the cobra-virus, may be prolonged for many hours by artificial respiration, and it is, therefore, possible that, if respiration be artificially continued for a sufficient length of time, life might be altogether preserved. In experiments performed upon the fowl and rabbit, after the most complete development of the physiological action of the poison, amounting to total paralysis and convulsions—conditions which immediately precede death—the convulsions

* *Vide* Appendix iii.

ceased, and in one case the heart was kept beating vigorously for about nine hours (and probably then failed from imperfect respiration carried on in the cold)—a result never before attained by any means that I am aware of."

2. The results obtained by artificial respiration, in animals subjected to the action of the curara or wourali poison, were calculated to encourage Dr. Fayrer to hope that similar treatment might, possibly, succeed in restoring to health animals almost dead from snake-poisoning. He says—" There is apparently a strong analogy between the action of the cobra-virus and that of the curara or wouralipoison of South America. It has been ascertained that an animal poisoned by this agent may, after apparent death for many hours, be restored, if artificial respiration be carefully and continuously applied for a sufficient length of time, the temperature of the animal being at the same time sustained at blood-heat by artificial warmth. Curara, it is believed, kills by paralysing the peripheral distribution of the motor nerves, thus inducing asphyxia by involving the muscles of respiration in general paralysis. If, however, the heart's action can be sustained by artificial respiration, during a sufficient length of time to allow of elimination of the poison through the excretory organs, (for whilst the heart acts they continue to perform their functions) the paralysed muscles regain their power, and life is slowly but certainly restored. I am not prepared to assert that the cobra-poison kills in exactly the same way as curara; I am inclined to the belief that it does not; but still analogy and the results of experiments support, or, perhaps, rather suggest the idea that, if artificial respiration be sustained in a case of cobra-poisoning, and life be thus artificially supported for a sufficient length of time, it might be for days, elimination of the poison may occur, and recovery may result. *It is, however,* (the italics are ours) *I fear, only too probable that, during its sojourn in the system, the poison may have, in the case of the cobra virus, done irreparable mischief to the nerve centres, or to the peripheral distribution of the nerves, even when life has been artificially supported; but there is no proof, as yet, that such is the case, and, therefore, I am of opinion that further most careful, often-repeated, and sustained experiments, should be made to test this very important subject.*"

3. As, however, it was impossible to conduct a series of detailed experiments to test the value of artificial respiration in England, for want of an adequate supply of snake-poison,

Dr. Fayrer considered it desirable to have the matter investigated by a Commission in Calcutta. The result was our appointment, and we have now the pleasure to submit the results of our inquiries for transmission to Her Majesty's Secretary of State for India.

4. At the outset, it was arranged that the method suggested by Dr. Fayrer should be tried, in graduated quantities of the cobra-poison. Above all, it seemed that the first point to be determined was the effects of artificial respiration on animals subjected to the whole of the poison emitted during the bite of a full-grown and vigorous cobra. When convulsions, general paralysis, and cessation of respiration, were fully developed, a canula was quickly inserted into the trachea. To the external end of the canula about a foot of India-rubber tubing was attached; and into the free extremity of this the nozzle of the bellows was fitted. The canula, tubing, and bellows,—specially constructed for the purpose of avoiding clogging with mucus,—were all connected and ready for use before the performance of the operation of tracheotomy was ever attempted. This was a necessary precaution, inasmuch as valuable time would have been lost had the connexions between the different parts of the apparatus been always made after the trachea had been opened. Care was also taken to see that the channels, through which the respiration was to be carried on artificially, were clean and patent. To the canula was also attached a supplementary side tube, provided with a stop-cock, to admit of the escape of respired air, whenever we found that it was not being rapidly enough discharged by the side of the tube, through the mouth. The elastic recoil of the lungs and atmospheric pressure were generally sufficient to accomplish the act of expiration. Whenever these were deemed inadequate to empty the lungs, the opening of this stop-cock, and compression of the chest with the hands, were employed to secure efficient expiration, whilst the pumping in of air was in no way interrupted for a single instant. The animal experimented upon was placed on its side on a strong table about two feet high, and the apparatus rested near the end of the same, to facilitate, in carrying out the system as much as possible, the imitation of the rythmic action of the respiratory process. We had command of any amount of labor to work the bellows. Dr. J. Campbell Brown, c.n., the Surgeon-General of the Medical Department, readily responded to our application for skilled aid, and placed at our disposal,

for a time, four native doctors. Mr. Vincent Richards, without whose assistance the Commission could not have undertaken these investigations, personally conducted every experiment from the beginning to its termination. In order to preserve uniformity, and avoid sources of fallacy, dogs were selected for experiment. Whenever the temperature of the animal seemed to be diminishing, artificial warmth was employed.

5. Mr. Richards has found, after repeated trials, that the quantity of poison expelled at each bite of the cobra in full vigour, amounts to upwards of thirteen grains of the liquid, and five grains of the dried virus. In the first twelve experiments, a dog was in each instance bitten in the fold of the groin, so that the poison was only injected into the cellular tissue. As care was taken to have each animal poisoned by a fresh snake, or, at any rate, by one in which ample time had always been allowed for the secretion of a full supply of the virus, it may be assumed that upwards of thirteen grains of the liquid poison were inserted in the meshes of the areolar tissue, in each dog experimented upon.

The cardinal results of these twelve experiments (Appendix, pp. i—viii), are brought into relief in the subjoined tabular statement:—

| Number. | | | From the bite to the commencement of artificial respiration. | | From the commencement of artificial respiration to the period of death. | | From the bite to the occurrence of death. | |
|---|---|---|---|---|---|---|---|---|
| | | | Hrs. | Ms. | Hrs. | Ms. | Hrs. | Ms. |
| 1 | ... | ... | 0 | 45 | 16 | 50 | 17 | 35 |
| 2 | ... | ... | 0 | 29 | 3 | 10 | 3 | 39 |
| 3 | ... | ... | 0 | 45 | 7 | 27 | 8 | 12 |
| 4 | ... | ... | 0 | 44 | 17 | 6 | 17 | 50 |
| 5 | ... | ... | 1 | 10 | 7 | 20 | 8 | 30 |
| 6 | ... | ... | 0 | 26 | 5 | 37 | 6 | 3 |
| 7 | ... | ... | 0 | 25 | 12 | 40 | 13 | 5 |
| 8 | ... | ... | 1 | 3 | 7 | 15 | 8 | 20 |
| 9 | ... | ... | 0 | 35 | 4 | 15 | 4 | 50 |
| 10 | ... | ... | 0 | 31 | 17 | 2 | 17 | 33 |
| 11 | ... | ... | 0 | 50 | 14 | 50 | 15 | 40 |
| 12 | ... | ... | 0 | 40 | 14 | 50 | 15 | 30 |
| | Total | ... | 8 | 25 | 128 | 22 | 136 | 47 |
| Average | ... | | 0 | 42 | 10 | 41 | 11 | 23 |
| Maximum | ... | | 1 | 10 | 17 | 6 | 17 | 50 |
| Minimum | ... | | 0 | 25 | 3 | 10 | 3 | 39 |

Death from snake-poisoning is preceded by general muscular paralysis, induced by interference with the actions of the spinal cord, medulla oblongata, and, it may be, the central ganglia of the encephalon; convulsions; unconsciousness, and absolute cessation of respiration. The rythmic action of the heart continues for about three or four minutes longer. In these experiments, the time selected for the commencement of artificial respiration in the manner already indicated, was the exact period when the breathing had ceased, and about three or four minutes prior to the stoppage of the beating of the heart.

6. The second column of the statement gives a tolerably accurate idea of the rapid tendency to death in animals subjected to the influence of an effective bite from a fresh and fully developed cobra. The average lapse of time between the infliction of the bite and the cessation of the respiratory process was only *forty-two minutes*, the maximum and minimum having been *one hour and ten minutes*, and *twenty-five minutes*, respectively. A cobra does, however, sometimes kill in a much shorter time.

7. The powerful influence of artificial respiration, in supporting and prolonging life, is well illustrated in the figures contained in the third column. Life was thus prolonged, on an average, *ten hours and forty-one minutes*, the maximum having reached *seventeen hours and six minutes*, and the minimum *three hours and ten minutes*.

8. Although the animals were almost at the point of death when artificial respiration was begun, as was demonstrated by universal convulsions, complete unconsciousness, and arrest of the respiration, and would have been dead in three or four minutes more, by the addition to these mortal conditions of the cessation of the heart's action; yet somatic death was marvellously postponed by the mechanical and artificial supply of atmospheric air regularly to the air cells of the lungs.

9. There is evidence to prove that the great shock of the poison is first felt in the nerve centres of the cord, gradually involving those of the medulla and the ganglia of the mesocephale; and lastly, implicating the functional integrity of the hemispheres of the brain. Firstly, in the rapid paralysis of the limb into which the poison is injected; secondly, the general paralysis of the voluntary and respiratory muscles; thirdly, arrest of respiration; fourthly,

the more or less general convulsions which immediately precede a fatal result; fifthly, the almost contemporaneous or consecutive supervention of complete insensibility.

From the delay which afterwards takes place in the cessation of the action of the heart, it may be reasonably concluded that the organic system of nerves is the last to suffer. It is also clear, from the augmented frequency of the pulsations of the heart, after the respiration has ceased, that the inhibitory or regulating power of the pneumogastric nerves over the central organ of circulation, has been partially annulled or materially disturbed. Still, notwithstanding the removal of this influence, the comparative freedom of the sympathetic system of nerves from implication—until respiration has ceased, either from paralysis of the central ganglia which preside over and regulate this function, or paralysis of the peripheral distribution of the excitor or motor nerves, or all together—renders it possible to prolong life for a considerable period, even when animals have been subjected to an overwhelming quantity of the poison. Hence, owing to the great freedom of the sympathetic ganglia and nerves which preside over the organs of circulation, secretion, excretion, from the primary action of the poison, their functions can be maintained for varying periods, even after the apparent death of the cerebro-spinal nervous system.

10. It is manifest from these experiments that, if the poison exerted the same deleterious influence on the organic, as it does on the cerebro-spinal system of nerves, it would be impossible to restore the function of the lungs and to continue that of the circulation, secretion, excretion, and, it may be for anything we know to the contrary, nutrition also, to a limited extent. That secretion and excretion are continued during the process of maintaining the circulation by means of artificial respiration was constantly noticed in the shedding of tears, in the expulsion of saliva, and of the urine, sometimes with, sometimes without, the application of galvanism. Further, the movements of the irides in response to galvanism probably support the view herein enunciated.

11. The frequent vomiting and defæcation as early symptoms of poisoning, the excessive flow of urine and saliva later on, all indicate an attempt on the part of nature to eliminate the poison from the body. Whether nature ever succeeds, except to a very partial extent in excreting much of the virus, it is difficult to say. All that can be declared at

present is that although the functions of the lungs, salivary glands, the excretory glands of the intestines, and of the kidneys, were fairly kept going, in one instance, for upwards of seventeen hours and six minutes, there was no positive evidence to show that the poison had ever lost its lethal hold on the cerebro-spinal ganglia.

12. It is true that the convulsions ceased (experiment No. 4) immediately on the commencement of artificial respiration ; but that, we take it, was due rather to the arterialization of the blood and the re-institution of nutrition in the nerve centres, than to any modification of the real influence of the poison itself. It is evident that this is the true explanation of the arrest of the convulsions, inasmuch as sufficient time had not elapsed for elimination of any quantity of the poison. Moreover, we found that the withdrawal of the artificial respiration was soon followed by recurrence of general convulsions ; whilst the restoration of the process was as quickly succeeded by their disappearance. The animal, perfectly insensible at 7.58 A.M., "appeared to be sensible" at 7.59 A.M., or a minute afterwards, on the re-establishment of artificial respiration ; but, notwithstanding the assiduous continuation of the process, no similar indication of restoration to consciousness was observed. The convulsive movements at 8.24 A.M. and 8.47 A.M. in the hind quarters were doubtless also due to imperfect local arterialization of the blood supplied to their nerve centres.

13. As time passed on, galvanism failed to excite even the irides and muscular structure of the bladder to contract, and eventually, in spite of the supply of abundance of air to the lungs, the organic system of nerves perished and the circulation could no longer be sustained.

14. It will be observed, by a glance at the second column of the above statement, that in each experiment the poison must have been extravasated into the cellular tissue only. The variation in the rate at which poisoning up to the destruction of the natural functions of the cerebro-spinal system and respiration supervened, was probably due to the difference—(1) in the quantity of the poison injected ; (2) in the proximity of the same to the venous radicles and lymphatics ; (3) in the rate at which venous and lymphatic absorption were carried on ; and (4) in the size, age, and strength of the constitution of the animals employed for experiment.

15. The *second series* consists of *six* detailed experiments (Appendix, page viii—xiii), showing the effects of artificial respiration on dogs poisoned with about a half of the ordinary quantity of the virus shed at one bite of a full-grown and fresh cobra. In these experiments the poison was inserted into the cellular tissue of the fold of the groin by means of the hypodermic syringe. The main features of these experiments are tabulated below :—

| Number. | From the injection to the commencement of artificial respiration. | | From the commencement of artificial respiration to death. | | From the injection to death. | |
|---|---|---|---|---|---|---|
| | Hrs. | Ms. | Hrs. | Ms. | Hrs. | Ms. |
| 13 | 1 | 20 | 26 | 15 | 27 | 15 |
| 14 | 0 | 49 | 14 | 47 | 15 | 36 |
| 15 | 0 | 50 | 20 | 25 | 21 | 15 |
| 16 | 0 | 50 | 18 | 0 | 18 | 50 |
| 17 | 1 | 15 | 12 | 50 | 14 | 5 |
| 18 | 2 | 9 | 14 | 5 | 16 | 5 |
| Total | 7 | 4 | 106 | 22 | 113 | 26 |
| Average | 1 | 10 | 17 | 44 | 18 | 54 |
| Maximum | 2 | 0 | 26 | 15 | 27 | 35 |
| Minimum | 0 | 49 | 12 | 50 | 14 | 5 |

Although the action of the poison on the nerve centres with the diminished quantity of the fresh poison used in these experiments was slower than in the first series in which the cobra was allowed to inject the full quantity contained in the recesses of its poison glands, the physiological effects were identically the same in both; and though the prolongation of life by artifical respiration was, on the whole, increased, the eventual termination in death took place in every case with unerring and appalling certainty. Thus the average period from the hypodermic injection to the occurrence of general convulsions, and arrest of the normal breathing, when artificial respiration was begun, was *one hour and ten minutes,* the maximum and minimum having been *two hours* and *forty-nine* minutes respectively. Again, the average period over which life was extended from the commencement of artifical respiration to the supervention of a fatal result was *seventeen hours and forty-four minutes,* whilst the maximum and minimum reached *twenty-six hours and fifteen minutes* and *twelve hours and fifty minutes.*

16. In the *third series* (Appendix, pp. xiii—xvii) the dogs were experimented upon with only one grain of the cobra-virus: the results were slowly manifested; death rapidly followed when once a sufficient quantity had been absorbed, in spite of the uninterrupted application of artificial respiration. These facts are demonstrated succinctly in the subjoined statement :—

| No. | | From the injection to the commencement of artificial respiration. | | From the commencement of artificial respiration to death. | | From the injection to death. | |
|---|---|---|---|---|---|---|---|
| | | Hrs. | Ms. | Hrs. | Ms. | Hrs. | Ms. |
| 19 | ... | 0 | 35 | 9 | 45 | 10 | 20 |
| 20 | ... | 1 | 45 | 17 | 10 | 18 | 55 |
| 21 | ... | 1 | 45 | 9 | 50 | 11 | 35 |
| 22 | ... | 2 | 57 | 9 | 20 | 12 | 17 |
| 23 | ... | 1 | 10 | 9 | 25 | 10 | 35 |
| 24 | ... | 1 | 0 | 14 | 30 | 15 | 30 |
| Total | ... | 9 | 12 | 70 | 0 | 79 | 12 |
| Average | ... | 1 | 32 | 11 | 40 · | 13 | 12 |
| Maximum | ... | 2 | 57 | 17 | 10 | 18 | 55 |
| Minimum | ... | 0 | 35 | 9 | 20 | 10 | 20 |

The average period from the injection to the commencement of artificial respiration was *one hour and thirty-two minutes*, the maximum and minimum having been *two hours and fifty-seven minutes* and *thirty-five minutes* respectively. The average time from the commencement of artificial respiration till death supervened was *eleven hours and forty minutes*, the maximum having been *seventeen hours and ten minutes* and the minimum *nine hours and twenty minutes*. It is apparent, from a careful review of these experiments, that, owing to the diminution of the dose, the period required for the development of the symptoms heralding a fatal result was prolonged; but when the poison once took effect, the end was much expedited by the smallness of the dogs at that time available, and their consequent comparative feebleness of constitutional power.

2

17. In the *fourth series* (Appendix, pp. xvii—xix) only *half a grain* of the cobra-poison was hypodermically injected. The chief results are portrayed in the following statement:—

| No. | | | From the injection to the commencement of artificial respiration. | | From the commencement of artificial respiration to death. | | From the injection to death. | |
|-----|---|---|---|---|---|---|---|---|
| | | | Hrs. | Ms. | Hrs. | Ms. | Hrs. | Ms. |
| 25 | ... | ... | 2 | 10 | 30 | 25 | 32 | 35 |
| 26 | ... | ... | 1 | 44 | 22 | 10 | 23 | 54 |
| 27 | ... | ... | 4 | 20 | 26 | 20 | 30 | 40 |
| Total | | ... | 8 | 14 | 78 | 55 | 87 | 9 |
| Average | .. | ... | 2 | 45 | 26 | 18 | 29 | 3 |
| Maximum | ... | ... | 4 | 20 | 30 | 25 | 32 | 35 |
| Minimum | ... | ... | 1 | 44 | 22 | 10 | 23 | 54 |

The postponement of the urgent symptoms, and the increased prolongation of life by means of artificial respiration, are well shown in these columns, doubtless due to the moderate quantity of the poison introduced into the cellular tissue. The average time occupied from the injection to the commencement of artificial respiration was *two hours and forty-five minutes ;* the maximum was *four hours and twenty minutes,* and the minimum *one hour and forty-four minutes*. From the time when artificial respiration was begun the average extension of life was *twenty-six hours and eighteen minutes*. The maximum period was *thirty hours and twenty-five minutes,* whilst the minimum was *twenty-two hours and ten minutes*.

18. In experiments 25 and 26 there was the usual cessation of the convulsions; but in 27, in which the artificial respiration was commenced at noon, four hours and twenty minutes after the injection, the dog was at that time convulsed, and perfectly insensible. The effects of sustaining the breathing artificially were very remarkable. The animal immediately became conscious, took notice when called, began to wag its tail, and endeavoured to get up from the table. At 12.30 P.M. it was in the same state and perfectly sensible. A certain amount of convulsive tremor was manifested, particularly in the hind-quarters. Consciousness remained under artificial respiration till about 2.50 P.M., after which it had entirely disappeared. The animal

succumbed even to this small quantity of the poison, notwithstanding the persevering application of artificial respiration, in *twenty-six hours and twenty minutes* from the time of its commencement, or *thirty hours and forty minutes* from the hypodermic injection of only *half a grain* of the virus.

19. The result of the *fifth series* (Appendix, pp. xx—xxi) in which only a *quarter of a grain* of cobra-poison was hypodermically injected, is tabulated below:—

No. 28.

|  | Hrs. | Ms. |
|---|---|---|
| From the injection to the commencement of artificial respiration ... ... | 4 | 2 |
| From the commencement of artificial respiration to death ... ... ... | 37 | 50 |
| From the injection to death ... ... | 41 | 52 |

Thus, it took four hours and two minutes until artificial respiration was resorted to. In four minutes more, in the absence of this system, this animal's heart would have ceased to beat and somatic death been complete. But by its steady application, life was extended to *forty-one hours and fifty-two minutes*. Breathing was not absolutely stopped when the method was adopted, though nearly so, but the animal was decidedly unconscious. Yet, even with the very small injection of a quarter of a grain, death resulted, without the slightest restoration of consciousness.

20. The power of artificial respiration in supporting the respiratory process; in maintaining the action of the heart, and the circulation of the blood to all parts of the body; in effecting the arterialization of the blood; in sustaining the life of the secreting and excreting organs, and that of the organic system of nerves; and in probably keeping up an imperfect form of nutrition of the tissues to which arterialized blood is supplied in abundance, for periods of time varying, to a great extent, according to the quantity of poison introduced into the system through the absorbent channels of the body, is, therefore, placed beyond all question.

But its influence in saving life, even where very small quantities of the poison have found entrance into the juices, is extremely problematical. It occurred to us that there might be hope in preserving life if the method were employed in conjunction with certain drugs. And though that hope was, from our previous experience of the mortal nature of the poison over animal life, very faint, we resolved to try artificial respiration with the exhibition of medicines, and in a few instances with transfusion of blood from a healthy dog into dogs poisoned with the virus of the cobra.

21. The results of artificial respiration with the exhibition of various powerful drugs and transfusion in animals subjected to varying degrees of snake-poison will now engage our attention.

22. The leading characteristics in dogs which have been bitten by fresh and vigorous cobras, and afterwards treated by the undermentioned drugs in association with artificial respiration, are demonstrated in the table given below :—

| Number. | DRUGS AND TRANSFUSION. | From the bite to the commencement of artificial respiration. | | From the commencement of artificial respiration to death. | | From the bite to death. | |
|---|---|---|---|---|---|---|---|
| | | Hrs. | Ms. | Hrs. | Ms. | Hrs. | Ms. |
| 1 | Liq. Ammoniæ ... ... | 0 | 49 | 0 | 35 | 1 | 24 |
| 2 | Liq. Ammoniæ ... ... | 0 | 49 | 6 | 21 | 7 | 10 |
| 3 | Liq. Ammoniæ ... ... | 0 | 30 | 0 | 35 | 1 | 5 |
| 5 | Morphia ... ... | 0 | 39 | 9 | 20 | 9 | 59 |
| 6 | Transfusion... ... ... | 0 | 30 | 0 | 5 | 0 | 35 |
| 7 | Strychnine ... ... | 0 | 27 | 3 | 0 | 3 | 27 |
| 8 | Strychnine ... ... | 0 | 27 | 1 | 18 | 1 | 45 |
| 21 | Transfusion... ... ... | 0 | 32 | 6 | 3 | 6 | 85 |

Thus, if a comparison be made between these results and those represented in the table in paragraph 5, it will be apparent that, on the whole, the administration of drugs or transfusion is far from encouraging. In order to facilitate the conception of this comparison, the period which elapsed from the commencement of artificial respiration to the occurrence of death *without* and *with* medicines and transfusion in eight experiments of each series, are placed in juxtaposition in the statement given below :—

| Number. | | Periods which elapsed from the commencement of artificial respiration till death without drugs, &c. | | Number. | Drugs and transfusion. | Periods which elapsed from the commencement of artificial respiration till death with drugs and transfusion. | |
|---|---|---|---|---|---|---|---|
| | | Hrs. | Ms. | | | Hrs. | Ms. |
| 1 | ... | 16 | 30 | 1 | Liquor Ammoniæ ... | 0 | 35 |
| 2 | ... | 8 | 10 | 2 | Liquor Ammoniæ ... | 6 | 21 |
| 8 | ... | 7 | 27 | 3 | Liquor Ammoniæ ... | 0 | 35 |
| 4 | ... | 17 | 6 | 5 | Morphia ... ... | 9 | 20 |
| 5 | ... | 7 | 20 | 7 | Strychnine... ... | 3 | 0 |
| 6 | ... | 5 | 37 | 8 | Strychnine... ... | 1 | 18 |
| 7 | ... | 12 | 40 | 6 | Transfusion ... | 0 | 5 |
| 8 | ... | 7 | 15 | 21 | Transfusion ... | 6 | 3 |
| Average | ... | 9 | 40 | | | 3 | 24 |

The truth is, that the employment of liquor ammoniæ, morphia, strychnine, and transfusion, does not appear to have improved the chances of prolonging or preserving the lives of the animals experimented upon.

23. The statement submitted herewith is intended to show the results of the association of transfusion of blood with ammonia; the administration of strychnine, phosphoric acid, and acetic acid, with artificial respiration in the treatment of dogs poisoned by from two to three grains of the dried cobra-virus hypodermically injected into the cellular tissue :—

| Number. | Drugs, &c. | From injection to the commencement of artificial respiration. | | From the commencement of artificial respiration till death. | | From injection to death. | |
|---|---|---|---|---|---|---|---|
| | | Hrs. | Ms. | Hrs. | Ms. | Hrs. | Ms. |
| 4 | Transfusion with ammonia ... | 1 | 5 | 14 | 35 | 15 | 40 |
| 9 | Strychnine ... ... ... | 0 | 27 | 4 | 23 | 4 | 50 |
| 15 | Phosphoric acid ... ... | 0 | 35 | 9 | 20 | 9 | 55 |
| 6 | Acetic acid ... ... ... | 0 | 22 | 24 | 50 | 25 | 12 |
| | Average ... ... | | 37 | 13 | 17 | 13 | 54 |

Thus, when about half of the ordinary quantity of the poison which the cobra is capable of emitting is hypodermically injected into the areolar tissue of a dog which is subsequently treated both by artificial respiration and drugs, or by transfusion with ammonia, death is rather promoted than retarded. When the results in the third column of the statement in paragraph 15 are placed in juxtaposition with those contained in the fourth column of this table, the truth of this observation becomes manifest :—

| Without Drugs, &c. | | | With Drugs, &c. | | |
|---|---|---|---|---|---|
| Number. | Period which elapsed from the commencement of artificial respiration to death. | | Number. | Drugs, &c. | Period which elapsed from the commencement of artificial respiration to death. |
| | Hrs. | Ms. | | | Hrs. Ms. |
| 13 | 26 | 15 | 4 | Transfusion and ammonia | 14 35 |
| 14 | 14 | 47 | 9 | Strychnine ... ... | 4 23 |
| 15 | 20 | 25 | 15 | Phosphoric acid ... | 9 20 |
| 16 | 18 | 0 | 6 | Acetic acid ... ... | 24 50 |
| Average ... | 19 | 51 | | | 13 17 |

24. The subjoined statement shows the results obtained by combining several other drugs, in addition to strychnine, with artificial respiration, in dogs poisoned with half a grain of the cobra-poison injected hypodermically into the areolar tissue :—

| Number. | Medicines. | From the injection to the commencement of artificial respiration. | | From the commencement of artificial respiration to death. | | From the injection to death. | |
|---|---|---|---|---|---|---|---|
| | | Hrs. | Ms. | Hrs. | Ms. | Hrs. | Ms. |
| 11 | Sulphuric acid ... ... ... | 1 | 20 | 33 | 25 | 34 | 45 |
| 12 | Strychnine ... ... ... ... | 1 | 26 | 19 | 40 | 21 | 6 |
| 13 | Chloral hydrate ... ... ... | 1 | 20 | 22 | 25 | 23 | 45 |
| 14 | Strychnine ... ... ... ... | 2 | 10 | 28 | 0 | 30 | 10 |
| 17 | Tinc. Cannabis Indica ... ... | 2 | 30 | 25 | 0 | 27 | 30 |
| 18 | Emetine ... ... ... ... | 0 | 30 | 28 | 40 | 29 | 10 |
| 19 | Podophyllin ... ... ... | 1 | 15 | 31 | 0 | 32 | 15 |
| 20 | Atropine ... ... ... | 1 | 15 | 27 | 15 | 28 | 30 |
| 22 | Podophyllin ... ... ... | 1 | 15 | 31 | 0 | 32 | 15 |
| 23 | Tinc. of Iodine ... ... ... | 3 | 10 | 38 | 25 | 41 | 35 |
| | Average ... ... | 1 | 37 | 28 | 29 | 30 | 6 |

A comparison of these results with those in the table given in paragraph 17 leads to the inevitable conclusion that the continuance of life in the animals experimented upon was solely due to the artificial respiration resorted to, and not in the least degree to the drugs administered.

25. A great deal of misconception has always existed regarding the question of supposed remedies and antidotes. The following experiments were planned with a view to ascertain the minimum quantity of virus required to kill dogs, and also to show how, in the event of only a very small portion having gained access to the subcutaneous cellular tissue, death does not necessarily follow :—

Bite.

| Number. | Weight of dog. | From poisoning to death or recovery. | | Averages. | | Remarks. |
|---|---|---|---|---|---|---|
| | | | | Weight. | Time. | |
| | | Hrs. | Ms. | | Hrs. Ms. | |
| 1 | 24 lbs. ... ... | 0 | 50 | } 30 lbs. ... | 0 50 | Cobras kept a long time in captivity were used in these experiments. |
| 2 | 36 ,, ... ... | 0 | 50 | | | |
| | | Injection of from 2 to 2½ grains. | | | | |
| 3 | 33 ,, ... ... | 1 | 43 | } 29 lbs. ... | 1 43 | |
| 4 | 25 ,, ... ... | 1 | 43 | | | |

*Bite*—(Continued).

| Number. | Weight of dog. | From poisoning to death or recovery. | Averages. Weight. | Averages. Time. | Remarks. |
|---|---|---|---|---|---|
| | | Hrs. Ms. | | Hrs. Ms. | |
| | | Injection of 1 grain. | | | |
| 5 | 39 lbs. ... ... | 1 21 | | | |
| 6 | 28 „ ... ... | 1 42 | | | |
| 7 | 24 „ ... ... | 0 57 | 32½ lbs. ... | 1 56 | |
| 18 | 40 „ ... ... | 3 45 | | | |
| 24 | 44 „ ... ... | 0 52 | ...... | ...... | A goat. |
| | | Injection of ¾ of a grain. | | | |
| 8 | 35 „ ... ... | 1 32 | 35 lbs. ... | 1 32 | |
| | | Injection of ½ a grain. | | | |
| 9 | 24 „ ... ... | 2 24 | 21½ lbs. ... | 2 11 | |
| | 19 „ ... ... | 1 58 | | | |
| | | Injection of ¼ of a grain. | | | |
| 11 | 20 „ ... ... | 4 20 | | | |
| 12 | 41 „ ... ... | 8 0 | 30½ lbs. ... | 6 10 | |
| 13 | 44 „ ... ... | Recovered. | | | |
| | | Injection of ⅛ of a grain. | | | |
| 17 | 14 „ ... ... | 4 28 | 14 lbs. ... | 4 28 | |
| | | Injection of 1/6 of a grain. | | | |
| 14 | 18 „ ... ... | 11 30 | 18 lbs. ... | 11 30 | |
| 15 | 30 „ ... ... | Recovered. | | | |
| 30 | 38 „ ... ... | Ditto. | | | |
| | | Injection of 1/12 of a grain. | | | |
| 19 | 41½ „ ... ... | Recovered... | ...... | ...... | Much affected. |
| 23 | 15 „ ... ... | Ditto ... | ...... | ...... | Ditto. |
| 31 | 29 „ ... ... | Result unknown | ...... | ...... | Bolted. |
| | | Injection of 1/16 of a grain. | | | |
| 20 | 17 „ ... ... | 31 25 | 17 lbs. ... | 31 25 | |
| 32 | 40 „ ... ... | Recovered. | | | |

It thus appears that when dogs were effectually bitten by the cobra, death resulted in fifty minutes, doubtless having been postponed on account of the long time the snakes had been detained in captivity. When the poison was hypodermically injected in from two to two and a half grains, one grain, three-quarters of a grain, and half a grain, death took place, on an average, in one hour and forty-three minutes; one hour and fifty-six minutes; one hour and thirty-two minutes; two hours and eleven minutes. Out of three dogs poisoned by a quarter of a grain, one died in four hours and twenty minutes; one died in eight hours; one recovered after having pined, through marked symptoms of snake-poisoning. The part of the leg into which the poison had been injected became much swollen, very painful to the touch or pressure, and ultimately suppurated. This dog was large and powerful, and there can be no doubt that it was owing to this, and its natural strength of constitution, that recovery was to be attributed.

A dog weighing 14℔s succumbed in four hours and twenty-eight minutes to the eighth of a grain of the virus. The tenth of a grain killed a dog weighing 18℔s in eleven hours and thirty minutes; but two dogs weighing 30 and 38℔s, although evidently affected, ultimately survived after a similar dose of the poison. Of three dogs into which the twelfth of a grain had been injected, two were known, after being much oppressed, to have recovered, whilst the third bolted and probably recovered also. The hypodermic injection, however, of only the sixteenth of a grain proved fatal to a dog weighing 17℔s in thirty-one hours and twenty-five minutes, but another weighing 40℔s recovered after being evidently affected for a whole day.

26.  In experiment 33 (Appendix, p. xlii) the injection of the twentieth of a grain of the cobra-virus beneath the skin of a dog weighing 26℔s, produced drowsiness and vomiting, but the animal recovered.  In 34 (idem, p. xlii) the fortieth of a grain was hypodermically injected into a dog weighing 29℔s; it did not show any recognizable indications of poisoning.  In 35 the sixty-fourth of a grain was inserted beneath the skin of a dog weighing 29℔s, without producing any apparent symptoms.

27.  In experiment 36 the tenth of a grain of cobra-poison placed in the peritoneal cavity of a dog weighing 16℔s proved fatal in three hours and twenty-nine minutes. In 37, the thirty-second part of a grain placed in the peritoneal cavity of a dog weighing 12℔s produced all the symptoms of snake-poisoning, and eventually killed it in forty-nine hours and twenty minutes.  Three grains (experiment 38) put in the same situation, killed a small dog in twenty-five minutes.

28.  It is evident that the above experiments will explain many of the favourable results obtained from reputed antidotes.  When a quantity too small to kill, but large enough

to produce marked depression of the cerebro-spinal system of nerves, the successful resistance of the vital powers of the constitution against the inroads of the poison may be easily enough put down to the supposed antidotal influence of any drug which may have been employed. In the human subject a mere scratch from a poisonous snake, or a bite from one exhausted by previous exercise of its offensive and defensive weapons, is sometimes followed by symptoms simulating those of snake-poisoning. Here fear, derived from the popular knowledge of the fatal character of snake-bite which has been effectual as regards penetration and consequent poisoning, has much to say to the nervous oppression which follows. One of our members, Mr. Richards, and one of our snake manipulators, were both accidentally scratched by snakes which were known to be charged with poison to a dangerous degree, and both suffered from nervous depression for some time afterwards, but without further ill effects. In neither of these cases was there any reason to believe that any poison had been injected underneath the skin. It is also well known now that persons bitten by innocuous snakes, but who believe themselves to have been attacked by poisonous ones, often suffer from the most intense nervous oppression and syncopal depression of the heart. It is greatly owing to this fallacy that some "antidotes" have gained much unmerited reputation for their supposed power in preserving life from poisoning by the virus of poisonous snakes.

29. There is reason to believe that the virus of the daboia, or Russell's viper, is not quite so rapidly fatal as that of the cobra. The experiments undertaken with a view to determine this point are tabulated below:—

*Daboia-Poison.*

| No. | Weight of Dogs. | From injection to death. Hrs. Ms. |
|---|---|---|
| | Injection of ½ of a grain. | |
| 25 | 36lbs | 9½ 0 |
| | Injection of ⅓ of a grain. | |
| 26 | 39lbs | 21 28 |
| | Injection of ¹⁄₁₈ of a grain. | |
| 27 | 18lbs | Very slightly affected. |

Thus, quantity for quantity, the poison of the daboia is not so powerful in its action as that of the cobra, and even

3

in fatal doses its operation is certainly slower. Daboia poison, however, gives rise to more local mischief than cobra poison.

30. The Commission undertook the subjoined series of experiments in order to determine, as far as possible, whether any of the means employed possessed any antidotal power over animals poisoned by varying quantities of the cobra virus:—

*Bite.*

| Number | Antidote | Weight of dog. | From bite or injection to death. | Averages. Weight. | Averages. Time. | Remarks. |
|---|---|---|---|---|---|---|
| | | | Hrs. Ms. | | Hrs. Ms. | |
| 1 | Brandy and opium | ...... | 11 27 | | | Cobra weak. Exclusive of No. 1, average is 26 minutes. |
| 2 | Opium ... | ...... | 0 25 | | 2 38 | |
| 5 | Brandy and opium | ...... | 0 25 | | | |
| 7 | Epsom salts ... | ...... | 0 9 | | | |
| 8 | Strychnine ... | ...... | 0 45 | | | |
| | | | 3 grains. | | | |
| 9 | Strychnine ... | 21 lbs | 1 4 | 21 lbs | 1 4 | |
| 4 | Opium ... | ...... | 2 0 | | | |
| 16 | Baptisin ... | ...... | 0 55 | | 1 33 | |
| 7 | India ... | ...... | 1 44 | | | |
| | | | ¼ a grain. | | | |
| 6 | Morphia ... | ...... | 1 50 | | | |
| 14 | Liquor Arsenicalis | 35 lbs | 2 11 | | | |
| 18 | Leptandrin ... | 29½ „ | 0 55 | | | |
| 19 | Nicotin ... | 30 „ | 1 55 | | | |
| 20 | Cannabis Indic a... | 29 „ | 12 55 | | | Sustained by artificial respiration. |
| 22 | Bichloride of mercury ... | 13 „ | 1 45 | 31 lbs | 1 39 | Excepting expt. 30 |
| 24 | Acid, Sulphuric ... | 19 „ | 1 41 | | | |
| 25 | „ Nitric ... | 34 „ | 2 30 | | | |
| 26 | „ Nitric ... | 24 „ | 2 50 | | | |
| 28 | „ Acetic ... | 23 „ | 1 40 | | | |
| 29 | „ Phosphoric | 44 „ | 2 13 | | | |
| 30 | „ Acetic ... | 22 „ | 0 42 | | | Andaman cobra. |
| | | | ¼ of a grain. | | | |
| 10 | Strychnine ... | 33 „ | 0 43 | | | |
| 11 | Ditto ... | 25 „ | 1 7 | | | |
| 12 | Ditto ... | 19 „ | 1 5 | | | |
| 13 | Ditto ... | 16 „ | 1 50 | 20½ lbs | 1 31 | |
| 23 | Bichloride of mercury ... | 15 „ | 1 45 | | | |
| 27 | Acid, Hydrochloric | ...... | 2 38 | | | |
| 31 | „ Phosphoric | 18 „ | 1 34 | | | |
| | | | ¹⁄₁₆ of a grain. | | | |
| 15 | Chloral hydrate... | 25 „ | 3 35 | 25 lbs | 3 35 | |
| | | | ½ of a grain. | | | |
| 21 | Bichloride of mercury ... | 21 „ | 27 50 | 21 lbs | 17 50 | |

An attentive analysis of these experiments shows that none of the drugs employed possessed the power of extending or preserving life.

31. No agent with which we are acquainted has claimed so much attention in modern times, as a remedy or antidote in snake-poisoning, as the Liquor Ammoniæ of the British pharmacopœia. More than two hundred years ago, Italian physicians extensively employed it in a diluted form, either as an intravenous injection, or externally, or by the mouth, for the treatment of man infected by the viperine snakes of Italy. With reference to this treatment the distinguished physiologist and naturalist, Fontana,* says: "It is very true that our Italian journals report several cases by *ammonia injected into the veins of persons bitten by the viper;* and it is also true that these cases partake of the marvellous and almost the miraculous. It appears, moreover, that certain individuals have had great pleasure in assuring the public that a true specific against that poison has been discovered—that which I had sought in vain for many years, and which, with philosophical candour, I had declared the inability of searching for. * * * *

"I have experimented with lambs and rabbits. The lambs have been bitten two or three times, but the rabbits twice only in the thigh, and the ammonia has been injected into the jugular vein immediately after the bites were inflicted. The doses used were from twenty to forty drops, not sufficient, as I had ascertained by experiment, to destroy the animals, for larger quantities might have been hurtful. These lambs were thus treated, and they all died—two in less than two hours, one in a few minutes. Of several rabbits that were bitten, only two lived for ten hours, the rest died in less than an hour. Twelve experiments, I know, may not be sufficient to prove the absolute inutility of the ammonia in the treatment of viper bite, but they are sufficient to prove that the fluid is not as specific as it is reported. And they show, moreover, that one should not place any confidence in the few favourable cases that are quoted by the supporters of that remedy." Again, with regard to the use of ammonia as an external application or administered by stomach, Fontana observes (p. 111, on Poisons): "It is then a fact proved that ammonia is entirely useless, whether applied simply to

* Extract from a letter from F. Fontana to M. Gibelin, Aix-m-Provence (" Opusculi scientifici di Félice, Fontana, p. 125, dated Florence, July 10th, 1782.; Translated from the Italian).

the bitten part, or whether taken internally, and *there is every reason to suspect that it was hurtful.*"

32. Professor Halford, in ignorance of the unfavourable results of the treatment of snake-bite in Italy by ammonia given by the stomach, applied to the surface of the wounded part, or injected, in strong doses, directly into the venous side of circulation, has resuscitated the method of combating the effects of snake-poison upon persons in Australia by means of the intravenous injection of this volatile alkali. He, however, does not regard ammonia thus introduced directly into the venous side of the circulation as an antidote capable of so destroying or altering the constitution of the poison as to render its action nugatory or inoperative for evil upon the lower animals or man. He rather regards the intravenous injection of the alkali "as a mode of treatment." In October 1868, Staff Surgeon Lewin recommended him to deluge the animal (dog) with it by giving it, in large doses, internally, and making the animal breathe and smell it so far as the spasm of the glottis will allow. Halford says that, in conformity with this suggestion, he "tried to deluge dogs with ammonia, but discovered no means of effecting it till he hazarded its injection into the veins." He continues, " The results of my first experiments were that, in all stages of snake-poisoning, dogs were improved by it; in many the symptoms instantly stopped, and if they returned, were again checked by another injection." Thus, it will be perceived that Dr. Halford's experiments with intravenous injection of ammonia in snake-bite were first tried on dogs. From the favourable results which he obtained in experimenting on these animals he recommended its adoption in cases of snake-poisoning in the human subject.

33. Dr. Halford has published the results of this practice in the *Medical Times and Gazette* (October 15th, November 22nd, and December 27th, 1873). He there gives 21 cases of persons of varying ages who were either bitten or supposed to have been bitten by poisonous snakes, and subsequently treated by the intravenous injection of ammonia. Of these, No. 3, regarding which no authentic account could be obtained owing to the death of Dr. Irwin who treated it, and No. 10, which was a case of drunkenness produced by large doses of brandy given to a boy of 17, by Dr. Starke, for supposed snake-poisoning, must be excluded from our account. Nos. 8 and 19, the former that of a boy aged 9 years, and the latter that of a boy aged 7 years, both

terminated fatally, notwithstanding the intravenous injection of ammonia. Of the remaining 17 cases, some were more or less the subjects of snake-poisoning, mostly in a moderate degree, and some of fear to an extreme degree, and all would probably have recovered as well without as with the intravenous injection of ammonia. We think the following quotation singularly applicable to Dr. Halford's summary of cases: " The physician regards as a remedy for the disorder that medicament which has been followed by recovery, when in sound logic no other deduction can be drawn than that the vaunted remedy has not killed the patient; and we see that the physician quietly reasons and believes that the sick person would have certainly died had he not been treated by him, and with this supposes that which he does not know, and which is most likely untrue. And it is not sufficient that the patient has recovered, but he is further convinced that without the remedy he must have died." (Fontana, *op. cit.*)

34. The instantaneousness of the vaunted cures, when the patients were supposed to be on the verge of death, is of itself strong presumptive evidence to show that the poisoning of the nerve centres and the cerebrum could not have been of a very grave character, the descriptions of Dr. Halford and his contributors to the contrary notwithstanding. Thus, in *Case* 1, the injection of twelve minims of ammonia partly into the saphena vein, and partly hypodermically, affected the patient at once, and after the second injection he woke up and became sensible. In *Case* 2, we are told that the effects of the operation performed by Dr. Halford were wonderful, the patient reviving at once, consciousness returning, the pulse becoming full, and the pupils acting readily to the stimulus of light. By another account of this case, we are informed that " the symptoms of this case at 5.30 P.M., were, corneæ insensible to the touch; pupils possessed only the minutest power of contraction, and considerably dilated; limbs paralysed; pulse of large volume, weak, and about 70; countenance rather approaching a livid hue; features swollen; breathing rather slow. In two or three minutes after the injection the patient awoke as from a deep sleep. The countenance was expressive of great surprise; the pupils contracted, and dilated again and again, and then settled down into pupils of ordinary size. He answered questions deliberately and coherently; in fact the coma was replaced by consciousness, and the declining functions of life resumed almost at once their normal activity,

leading this poor fellow onwards to the happy termination of his misfortune in complete recovery." In *Case* 4, the patient had swallowed a bottle of brandy. "Twenty-five minims of liq. ammoniæ, diluted with water, were injected into a vein in the arm, and brandy and ammonia given at intervals of every half hour till recovery." Dr. O'Grady gives no particulars, but his opinion was that "but for the injection of ammoniæ, the man would have died." In *Case* 5, Dr. Bennett "injected fifteen minims of liq. ammoniæ into the median vein of the injured arm. In a few minutes, she (a girl aged 14) became conscious and violently excited, laughing, crying, singing, biting, and throwing herself about so much as to require two people to restrain her. After this, with occasional small doses of ammonia and brandy in water, she thoroughly recovered." This girl was bitten by another snake on the following day. The part was instantly excised by her mother, who also administered two ounces of gin and two drachms of aromatic spirits of ammonia. No symptoms of poisoning were observed by Dr. Bennett, who, "as a matter of precaution, injected fifteen minims of ammonia into a vein at the elbow," and in five minutes "asked her if she felt anything unusual ;" she replied "'No,' excepting a burning pain on the inside of the arm," in the course of the basilic vein. In another five minutes the same train of nervous symptoms set in as occurred yesterday, but not so violent. In *Case* 6, in which the patient is reported to have been "perfectly insensible, with the pupils dilated and fixed, thirty minims of liquor ammoniæ (B. P.) were injected into the basilic vein. In eight seconds, the pupils began to contract to the stimulus of light, and he presently became conscious. Then followed some tetanic spasms of the muscles of the neck and arms ; but these subsided in a few hours." With regard to this case Dr. Halford remarks—"This case is valuable, as showing the instantaneous recovery from the coma." He further observes that, in his opinion, the injection had nothing to say to the spasms which followed. But in our experiments on dogs, we have found that the injection of ammonia into the veins very frequently produces general tremor, and convulsive spasms of a more or less severe character. With this knowledge, well-known to all careful experimenters, we are disposed to attribute the spasmodic action of the muscles both in this and the preceding case, not to the small amount of poisoning that may have existed, but to the immediate action of the ammonia on the cerebro-spinal nerve centres.

In *Case* 7, two druggists, Messrs. Stillman and Henshall, finding that "the boy was evidently sinking, they, at 9 P.M., decided upon using the injection as recommended by Professor Halford. A half-ounce glass syringe having been carefully charged with diluted ammonia, in the proportion of two parts of strong ammonia to ten of water, Mr. Stillman opened a vein at the bend of the elbow, from which dark, thick blood oozed slowly. Mr. Henshall inserted the nozzle of the syringe, and slowly injected upwards towards the shoulder about half the contents of the syringe. The effect was instantaneous: the boy, who had been in a state of stupor, at once rallied." In *Case* 8, although ten minims of ammonia were injected at two operations into the venous circulation of a boy aged 9 years, "no apparent effect followed the use of the remedy, and the child died, remaining perfectly sensible to the last." In *Case* 9, "the median cephalic vein of the right arm was exposed, and twelve minims of liquor ammoniæ put in a drachm of warm water, carefully injected into the blood current by means of a hypodermic syringe. Within a minute indications of returning consciousness were apparent, and in about ten minutes he had sufficiently recovered to walk out in the open air unassisted." In *Case* 10, a boy aged 17 was ineffectually bitten. He was intoxicated with brandy and ammonia. "To be on the safe side, Dr. Hyde Starke injected twenty minims of liquor ammoniæ, first mixed with forty of water, into the median cephalic vein. Within half a minute he complained of great pain in the eyes and head. On being put to bed he recovered most unusally quickly from the drunkenness, and continued well."

In *Case* 11, sixty-nine minims of the liquor ammoniæ were injected at several operations. At the first operation "twenty minims of ammonia solution, strength two-thirds, strongest liquor ammoniæ, specific gravity 88, to one-third of water, were injected into the median basilic vein of the right arm. Almost immediately he (the patient, James C., *æt:* 33,) looked relieved, and said he felt better. In about ten minutes, Dr. Dowling injected another similar quantity. Within two minutes after this he looked up naturally and brightly, like one aroused and refreshed from a sleep, and said 'I feel all right now.'" Periodic clonic spasms having returned so as to become "a general and pretty constant convulsion shortly afterwards, another injection of a similar quantity of the ammonia solution was practised into the same vein, and almost instantaneously the vacant look disappeared, and the convulsions subsided into a more gentle spasm." The patient seemed to improve until the ligature placed between the bitten part and the heart was removed, and a few hours after the patient again complained of sickness, a drowsy sensation, and incessant muscular spasms. Dr. Dowling "now laid bare the median cephalic vein in the left arm, and injected twenty minims of a stronger solution of ammonia (liquor ammoniæ, fort. m. xxv, aquæ m. v). Hardly any perceptible effect was produced, so after waiting twenty minutes he injected another twenty minims, and in a few minutes he said he felt better, breathed freely, and looking cheerfully around, the spasms getting less and less." In *Case* 12, the patient, an old woman, when seen by Dr. Eedes, "was cold, pulseless, insensible, and apparently on the point of dying. Dr. Eedes injected fifteen minims of liquor ammoniæ put in one drachm and a half of water, and the pulse immediately became perceptible, and consciousness returned in twenty minutes. After this she was allowed to sleep, and upon waking was quite well." In *Case* 13, "a woman having been bitten, ammonia was injected both into a vein and also subcutaneously, by Drs. Cooke and Hutchinson. This had the effect of reviving her, but the subcutaneous injection produced afterwards very ugly sores." In *Case* 14, a woman having been bitten by a snake, and subsequently becoming drowsy, cold, and clammy, with diluted pupils, twelve minims of liquor ammoniæ fort., diluted with twice as much water, was injected into a vein in the forearm. The patient roused at once, and said, "'I do not feel a bit sleepy now.'" In a few seconds the veins of her forehead became distended, she broke out into a perspiration, and complained of headache and burning hands; she retched a little, but soon said she felt quite well, and, in fact, walked up and down the ward without help. In the morning she took her breakfast and returned to her home."

In *Case* 15, a boy having been bitten, "the part was freely excised and brandy given pretty frequently. In an hour he became comatose, with eyes fixed and glassy, and the pulse scarcely perceptible. After waiting an hour and a half, and still giving brandy and ammonia, six drops of liquor ammoniæ fort. with two drachms of water were injected into a vein of the forearm by Dr. Walpole. Consciousness at once returned, the pulse became good, and recovery soon followed." In *Case* 16, a drachm and a half of ammonia was, in several increased graduated doses, injected into a vein in each arm

of a man four hours after he was bitten, and when he was reported to be perfectly comatose, and in a dying state, with the
pupils widely dilated and fixed, and surface of the body and
extremities cold. It is said that " improvement followed each
injection; the pulse and breathing were well restored; the
jaw, which had fallen, drew up; the pupils responded to the
stimulus of light; consciousness returned; and to the surprise
of everybody present, the man walked away unassisted two
hours after his arrival." In *Case* 17, a woman was bitten, and
after arriving at Winchelsea, a distance of fourteen miles,
she was completely comatose. During the injection of ten
minims of liq. ammoniæ fort. mixed with fifty minims of
water she was quite insensible; but " before half a minute had
elapsed she roused up into consciousness, the pulse became
fuller, and the temperature of the body sensibly increased;
and in a quarter of an hour she began to eat bread and
butter, and from that time rapidly recovered." In *Case* 18, a
woman was bitten: "ammonia was injected beneath the
skin, but by 5.30 P.M., or 8 hours and 20 minutes
afterwards, she had become quite helpless, pale, and nearly
insensible. Twelve minims of the liq. ammoniæ fort. mixed
with twenty-four of water, were injected into a vein of the
arm. It had almost an instantaneous and magical effect:
consciousness returned, the muscular power was restored,
and she became cheerful. This did not last long: she
became as bad as ever, the injection was twice repeated;
each time she improved, and after the last rapidly got
well."

In *Case* 19, a boy, aged 7, was supposed to have been
bitten by a snake in the morning. Symptoms came on
at 7.30. He was " pale, cold, and clammy, with widely dilated
pupils, very drowsy, but easily aroused, and able to answer
questions sensibly. Liq. ammoniæ was injected into the
median basilic vein. The child rallied, and was put to
bed quite easy and comfortable; pulse 90, skin warm, and
the pupils natural." When seen by Dr. Bennett the next
morning, the neck, cheeks and tongue appeared swollen.
At 1 P.M. he refused to swallow, the pupils were again
widely dilated, the extremities cold, pulse 130, and drowsiness constant. Injections into the vein were now made four
times, at intervals of a quarter of an hour each time; the
child improved very much; his colour returned, he could
drink easily, the pupils were less dilated, he became quite
sensible, now and again talking voluntarily to his mother.

4

Drs. Bennett and Keating left perfectly satisfied with the progress of the case, but on returning soon after 10·30 found him greatly changed: pulse 160; very weak. "I wished," says Dr. Bennett "to inject again, but the mother would not allow it, and I have only to regret that I did not enforce it." Soon afterwards the child died. In *Case* 20, a boy, aged 11, was bitten just above the ankle by a snake. Blood flowed from the punctures. A ligature was applied, and half a tumblerful of strong spirits was given in two doses; the symptoms increasing, ten minims of prepared ammonia were injected into a prominent vein at the bend of the elbow by means of a common syringe by a non-professional person. "The relief was almost instantaneous." As the foot became painful the ligature was removed, and it is reported that soon the worst symptoms of snake-poisoning returned, viz., total loss of power over the limbs; cold, clammy skin; breathing almost imperceptible, and fluttering pulse. Ten more minims were injected into the same vein; in two minutes the pulse could be again detected, a decided improvement set in, and by seven o'clock the same evening the boy was well, laughing as heartily as any one could wish."

In *Case* 21, a servant girl was bitten on the back of the hand by a large brown snake (*Diemenia superciliosa*) about 10 minutes before she was seen by Dr. Jackson. The woman was found in a state of extreme agitation, declaring that she had been bitten by a snake about four feet long! The bitten part was excised and the wound subjected to suction, and washed with a strong solution of ammonia. She was then placed in the recumbent position, and "still remained much agitated, though up to this time there were no symptons of snake-poisoning. In about twenty minutes nausea was complained of, with a feeling of internal distress at the epigastrium, followed by violent and persistent retching." Fifteen minims of the ammoniacal solution were injected into the median cephalic vein, vomiting ceased, and relief was experienced. The vomiting returned in half an hour. Another injection was used, which gave immediate relief. She remained quite comfortable for three-quarters of an hour, when vomiting recurred. "For the third time fifteen minims of ammonia were injected, when vomiting ceased as suddenly as before." At short intervals it was found necessary to inject the ammoniacal solution on two different occasions, "after which the woman gradually recovered, and is now in the enjoyment of perfect health."

35. There can, we think, be little doubt that in many of these cases the poisoning was very slight indeed, and that the symptoms alleged to be due to snake-poisoning were greatly attributable to brandy or other alcoholic stimulants, and fear. "Here," says Dr. Halford, "nearly all cases (of snake-bite) are soon seen by medical men, and they become a source of fearful anxiety on the part of everybody, the symptoms and the results of treatment being carefully noted." (*Medical Times and Gazette*, 10th January, 1874, p. 53.) To these undoubted sources of fallacy, excepting in the two fatal cases, and others in which there is no evidence of snake-poisoning at all, we find, on an analysis of his cases, that, *in fourteen* of the *twenty-one cases*, the extreme importance, in a scientific question of this kind, of determining whether the snake-bite was inflicted by a poisonous or non-poisonous snake, does not seem to have been worthy of serious consideration. Again, when it is borne in mind that a large number of the bites were experienced by women, girls, and boys, whose nervous organization is delicate and easily upset by the operation of the emotions, fear, &c., it will be readily understood why we regard his cases as generally wanting in that scientific precision and accurate observation of facts which alone must be allowed to carry conviction.

36. We nowhere find in Dr. Halford's writings that he has attempted to measure the exact quantity of poison which any of the poisonous snakes of Australia is capable of shedding during one effective bite. We, therefore, conclude that he has not the slightest idea as to the quantity necessary to destroy dogs and man, and the minimum quantity which can be resisted either by dogs or man with comparative impunity. It was to determine this vitally important point, and to illustrate the fallacy which must underlie partial or ineffective bites, that we undertook the graduated series of experiments, the leading points of which are tabulated in paragraph 25, and commented upon in the two succeeding paragraphs, 26 and 27. It is there shown that the time taken to kill dogs varies strictly according to the quantity of virus inserted, either by bite or by means of a hypodermic syringe, into the areolar tissue of a dog; that one large dog recovered after being much affected from an injection of a fourth of a grain; that the eighth of a grain proved mortal to a small dog; that the tenth of a grain killed a small dog, but failed to kill two larger dogs; that though two out of three dogs were much affected by an injection of the twelfth of a grain, they

both ultimately recovered; and that the injection of the sixteenth of a grain proved fatal to a dog weighing seventeen pounds, whilst the same quantity had little or no effect on a dog weighing forty pounds.

37. We have further been at some pains to determine the average quantity of poison shed by a full-grown, fresh, and active cobra. We have, after numerous trials, ascertained that this amounts to about thirteen grains of liquid poison, giving from four to five grains in the dried state, and that at each successive bite the poison becomes less and less, until the liquid shed is not sufficiently potent to destroy dogs or fowls.

38. On the receipt of the twenty-four Australian snakes obtained by the Commission through the Governments of India and Melbourne, one of the first things which we undertook was a series of carefully conducted observations with a view to determine the exact quantity of poison which each snake was capable of shedding when angry, in a fresh and vigorous condition. As one of our members, Dr. Richards, can handle poisonous snakes with more ease and fearlessness than any professional snake-man, we had no difficulty whatever in conducting this part of our enquiry with the same precision and exactitude as we ascertained, through his valuable assistance, the quantity usually shed by a fully-developed cobra.

39. On arrival, these snakes (*Pseudechis porphyriacus* and *Hoplocephalus curtus*) were mostly very active; a few were seedy and thin, but these also soon recovered their activity and viciousness. As a rule, we found that the yield of poison at one vigorous bite through a plantain leaf into a spoon amounted only to a grain and a half. In a few instances, however, the quantity amounted to two grains. Another peculiarity is that these snakes secrete the poison much more slowly than the Indian cobra. Sometimes the poison is thick and amber coloured, at others thin and watery. In this it resembles the cobra-poison. In the process of drying the former variety, the loss by mere evaporation is small, but in the thin, it is over 75 per cent.

40. Quantity for quantity, we have arrived at the conclusion from experimental observation, that there is some difference of power between the poisons of the cobra and the *Pseudechis porphyriacus* and the *Hoplocephalus curtus*. The poison of the two latter is weaker in its action than that of the former. But one grand source of fallacy underlying

many of Dr. Halford's experiments is the belief that he
was operating on dogs (and recording results in man)
poisoned by snakes which he had declared to be quite as
poisonous and deadly (snake for snake) as the Indian cobra.
He says : " I would also add that in my first communication to
you on snake-poisoning (July 26th, page 91) I endeavoured
to show that the strength of the poison of our snakes equalled
at least that of the cobra di capello."—(*Medical Times and
Gazette*, January 10th, 1874, page 54.)  So far from this
being true, the fact is, that while a full-grown cobra will
expel thirteen grains of fluid poison through a plantain leaf
into a spoon, the Australian tiger snake, the most venomous
reptile on that continent, can only produce on an average a
grain and a half.  In other words, one cobra, as a rule, will
produce at one bite as much poison as the aggregate of the
bites of eight tiger snakes.  And when the amount of
poison emitted by tiger snakes is one or two grains, one
cobra can produce as much poison as thirteen, or six tiger
snakes respectively.  Here, there is an unmistakeable source
of many of the errors committed, doubtless quite uncon-
sciously, by Professor Halford, in his experiments, and in
the conclusions he draws from the results of the intravenous
injection of ammonia diluted with water, in dogs and men
poisoned by any of the poisonous snakes of Australia.

41.  We propose now to address ourselves to the results
obtained by poisoning dogs with graduated doses of the virus
of the Indian *cobra* and *duboia*, and the Australian tiger snake
*Hoplocephalus curtus*, and the *Pseudechis porphyriacus*, and
afterwards subjecting them to treatment by the intravenous
injection of the diluted liquor ammoniæ fort. of the British
Pharmacopœia.  The results obtained in cobra and daboia
poisoning and intravenous injection of ammonia are submitted below :—

| Number. | Weight of Dog. | From time of poison-ing till death. | | AVERAGES. | | Quantity of ammonia injected. |
|---|---|---|---|---|---|---|
| | | | | Weight. | Time. | |
| | | Hrs. | Ms. | Bite. | Hrs. Ms. | |
| 1 | | 0 | 34 | | | 70 minims. |
| 2 | Not noted ... | 0 | 15 | Not noted | 0  23 | 20   „ |
| 3 | | 0 | 22 | | | 30   „ |
| | | Injection of a grain and a half. | | | | |
| 11 | 25lbs | 0 | 22 | | | 15   „ |
| 12 | | 2 | 4 | Not noted | 1  20 | 20   „ |
| 13 | Not noted ... | 1 | 41 | | | 20   „ |
| 14 | | 1 | 40 | | | 20   „ |

| Number. | Weight of Dog. | From time of poison- ing till death. | | Averages. | | | | Quantity of ammonia injected. |
|---|---|---|---|---|---|---|---|---|
| | | | | Weight. | | Time. | | |
| | | Hrs. | Ms. | | | Hrs. | Ms. | |
| | Injection of three-quarters of a grain. | | | | | | | |
| 10 | Not noted ... | 0 | 48 | Not noted | | 0 | 48 | 20 minims. |
| | Injection of half a grain. | | | | | | | |
| 6 | 27lbs ... ... | 1 | 25 | | | | | 35 " |
| 7 | 30 " ... ... | 1 | 15 | 27lbs ... | | 1 | 29 | 30 " |
| 8 | 32 " ... ... | 1 | 30 | | | | | 40 " |
| 9 | 19 " ... ... | 1 | 47 | | | | | 20 " |
| | Injection of one-third of a grain. | | | | | | | |
| 17 | 42lbs ... | 1 | 15 | 42lbs ... | | 1 | 15 | 60 " |
| | Injection of a quarter of a grain. | | | | | | | |
| 5 | 29lbs ... ... | 1 | 40 | 29lbs ... | | 1 | 40 | 20 " |
| | Injection of an eighth of a grain. | | | | | | | |
| 4 | 27lbs ... ... | 3 | 43 | 27lbs ... | | 3 | 43 | 35 " |
| | Injection of a quarter of a grain into the peritoneal cavity. | | | | | | | |
| 18 | 22lbs ... .. | 0 | 40 | 22lbs ... | | 0 | 40 | 30 " |
| | Injection of one and a half grains of Daboia-poison. | | | | | | | |
| 15 | Not noted ... | 5 | 31 | Not noted | | 6 | 0 | 10 " |
| 16 | | 6 | 29 | | | | | 10 " |

By a comparison of these results with those contained in the table given in paragraph 25, the conclusion that the ammonia—though administered with great care by means of a hypodermic syringe used for no other purpose—hastened death, is irresistible. A few of these results are compared in the subjoined statement:—

| Number. | Time from poisoning till death in the absence of remedies (para. 25.) | | Number. | Time from poisoning till death in cases when ammonia was administered. | |
|---|---|---|---|---|---|
| | Hrs. | Ms. | Bite. | Hrs. | Ms. |
| 1 | 0 | 50 | 1 | 0 | 34 |
| 2 | 0 | 50 | 2 | 0 | 15 |
| | Injection of half a grain. | | | | |
| 9 | 2 | 24 | 6 | 1 | 25 |
| | 1 | 58 | 7 | 1 | 15 |
| | Injection of a quarter of a grain. | | | | |
| 11 | 4 | 20 | 5 | 1 | 40 |
| | Injection of one-eighth of a grain. | | | | |
| 17 | 4 | 28 | 4 | 3 | 43 |

42. The injection of ammonia into the veins doubtless produces a stimulant effect upon the heart and nervous system. But a careful review of the experiments as detailed in the Appendix will afford convincing evidence to prove that the sudden injection of an unusual quantity of free ammonia, a portion of which probably becomes carbonate of ammonia immediately it has been mixed with blood surcharged with free carbonic acid, over-stimulates the cerebro-spinal and sympathetic ganglia, inducing tremors and promoting the development of the convulsions and general paralysis, which are the precursors of a fatal termination in cases of snake-poisoning. There is, perhaps, another explanation of what we must regard as its deleterious action, and that is, that the circulation of a quantity of carbonate of ammonia in the blood stimulates the nerves which preside over the functions of the lymphatics and smaller veins, and thereby promotes the absorption of the poison into the blood.

43. The well-known power of ammonia as a diffusible stimulant, so far from prolonging, when injected into a vein of a dog poisoned with the virus of the cobra, is rather calculated to shorten life. That it possesses no real antidotal power over animals poisoned with the virus of the cobra or daboia, is placed beyond a doubt by these experiments.

44. The poison has been mixed with ammonia, and then this mixture has been hypodermically injected: the ammonia has been employed by intravenous injection prior to the poisoning of an animal by the snake virus; it has been used immediately after the animal has been poisoned, and in all these cases (exemplified in the experiments of Dr. Fayrer and our own), the animals were subsequently treated by repeated intravenous injections of the alkali, without the slightest apparent benefit.

45. That the intravenous injection of ammonia diluted with an equal quantity of water must have shortened life is plain from the comparative statement given in paragraph 40. In two dogs bitten by a fresh cobra, and for which no treatment was adopted, death took place after the usual symptoms and in the usual manner, in fifty minutes; whilst in two dogs, also bitten by a fresh cobra, and for the treatment of which ammonia was freely and directly introduced into the circulation, according to the method recommended by Professor Halford, death supervened in *thirty-four minutes* and *fifteen minutes respectively.* In two dogs poisoned by the hypodermic injection of *half a grain* of cobra-poison, and for which

no treatment was had recourse to, death occurred in *two hours and twenty-four minutes* and in *one hour and fifty-eight minutes ;* whereas in two dogs, poisoned in the same manner and with the same quantity of virus, and subsequently treated with the intravenous injection of ammonia, death happened in *one hour and twenty-five minutes* and in *one hour and fifteen minutes.* Again, a dog was poisoned with a *quarter of a grain* of the cobra virus. No treatment was adopted. It died in *four hours and twenty minutes.* But another dog similarly poisoned and afterwards freely treated with the intravenous injection of ammonia, died in *one hour and forty minutes.* Further, the eighth of a grain of virus was hypodermically injected into a dog. It died in *four hours and twenty-eight* minutes without treatment. But the injection of the same dose of the poison into the cellular tissue of a dog proved fatal in *three hours and forty-three* minutes, notwithstanding the adoption of the ammonia treatment.

46. The following table demonstrates the leading results in dogs poisoned by the bite of the Australian snakes (*Hoplocephalus curtus and Pseudechis porphyriacus*) and also by the hypodermic injection of definite quantities of the virus, and their subsequent treatment by the intravenous injection of liquor ammoniæ (B.P.):—

| Number of experiment. | Serial number of experiment. | Mode of poisoning. | Weights of dogs. | Time from poisoning till death. | | Recovery. | Quantity of ammonia used. | REMARKS. |
|---|---|---|---|---|---|---|---|---|
| | | | | Hrs. | Ms. | | Minims. | |
| 2 | 1 | Bite ... | 16lbs | 1 | 42 | ....... | 63 | |
| 14 | 2 | „ ... | 38 „ | 2 | 10 | ....... | 76 | |
| 15 | 3 | „ ... | 18 „ | 0 | 0 | 1 | 30 | Unaffected. |
| 16 | 4 | „ ... | 20 „ | 0 | 0 | 1 | 60 | Unaffected. |
| 17 | 5 | „ ... | Not stated | 3 | 60 | ....... | 40 | |
| 18 | 6 | „ ... | 31lbs | 2 | 17 | ....... | 30 | |
| 19 | 7 | „ ... | 35 „ | 12 | 20 | ....... | 30 | |
| 20 | 8 | „ ... | 33 „ | 2 | 43 | ....... | 50 | |
| 21 | 9 | „ ... | 18 „ | 2 | 23 | ....... | 10 | |
| 22 | 10 | „ ... | 39 „ | 5 | 16 | ....... | 40 | |
| 24 | 11 | „ ... | 33 „ | 59 | 58 | ....... | 80 | |
| | | | Hypodermic Injections. | | | | | |
| 4 | 12 | ⅛ grain | 32lbs | 4 | 4 | ....... | 80 | |
| 11 | 13 | ¼ „ | 35 „ | 6 | 59 | ....... | 140 | |
| 10 | 14 | ¼ „ | 30 „ | 16 | 0 | ....... | 40 | |
| 12 | 15 | ¼ „ | 16 „ | 4 | 35 | ....... | 30 | |
| 8 | 16 | ¼ „ | 14 „ | 0 | 27 | ....... | 10 | |
| 5 | 17 | ⅕ „ | 34 „ | 23 | 57 | ....... | 50 | |

If the data contained in this statement be compared with those portrayed in the table given in paragraph 41, it will appear manifest that the bite of these Australian snakes is slower in proving fatal than that of the cobra, and that injections of similar quantities of the poison beneath the skin is also more rapidly fatal in the case of the Indian than the Australian snakes. Thus, in the three dogs bitten by the cobra, and afterwards treated with injections of ammonia into the veins, death took place in 34, 15, and 22 minutes. But in the above eleven dogs, bitten by Australian snakes, two were never affected, excepting by the ammonia injected into their veins, and in the others, death took place in spite of the introduction of ammonia into the venous circulation, in from 1 hour and 42 minutes to 59 hours and 56 minutes. That this difference in the rate of the fatal effects of these poisons is due in great part to difference in the quantity injected at each bite, we have proved by weighing the amount of virus expelled by an effective bite of each kind of snake. But a further comparison of the results of hypodermic injections of equal quantities of the cobra and tiger snake-poisons, warrant the Commission in concluding that the cobra-poison is somewhat more powerful and mortal. Thus, a reference to the statement in paragraph 41 will show that four dogs, each poisoned by half a grain of cobra-poison injected under the skin and subsequently treated by intravenous injection of ammonia, died in 1 hour and 25 minutes, 1 hour and 15 minutes, 1 hour and 30 minutes, and 1 hour and 57 minutes. But the hypodermic injection of half a grain of the tiger snake-poison into a dog, similarly treated by the intravenous injection of ammonia, did not prove fatal until 4 hours and 4 minutes had elapsed. Again, a quarter of a grain of cobra-poison, hypodermically injected, killed a dog in 1 hour and 40 minutes; but a similar injection of the Australian snake-poison only proved mortal in 6 hours and 59 minutes. Further, the hypodermic injection of an eighth of a grain of cobra-poison killed a dog in 3 hours and 43 minutes, notwithstanding the intravenous administration of ammonia; but the injection hypodermically of the same quantity of Australian snake-poison into two dogs, which were also treated by ammonia, did not prove fatal till the lapse of 16 hours, and 4 hours and 35 minutes.

47. We have already adverted to the uncertainty as to the effectuality of the bite of the Australian snakes, and the slowness with which fresh relays of poison are secreted

after the poison glands have once been emptied of their contents. This is well illustrated in the subjoined statement, whilst the great mortality from hypodermic injections is equally well demonstrated :—

*Cases in which no Ammonia was used.*

| Number of experiment. | Serial number of experiment. | Mode of poisoning. | | | | Weight of dogs. | Time from poisoning till death. | Recovery. | Unaffected. |
|---|---|---|---|---|---|---|---|---|---|
| | | | | | | lbs. | Hrs. Ms. | | |
| 1 | 1 | Bite | ... | ... | ... | 26 | 2  40 | ...... | ...... |
| 23 | 2 | Ditto | ... | ... | ... | 34 | 2  55 | ...... | ...... |
| 25 | 3 | Ditto | ... | ... | ... | 26 | ...... | ...... | 1 |
| 26 | 4 | Ditto | ... | ... | ... | 16 | ...... | ...... | 1 |
| 27 | 5 | Ditto | ... | ... | ... | 41 | ...... | 1 | ...... |
| 28 | 6 | Ditto | ... | ... | ... | 18 | ...... | ...... | 1 |
| 29 | 7 | Ditto | ... | ... | ... | 23 | ...... | ...... | 1 |
| 30 | 8 | Ditto | ... | ... | ... | 42 | ...... | ...... | 1 |
| | | Hypodermic Injections. | | | | | | | |
| 13 | 9 | Poison of 1 snake | ... | ... | 44 | ...... | ...... | 1 |
| 3 | 10 | ¼ grain | ... | ... | ... | 28 | 7  15 | ...... | ... |
| 6 | 11 | ¼ ditto | ... | ... | ... | 9¼ | 2  23 | ...... | ...... |
| 9 | 12 | ¼ ditto | ... | ... | ... | 34 | 49  5 | ...... | ...... |
| 7 | 13 | ¼ ditto | ... | ... | ... | 12¼ | 0  51 | ...... | ...... |

When the poison of the Australian snakes was injected even in very small doses there was no recovery after the intravenous injection of ammonia. But here, when ammonia was not used, a large dog remained unaffected by the poison of one snake extracted in the ordinary way and inserted underneath the skin by means of a hypodermic syringe.

48. There can be no doubt about the poisonous character of the Australian snakes, but there can also now be no doubt that they are not nearly so fatal as the Indian cobra, partly and principally because the quantity of poison secreted at any one time is much less, and partly because the poison, quantity for quantity, is not quite so inimical to animal life. Even in dogs the above statement shows 75 per cent. of recoveries from the bites, and 20 per cent. from the injections. How different is this result from that which has been obtained from experiments with the virus of Indian snakes, as illustrated in the foregoing pages of this report.

49. Still, when dogs are effectively poisoned by the Australian snake-poison, even with small quantities of it, it generally proves fatal with or without the intravenous

injection of ammonia. We have not found that in cases of geniune poisoning, ammonia does the slightest good. It probably does harm rather than good. It certainly increases the nervous excitement, producing spasms and increasing the convulsions. It is a noteworthy fact that in none of the cases in which the poison was hypodermically injected, and the intravenous use of ammonia subsequently had recourse to, did the animals recover. But a large dog into which was injected the whole of the poison just extracted from a tiger snake, and which was not treated by ammonia, actually recovered without any important symptoms.

50. Seeing, therefore, that an effective poisoning after the bite of an Australian snake, is rather the exception than the rule, it would be easy to understand how any antidote or remedy might gain temporary notoriety.

To sum up:

1. The result of our experiments on dogs goes to show that the intravenous injection of ammonia possesses no antidotal or remedial power.

2. That the intravenous injection of ammonia, probably by promoting the absorption of the poison, rather expedites than retards the tendency to death.

3. That the Indian cobra is from six to thirteen times more poisonous than the snakes of Australia.

4. That a given quantity of the cobra-poison is more powerful and more rapidly mortal than the same quantity of Australian snake-poison.

5. That a large proportion of the bites of the two kinds of Australian snakes with which we experimented were, under the usual conditions, altogether ineffective.

6. That the facts alluded to in 3, 4, and 5, are sufficient to account for the unmerited recognition of the intravenous use of ammonia as an antidote or a mode of treatment, in poisoning from Australian snakes.

51. The trials which have been made of the intravenous injection of ammonia in persons poisoned by venomous snakes in India have been uniformly unsuccessful. To illustrate this point we cite below two recent cases by Dr. Hilson, and one case by Assistant Surgeon Jadub Kristo Sen, both distinguished for their zeal in the cause of scientific progress.

Two Cases of Snake-bite treated by Injection of Liquor Ammoniæ into the Veins. — *(Indian Medical Gazette, October 1873.)*

By A. H. HILSON, M.D., *Officiating Civil Surgeon, Moradabad.*

CASE I.—On the night of the 19th June, last year, at about half past 12 o'clock, Dabee, a Hindoo punkah-coolie, aged 40 years, while sleeping in the verandah of my house, was bitten on the shoulder by a snake.

The night being hot and close, he was lying without any covering on the upper part of his body, so that nothing intervened between his skin and the fangs of the reptile; and as there was bright moonlight at the time, he was able to see his assailant, which he described as being more than a yard long, and black.

The noise and confusion that followed awoke me, but, unfortunately, about five minutes elapsed before I could get a candle lighted, so as to enable me to render him assistance.

On inspecting the wound, there were found over the prominence of the right deltoid muscle, and about three-quarters of an inch apart, two large drops of a clear serous-like fluid tinged with blood, which had apparently oozed from two small punctures, so minute that they could not be perceived with the naked eye.

A burning pain was complained of in the neighbourhood of the bite, which rapidly increased in intensity, and extended so as to affect a circular portion of the integument of the size of an ordinary saucer, and judging from the description given of it by the patient, I concluded it was very similar in character to that produced by the sting of a scorpion.

Having learnt from the report of Dr. Fayrer's experiments that local treatment in such cases, unless instantaneously resorted to, is of no avail, I determined to give Professor Halford's remedy a trial.

The hypodermic syringe necessary for this purpose I had with me, but unfortunately there was no ammonia in my house, and some had to be obtained from the jail hospital, about a quarter of a mile distant.

While waiting for the ammonia, I had the patient walked up and down, and small quantities of brandy and water administered to him.

At 12.45, or about a quarter of an hour after being bitten, he complained of the pain in the shoulder shooting towards his throat and chest, and said he was beginning to feel intoxicated (nasha نشا), but there was nothing in his appearance at this time to indicate that he was in any way under the influence of the poison.

On the contrary, he was quite calm and collected, and answered all questions intelligently, while at the same time he was fully alive to the danger of his condition. "A person bitten by a black snake never recovers," he replied to one of his friends, who suggested, by way of consoling him, that the snake might possibly have been a non-poisonous one.

His pupils were not dilated, and they contracted when exposed to the light of a candle; the pulse was normal, and there was no embarrassment of the respiration.

About five minutes afterwards he began to lose control over the muscles of his legs, and staggered when left unsupported.

At about 1 o'clock the paralysis of the legs having increased, the lower jaw began to fall, and frothy and viscid saliva to ooze from the mouth.

He also spoke indistinctly, like a man under the influence of liquor.[*]

At 1.10 A.M. he began to moan and to shake his head frequently from side to side. The pulse was now somewhat accelerated, but was beating regularly. The respirations also were increased in frequency. He was unable to answer questions, but appeared to be quite conscious.

His arms did not seem to be paralysed.

At 1.15 A.M., the liquor ammoniæ having been brought to me (strength of the British Pharmacopœia), 25 minims of it were rapidly injected under the skin of the forearm; but as this produced no result, the left basilic vein was laid bare and 25 minims injected into it.

Having no skilled assistant with me, I had not time to observe what effect the operation had on the circulation, but it certainly caused no amelioration of the symptoms, and it was evident that the condition of the patient was fast becoming critical.

He continued to moan and to shake his head from side to side, as if trying to get rid of viscid mucus in the throat.

The respirations were labored but not stertorous.

The external jugular vein of the left side was next exposed, and 25 minims of the liquor ammoniæ injected into it, but without producing any good effect.

The breathing gradually became slower and slower, and finally ceased at 1.44 A.M., while the heart continued to beat for about one minute longer.

No convulsions preceded dissolution, which took place in one hour and five minutes after the infliction of the bite.

*Post-mortem Examination at 6 A.M., or five hours after death.*

*Rigor mortis* well marked; countenance placid. Nothing abnormal could be noticed externally, except a slight tumefaction of the bitten shoulder. The apertures formed by the fangs of the snake could not be seen with the naked eye, but on removing the skin extensive ecchymosis of the cellular tissue was disclosed around the bitten part. The blood was everywhere fluid and of a peculiar claret-like colour.

The large thoracic and abdominal veins were gorged, and all the cavities of the heart were distended with fluid blood.

Both lungs were much congested, and on making a section, blood flowed freely from them.

The liver, spleen, and kidneys, were of a deeper colour than usual, but otherwise they were healthy.

The membranes of the brain were much congested, but only a small quantity of serum was found either external to that organ or in its ventricles. The brain substance was nowhere softened or diseased, but a section displayed numerous *puncta cruenta*.

The *post-mortem* appearances, in short, were identical with those seen in the lower animals after cobra bite, except that the blood did not coagulate on exposure to the air. On examining this fluid with a

---

[*] Paralysis of the tongue is a constant symptom of snake-poisoning.—(Commission.)

microscope, magnifying 500 diameters, I was unable to observe any of the peculiar cell formations which are said by Professor Halford to be discernible in it after death from snake-bite. The white cells were not increased in numbers, while the red corpuscles were, to a great extent, broken up and had coalesced, so as to form bright red amorphous masses. Many of them, however, had undergone no change.

Case II.—On the 11th September last, at 4 P.M., one of my grass-cutters, named Futwah, a healthy young man, about 22 years of age, while taking his pipe out of a hole in the stable wall, was bitten by a snake on the end of the middle finger.

I saw him about ten minutes after the occurrence, when I found that a ligature had been put round the finger, from the end of which blood was oozing freely. The epidermis being rough and horny, no distinct punctures could be seen. Pain was complained of in the finger, but there was no swelling beyond what was due to the ligature.

The statement of the man regarding the appearance of the animal that had bitten him was at first rather puzzling, for he assured me most positively that he had seen it, and recognized it to be a *biscobra*, a species of lizard, the bite of which is universally believed by natives to be more deadly than that of the cobra itself; but the fallacy of this supposition need scarcely be pointed out, because it is well known that none of the Saurian reptiles possess poisonous properties.

On questioning him further, and after examining the hole in the stable wall, it became evident that he could not possibly have seen more than a very small part of the animal; and, judging from the absence of pain in the arm and the quantity of blood flowing from the wound, I concluded he had been bitten by some non-venomous species of snake, probably a dhamin.

As there was some doubt, however, on this point, the ligature was tightened and an escharotic applied, after which I left him.

One hour afterwards, or about a quarter past 5 o'clock, I saw him again, when he said he was feeling intoxicated, and his appearance did not belie his statement.

His eyelids drooped, but he could raise them on making an effort to do so; he was unsteady on his legs, although he could still walk in a staggering sort of way; he could speak with difficulty, and complained of a choking sensation in his throat and of a pain shooting up the bitten arm and extending all over the body, as he expressed it. The pupils were slightly dilated, and they contracted on the application of light; the pulse beat steadily, without intermission, and its rate and force showed no deviation from the normal standard.

There was perfect consciousness, and the patient being aware of his dangerous condition, begged that one of his relatives, living a short distance off, might be sent for.

The paralytic symptoms gradually increased until he could not walk; the choking feeling in the throat became intensified until it prevented him speaking or swallowing; but the pulse remained good, and he breathed freely, although somewhat quicker than usual.

At 6 o'clock, while he was in this condition, I laid bare the basilic vein of the left arm and injected into it 25 minims of the liquor ammoniæ of the strength of the British pharmacopœia.

The operation seemed to rouse him a little, and increased the force and frequency of the heart's action, but no beneficial change in the general symptoms could be observed.

Dr. Rutledge, of H. M.'s 5th Regiment, now saw him, and at his suggestion the actual cautery was applied to the back of the neck.

At about 6.30 the breathing began to be embarrassed by phlegm or mucus falling into the rima glottidis, and much relief was obtained by putting him on his side so as to allow the fluid to trickle from the mouth.

He made no attempt to clear his throat, from which I surmised he had not the power to do so.

Little change in the symptoms occurred until 7.15, when he became very restless and put his hands frequently to his throat.

The breathing began to be labored but not stertorous, while the pulse continued regular and of good force.

The pupils were slightly dilated, and they contracted slowly when a candle was brought near them. He was unable to speak, but appeared to be quite conscious, and waved his hand, in the native fashion, to indicate his dissent when told the injection of ammonia was about to be repeated.

He also put his hands to his knees when asked to try and raise his legs.

The latter seemed completely paralysed, while the arms could be moved with considerable freedom; and in this respect no difference could be noticed in the two arms.

I was unable to elicit any signs of pain or of reflex action by pinching or tickling the legs, but the sensibility of the upper part of the body and arms was retained to a great extent, which was proved by the patient wincing when the actual cautery was applied, and also when the skin was cut for the purpose of exposing the vein.

The sense of hearing remained intact almost to the last. Vision did not seem to be impaired; but from his losing the power of speech so soon, it was impossible to determine this point. The sense of taste was not tested.

At 7.30, although the state of the circulation did not seem to demand it, 25 minims more of the liquor ammoniæ were injected into the basilic vein without producing any effect.

Shortly after 8 A.M., saliva began to flow profusely from the mouth, the breathing became slower and slower, and at last stopped altogether.

Perceiving that he was on the point of death, I thrust the nozzle of the syringe through the wall of the thorax and injected 25 minims of liquor ammoniæ into the right ventricle of the heart, and, with the aid of attendants, kept up artificial respiration until that organ ceased to beat.

This occurred about two minutes after respiration had stopped.

Death took place in four hours after the infliction of the bite, and was not preceded by convulsions or any involuntary action of the bladder or bowels.

*Post-mortem Examination at 7 A.M. on the 12th, or 11 hours after death.*—Body well nourished; countenance placid; *rigor mortis* well marked; middle finger slightly swollen; no distinct punctures could be seen. On removing the skin of the bitten finger, extensive serous infiltration was discovered.

On opening the chest the venous system was found to be gorged. All the cavities of the heart were distended with dark-red fluid blood, which, when looked at against the side of a white porcelain cup, had a peculiar claret-like colour.

The lungs were deeply congested, and on making a section of them, blood poured from the cut surface as from a fresh wound.

The mesenteric veins were congested, and the liver and spleen were of a deeper colour than usual.

There was nothing remarkable about the other abdominal organs.

There was much congestion of the brain and its membranes, but more particularly near the sulci, between the convolutions.

The substance of the cerebrum, cerebellum, optic thalami, and medulla oblongata, was of normal consistence, and sections displayed numerous *puncta cruenta*.

There was some effusion of serum on the surface of the brain, and a considerable quantity was found in the ventricles.

The blood was everywhere fluid, and did not coagulate even when left exposed to the air for three days.

The contents of the right ventricle, into which the liquor ammoniæ was injected when the patient was *in articulo mortis*, were of a deep claret-colour, and after standing for five minutes, threw down a dark-colored precipitate, leaving the supernatant fluid quite clear.

I failed to see with the microscope the changes described by Professor Halford.

The white cells were not in abnormal numbers. Many of the red corpuscles had broken up and coalesced, while others preserved their usual rounded appearance with the characteristic central disc.

REMARKS.—It is unfortunate that in neither of these cases was the snake found; but I think there can be little doubt that the punkah-coolie, Dabee, was bitten by a cobra, which, judging from the statement of the man, and the distance by which the punctures on the shoulder were separated, must have been a large one.

The grass-cutter was probably killed by a small cobra or a krait (*Bungarus cœruleus*), but it could not be found, although a large part of the wall of the stable was pulled down in searching for it.

Many cobras and kraits were killed or seen in my own compound, and in those adjoining it, during the hot and rainy seasons of last year; while, as far as I am aware, no other poisonous species is met with in Moradabad or its neighbourhood.

---

A CASE OF SNAKE-BITE TREATED BY INJECTION OF LIQUOR AMMONIÆ INTO THE VEINS : DEATH.—(*Indian Medical Gazette, February* 1874.)

*By Assistant Surgeon* JADUB KRISTO SEN, *Gonda.*

THACOORPRASAD, Hindoo, male, age about 60 years, was bitten by a snake (krait) on the left index finger, at about 9 o'clock on the night of the 15th July, while he was sleeping in a room in the Bulrampore Maharajah's *cooty.*

He was admitted into hospital at 5 o'clock next morning, with the following symptoms :—Giddiness ; drowsiness ; incoherence of speech ; difficulty of breathing, and a choking sensation in the throat. Pulse 98 ; temperature normal ; conjunctivæ congested, pupils dilated, but acted on by light. Had had no stools since he was bitten, but passed urine several times. The left hand was livid, swollen, and painful, and its motion was much impaired, but not completely lost ; could not walk or sit up unsupported.

On washing off the paste of native medicines with which the finger was covered, two fang-marks, about ⅜ of an inch apart from each other, were observed on the dorsal aspect of the finger, about half an inch from its root.

There being no potent remedy known to meet the exigency of a case of this nature, Dr. Halford's method was adopted. Immediately after admission, liquor ammoniæ (ℳxxx diluted with ℳxx of water), was injected in the left basilic vein, and a similar dose with camphor water was given by the mouth : no effects.

6 A.M.—Parotids swollen ; complained of severe shooting pain in the left thigh ; vomited once : the vomiting consisted of tenacious mucus of a greenish tinge. Liquor ammoniæ ℳxxx undiluted was injected into the right basilic vein : no effects.

6.30 A.M.—Distressing nausea ; vomited three times ; voice became very low ; breathing very much oppressed. Became very restless ; complained of smarting pain in the left hand. Liquor ammoniæ ℳxxx, diluted with an equal quantity of water, was injected again into the left basilic vein, through the former puncture : no effects.

7 A.M.—Could not swallow medicines ; could not speak ; eyelids drooped ; constantly putting the right hand into the mouth. Spasmodic twitchings commenced in the muscles of the legs. Pupils acted on by light. Pulse fair. Ordered, Ammon. carb. gr. x., rum oz. i., as an enema, every half an hour.

7.15 A.M.—Vomited once ; no stool ; and urine. At 7.14 Dr. Heffernan saw the patient. He injected liquor ammoniæ ℳxxx, diluted with ℳxxx of water, into the left saphenous vein : no effects.

8 A.M.—Rattling noise in the throat ; respiration difficult ; passed urine in his clothes. Liquor ammoniæ, of the same dilution, was injected into the right saphenous vein : no effects.

8.30 A.M.—Breathing slow and noisy. Head turned on the left side ; viscid saliva dribbling from the mouth ; pulse fair ; extremeties cold. Injection was repeated into the left saphenous vein : no effects.

9 A.M.—Died in convulsions, in the presence of Dr. Heffernan, about 12 hours after the infliction of the bite.

*Post-mortem* was not allowed.

The snake which had bitten the man was caught on the spot, and brought to the dispensary alive. It was a vigorous krait upwards of three feet in length.

52. The physiological action of the poison of the Australian snakes does not differ from that of the poison of the Indian cobra, the symptoms following the bites of each being precisely the same.

ANALYSIS OF THE POISON OF THE COBRA.

53. We are indebted to Mr. Alexander Pedler, of the Presidency College, for the following report of his analysis of the poison of the cobra (*Naja Tripudians*), which he very kindly undertook at the request of the Commission :—

" I beg to hand you the results of my analysis of the cobra poison with which you supplied me.

" On opening the bottle containing the poison on the morning after receiving it, a slight escape of gas was observed, and a peculiar sickly odour noticed. It is possible that the evolution of gas was due to an incipient decomposition having taken place.

" Three portions of the liquid poison were taken and dried in three separate ways, so as to ascertain, if possible, if any other volatile matter excepting water was present. One sample was dried at the ordinary temperature in air kept dry by sulphuric acid ; the second sample was dried at the ordinary temperature *in vacuo*, over sulphuric acid ; whilst the third sample was dried at a temperature of 100° C. in an ordinary steam bath. It was found that in each case an almost indentical loss of weight took place. The samples dried in air and *in vacuo* were subsequently heated to 100°C., and in each case no appreciable loss of weight took place. This would indicate the probability that no other volatile matter excepting water is contained in the poison, and also shows the stability of the poison itself.

" 0·6792 gram of the liquid poison as received yielded 0·1884 gram of dried poison ; or, in other words, the liquid poison contains 27·74 per cent. of solid matter and 72·26 per cent. of moisture driven off at 100° C. The total quantity of poison sent yielded 0·4133 gram of dried poison. I am sorry the quantity was not larger, as it has only enabled me to estimate the amounts of carbon, hydrogen, nitrogen, and the amount of inorganic ash contained in it. I had not sufficient of the substance to make a dertermination of the percentage of sulphur present in the poison.[*] The dried poison was found to contain a considerable proportion of inorganic ash. A determination of the quantity was made, when 0·2051 gram of poison yielded 0·0137 gram of ash, or 6·68 per cent. This ash on being tested qualitatively contained magnesium, sodium, and potassium ; traces of aluminium, calcium, and silica were

---

[*] The Committee regret that it was not in their power to send Mr. Pedler the large quantity of poison he required.

also indicated, but the quantity of ash being very small these are not determined absolutely.

"The combustion of the carbon and hydrogen yielded the following results: 0·2051 gram of dried poison gave 0·1295 gram of water, and 0·3711 gram of carbon dioxide. Expressed as percentages, this will give (corrected for the amount of inorganic ash contained in the poison)—

"Carbon, 52·87 per cent.
"Hydrogen, 7·51 per cent.

"The nitrogen contained in the poison was also determined by the soda-lime process:

"0·0760 gram of dried poison yielded 0·1989 gram of ammonio platinic chloride.

"This when calculated gives the percentage (corrected for the ash in the poison) as nitrogen, 17·58 per cent.

"The composition of the poison free from ash as determined above will be—

"Carbon 52·87 per cent.; hydrogen, 7·51 per cent.; nitrogen, 17·58 per cent.

"The composition of albumen is usually taken to be—

"Carbon, 53·4 per cent.; hydrogen, 7·1 per cent.; nitrogen, 15·8 per cent.; sulphur, 1·8 per cent.; oxygen, 22·0 per cent.

"It will be seen, on comparing the above, that the cobra-poison contains a larger percentage of nitrogen than albumen, and also a somewhat larger percentage of hydrogen, but that there is less carbon.

"It is unfortunate that the quantity of substance did not permit of the sulphur being determined, to see if it bears any relation to the quantity contained in albumen.

"It is quite impossible to draw any deductions as to the nature of the poison. It is more than possible that the poison is a mixture of albuminous principles with some specific poison. To determine this would require a considerable amount of substance and the application of the most refined methods of analysis. In conclusion, I have to thank you for supplying me with the poison, and also to ask you to examine the physiological properties of a small sample I send with this. It is some of the dried poison which has been submitted to the action of ethylic iodide at 100° C."

54. As requested by Mr. Pedler, the following experiment was performed to test the poisonous power of the sample sent to us. At 4.35 P.M. the poison (which weighed ⅔ths

of a grain) diluted with water, was hypodermically injected into a dog weighing 33¼lbs. At 5 P.M. the animal remained unaffected; at 5·35 P.M. it was still uninfluenced by the poison, and continued in this condition until 9 P.M., when the symptoms of poisoning were developed. At 9.30 P.M. it became convulsed, and at 10 P.M. it was dead; *i.e.*, in 5 hours and 25 minutes. The physiological effects of this substance were in no way different from those witnessed in cases where the fresh or spontaneously dried poison has been used. But its fatal action was considerably delayed; for a dog weighing 35lbs. was killed in an hour and thirty-two minutes, by the hypodermic injection of ¾ths of a grain of spontaneously dried poison.

55. So far as we are aware, this is the first time that absolutely fresh cobra-poison has been submitted to ultimate analysis. It will be observed from a reference to the following tables, that the substance isolated and analyzed by Mr. Pedler is more nearly allied to albumen than that submitted to examination by Dr. Armstrong. The reason of this discrepancy may possibly be found to exist in the fact that the poison investigated by the former gentleman was fresh and pure, whilst that analyzed by the latter was already in a state of decomposition before it was analyzed :—

| | Armstrong.* | Pedler. | |
| | Crude poison (decomposing). | Pure and fresh poison. | Albumen. |
| --- | --- | --- | --- |
| Carbon ... ... | 43·55 | 52·87 | 53·4 |
| Nitrogen ... | 43·30 | 17·58 | 15·8 |
| Hydrogen ... | ...... | 7·51 | 7·1 |
| Sulphur... ... ... | ...... | Not ascertained | 1·8 |
| Oxygen... ... ... | ...... | ...... | 22·0 |

An exhaustive analysis of snake-poison is still a desideratum. The active principle upon which the poisonous property is dependent is yet to be discovered. It is certain that the viperine detected by Prince Lucien Buonaparte is not the really poisonous principle of the viper.

* *Proceedings of the Royal Society, No. 145, 1873, on the nature and physiological action of the poison of the Naja Tripudians and other Indian venomous snakes, by Doctors Brunton and Fayrer.*

56.  We now propose to deal with the physical change produced by snake-poisoning on the blood. From observations which have been made by Mr. Richards* and ourselves, we have arrived at the following conclusions :—

*The blood appears to remain fluid after death under the circumstances noted below : —*

1st.  When a large quantity of the cobra-poison has been directly injected into the circulation, as for example, into an artery or a vein.

2nd.  In cases where animals or man have been poisoned by the bite of vipers, such as the Russell's viper.

3rd.  In all cases of snake-bite, whether from the poisonous colubrine, or viperine genera in the human subject.

*The blood undergoes either partial or complete coagulation under the following conditions :—*

1st.  When a small quantity only of the cobra-poison has been injected into a vein or an artery.

2nd.  In cases where the lower animals have been bitten by the cobra.

57.  Why the admixture of a large and quickly fatal injection of the cobra-virus into the circulation of animals should produce comparatively permanent fluidity of the blood, or interfere with its ordinary coagulability soon after removal from the body or after death, and why the injection of a smaller and more slowly fatal quantity should interpose no obstacle to its speedy coagulation, are questions extremely difficult to account for or explain.  We can only state the fact that in the one case coagulation occurs speedily, and in the other this coagulation is retarded or altogether prevented by some cause at present unknown.

58.  Our colleague, Mr. Richards, thinks that the larger the quantity of the poison absorbed the nearer to fluidity will the blood be found after death ; that is to say, the fluidity of the blood is entirely dependent upon, and is in direct proportion to, the amount of the poison taken into the circulation. He says, the fact of the blood remaining fluid in the case of man being bitten by a cobra and coagulating in the case of an effective cobra bite in the lower animals, can probably be accounted for in this way.  The poison is probably absorbed in the human subject in a larger quantity before death supervenes, consequently the proportion of poison to blood

is greater than in the lower animals. Whether this be the true solution of the matter, he, of course, cannot positively assert, but at any rate, it appears to him to be a rational explanation of the problem.

59. We are much indebted to Drs. Lewis and Cunningham for the sub-joined microscopical examination of (1) layers of epithelium scraped from the roof of the mouth of a cobra; (2) mucus and epithelium cells from the mouth of a cobra; (3) fresh cobra-poison, with numerous corpuscles (identical in appearance with those visible in the ordinary inert mucus) imbedded in the meshes of fibrin precipitated by the addition of water; (4) crystalline bodies which gradually formed in cobra-poison; (5) blood from fowl killed by cobra-poison; (6) blood from dog killed by cobra-poison; and also for the excellent manner in which their observations have been figured in the accompanying illustrations. A brief description of these plates by Dr. D. D. Cunningham is herewith submitted.

### PLATE I, FIG. I.

The material, a portion of which is here figured, was obtained from the mucus membrane of the mouth of a living cobra. It consisted of two distinct layers of cells, the one layer being formed of irregularly rounded, nucleated, squamous, epithelium, whilst the other was formed of a layer of flattened polygonal cells, containing numbers of oil globules and granules.

### PLATE I, FIG. II.

This shows the various elements visible on microscopic examination of mucus from the mouth of a living cobra. The greater number of the cells present are evidently derived from the layer of squamous epithelium delineated in fig. I, but a pair of cylindrical epithelial cells and a few mucus corpuscles are also shown, together with active infusoria (a).

### PLATE II, FIG. III.

The material here figured formed portion of a small fibrinous coagulum precipitated from some perfectly fresh cobra-poison, on the addition of water to it. The basis of the coagulum consisted of fine fibrinous threads, and entangled among the meshes of these was a sprinkling of mucus corpuscles of various sizes and shapes.

### PLATE II, FIG. IV.

The crystals in this figure appeared in microscopic preparations of cobra-poison after they had been for some days under observation. The preparations in question were ordinary preparations in which the poison was mounted in thin layers beneath cover glasses. Other samples of the same poison mounted at the same time in the form of drops in wax cells did not show any formation of crystals, but after a considerable time became gradually filled with small oil globules.

### PLATE III, FIG. V.

This shows the appearances observed in the blood of a fowl killed by cobra-poison. It will be seen that nothing of an abnormal nature was present in the fresh blood, and this continued to be the case in specimens retained under observation for some time in wax cells.

### PLATE III, FIG. VI.

In the specimen of blood from a dog, from which this illustration is derived, the appearances were, just as in the case of the fowl, perfectly normal to the kind of blood, both immediately and during continued observation.

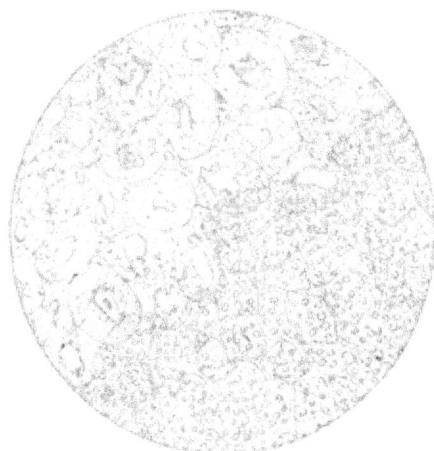

Fig. I                                          × (?)

**Layers of Epithelium** scraped from the roof of the Mouth of a Cobra

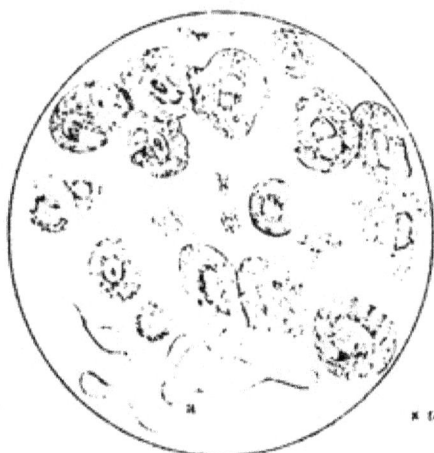

Fig. II

Mucus and Epithelium Cells from the Mouth of a Cobra;
moving among the Cells were numerous specimens of *Bodo intestinalis* (a)

MICROSCOPICAL APPEARANCES OF MUCUS FROM THE MOUTH OF A COBRA.
(Figured and Described by D. D. Cunningham M. B. and T. R. Lewis M. B.)

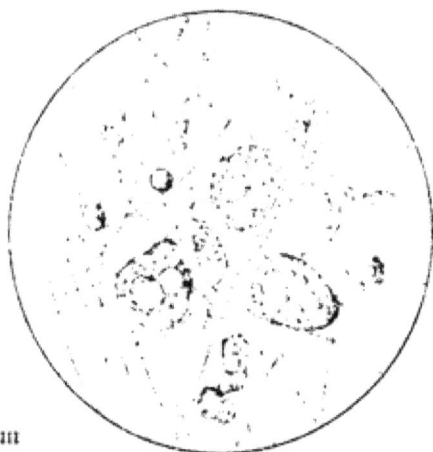

Fig III                                                    × 50

Fresh Cobra poison, with numerous Corpuscles identical in
appearance with those visible in the ordinary, inert, mucus involved
in the masses of Strin precipitated by the addition of water.

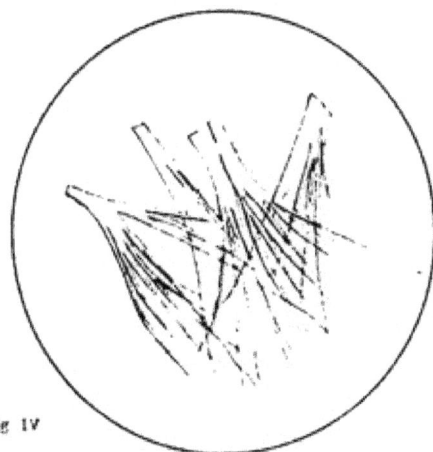

Fig IV                                                     × 50

Crystalline bodies which gradually formed in Cobra poison.

MICROSCOPICAL APPEARANCES OF SNAKE POISON.
(Figured and Described by D. D. Cunningham M. B. and T. R Lewis M B.)

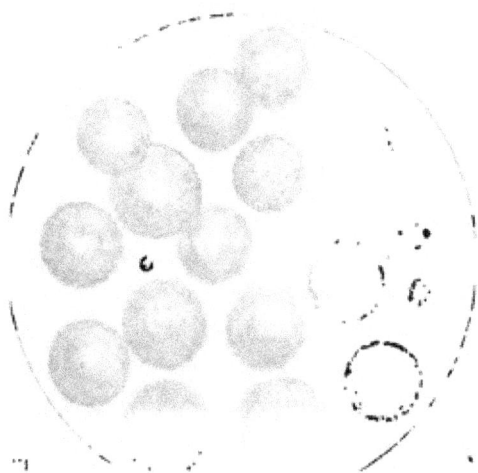

60. We have to express our obligations to Mr. Pedler, F.C.S., for having favored us with the absorption spectra of blood of chicken, and of chicken poisoned by cobra-poison. His description of the appearances presented is given below.

## Absorption Spectra of Blood of Chicken, and of Chicken poisoned by Cobra-poison. *By* ALEXANDER PEDLER, ESQ., F.C.S.

THE Commission investigating the effects of snake-poison on the lower animals, having suggested that it would be desirable to ascertain what effect the poisoning of an animal by cobra-poison had upon the coloring matter of blood, I have made a series of measurements of the absorption spectrum of the blood of a chicken killed with the poison. The absorption spectrum of blood is well known, and consists of a very dark broad band in the yellow part of the spectrum, and a second, not quite so dark but rather broader, in the yellowish green. These two bands are characteristic of solutions of blood from all sources, and are very well defined, so as to be readily recognizable. The spectrum of the blood of a healthy chicken was taken with the same spectroscope as used in the other experiments, and is represented in plate IV B, the red end of the spectrum being on the left hand and the violet end on the right. The positions of the bands may be easily recognized by reference to the Fraunhofer's lines of the solar spectrum (plate IV C), which are placed beneath for the purposes of comparison.

On taking the spectrum of the blood from the poisoned animal, very little difference was observed between the two prominent absorption bands and those of healthy blood, the only difference being that, in the case of the poisoned blood, the band in the yellow part of the spectrum (near D) was slightly widened. Indeed, throughout the whole spectrum of the poisoned blood, there was noticed rather more general absorption than is usual with blood spectra, the chief difference between the two spectra being the loss of light at the two ends in the case of the poisoned blood. The drawing of the spectrum of the poisoned blood will be found at plate IV A, and it will be seen that there is little difference between the two spectra excepting at the two ends.

A confirmation test was tried by taking two similar samples of a watery solution of blood, and treating one with 5 drops of cobra-poison diluted with water (strength ii grains to 3i); the cell containing the poisoned blood was kept in its position in front of the slit of the spectroscope, whilst (by reflection from a rightangled prism) the spectrum from the pure solution of blood was projected above the spectrum of the blood mixed with poison. The immediate effect of the addition of the poison was to throw down a whitish precipitate in the solution of blood, and this caused a considerable amount of general absorption throughout the whole spectrum, more particularly at each end, the two characteristic bands at the same time appearing slightly darker. On the settlement of the deposit, which occupied from 10 to 15 minutes, the spectrum cleared, and was found to resemble closely the spectrum of the natural blood, with the exception of the band in the yellow being slightly widened, and a certain loss of light at each end of the spectrum. The spectrum from this sample of blood was examined again at one and at eight hours after the addition of the poison, but no alteration was found, excepting that a rather larger quantity of the pinkish white precipitate had formed.

It appears, therefore, that the cobra-poison has practically very little effect on the coloring matter of blood, in so far as is shown by its spectrum; the production of the white precipitate on the addition of the poison to blood, appears to be worthy of further investigation.

61. We have to express our thanks to the following gentlemen, viz., Dr. Fayrer, c.s.i., for many valuable suggestions; Dr. Campbell Brown, c.b., Surgeon-General, and Dr. Buckle, c.b., Deputy Surgeon-General, for the readiness with which they at all times assisted in furthering our views; Surgeons D. D. Cunningham and Lewis, for their very able microscopical examination of snake-poison and snake-poisoned blood; Mr. Pedler for his careful chemical analysis of the poison and for his equally skilful spectrum analysis of the blood of a healthy chicken contrasted with that of the blood of a chicken poisoned with cobra-poison; Surgeon-Major Cowie, Surgeons Lawrie, Griffith, Mallins, and B. O'Brien, for kindly assisting in taking notes on various occasions; and

PLATE IV

# ABSORPTION-SPECTRA

of Blood of Chicken, and of Chicken Poisoned by Cobra Poison.

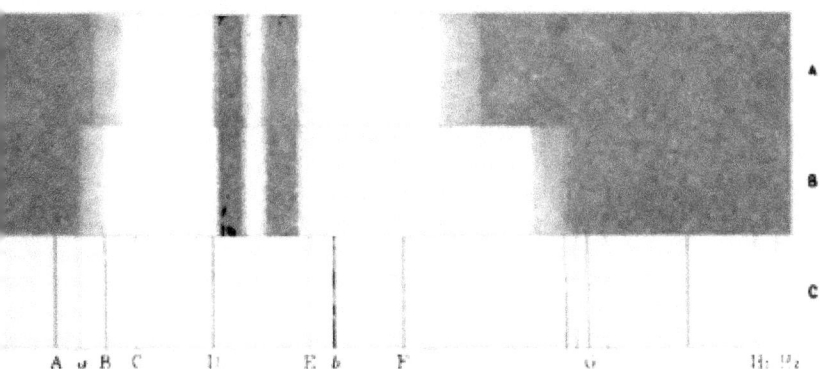

A. Spectrum of Blood of Poisoned Chicken

B. Spectrum of Blood of Chicken

C. Fraunhofer's Lines of Solar Spectrum

Figured and described by Alexander Pedler F. C. S., Fellow of the Chem. Soc. Berlin.

Professor Halford of Melbourne, for obtaining and forwarding the Australian snakes.

The Commission are also indebted to several other gentlemen, amongst whom are Messrs. T. Norman, c.s., H. L. Harrison, c.s., J. Lambert, Deputy Commissioner of Police, Calcutta, and E. I. Shuttleworth, District Superintendent of Police, Alipore, for assistance in obtaining snakes and animals for experimental purposes.

JOSEPH EWART, M.D., ... *President.*

VINCENT RICHARDS,

S. COULL MACKENZIE, M.D., ... } *Members.*

# PART II.

## Review of the Literature of Snake-poisoning for the past two Centuries.

MORE than two hundred years have elapsed since Francesco Redi—"a man of the widest knowledge and most versatile abilities, distinguished alike as scholar, poet, physician, and naturalist" (Huxley), and the originator of the doctrine of Biogenesis—first gave to Europe the result of his investigations into the nature of the venom of the viper. Previous to his time the grossest ignorance prevailed, not only regarding the nature of the poison, but even as to the organ by which the snake inflicted its deadly injuries. It is true this great man did little more than correct the principal fallacies which prevailed; still he it was who first directed men's minds to the subject, and collected by patient enquiry the crude material which Fontana, a century later, moulded into something like definite shape.

Physiology has, thanks to chemistry and mechanical art, made rapid progress. For example, the theory of "*omne vivum ex ovo*," which was only very roughly demonstrated by Redi, is now demonstrated (and by many considered *positively* proved) by the most elaborate processes. What was in Redi's time a rough outline, is now a well-filled-in picture, not quite complete in all its details, but a picture nevertheless; and the microscope has been the principal means by which the theory has been, and is still being, sifted to the most minute particular.

From time immemorial the viper has been the symbol of Divine Power, not only in Asia and Europe but in other parts of the world. It was as sacred to the Egyptians and Arabians as it is now to the Indian snake-charmer, and a man who could manipulate the reptile or was bitten without injury was honoured as a god. We have an instance of this in the history of St. Paul, who, after being shipwrecked off the island of Malta, was received by the "barbarous people" of the island, and while lighting a fire was attacked by a viper, which he shook off into the fire, whereupon "the people said that he was a god." The Psylli, an ancient nation of Africa, and the Marsi, in Italy, were supposed to be able to resist the fatal effects of the poison of the viper, and the most marvellous stories are related of them; but, as in the case of our Indian snake-charmers, there was evidently some trick at the bottom of their supposed immunity from the ill effects of the poison. Some supposed that the viper would not touch them, and it was said that this was made a test of the legitimacy of their children. We have observed that nothing will induce a snake-charmer to kill a cobra, especially if he happens to have been bitten by it. It is recorded that the king of Calicut actually had huts built in which snakes might take shelter during the rains, and that the punishment awarded to any one who harmed these reptiles was death.

the season of the year, the greater or less rage of the viper, the size of the reptile and animal bitten, and the depth of the wound, he proceeds to explain why snakes live so long without food. On this point he observes, " owing to the length of time the process of digestion takes, and to the fact that the blood of the snake is a grosser or more viscid fluid than that of most other animals, so that there is very little expense of it by transpiration, it is able to go without food for five or six months." Dr. Fayrer kept a *daboia* for one year without food or water, and it was vigorous, as regards its power to kill, up to the last. We have had one in our possession for seven months, and it has not partaken of either food or water during the whole time.

Mead's microscopical examination of snake-poison is most curious. He examined it in the following manner :—" I have oftentimes by holding a viper advantageously, and enraging it till it stuck out its teeth, made it bite upon somewhat solid so as to void its poison," which having put under the microscope, he proceeded to examine. " Upon first sight," he remarks, " I could see nothing but a parcel of small salts nimbly floating in the liquor; but in a very short time the appearance was changed, and these saline particles were now shot out, as it were, into crystals of an incredible tenuity and sharpness, with something like knots here and there, from which they seemed to proceed, so that the whole texture did, in a manner, represent a spider's net, though infinitely finer and more minute; and yet so rigid were these pellucid *spiculæ*, or darts, that they remained unaltered upon my glass for several months." What Mead really saw was nothing more nor less than the drying of the poison.

One would have imagined that the source from which the poison was derived could not have been very difficult to decide. It appears, however, to have been otherwise, for Mead tells us that he performed an experiment " with a view to the controversy between Redi in Italy and Charas in France." The former affirmed that " the venom of the viper lay in the yellow liquor of the gums." The latter, in opposition to this theory, espoused a notion, advanced first by Von Helmont, and " placed it altogether in the enraged spirits of the creature, calling this yellow liquor, a pure innocent saliva," and citing experiments in proof of his theory. But, as Mead very rightly observes, " there is a great deal of difference in the success of the same experiments when faithfully and judiciously made, and when they are cautiously and timorously managed, lest they should overthrow a darling hypothesis." Redi's conclusions were confirmed by Monsieur du Verney and Drs. Areskine and Mead.

The treatment recommended by Mead is suction of the wound, an emetic with oil and warm water, and *Axungia Viperinæ* or viper's fat. He did not believe in external management, " since it cannot prevent the sudden communication of the poison to the nerve." The following case in which suction of the wound was had recourse to, is well worth citing :—

" A man was bit on one of his fingers by a rattlesnake, just then brought over from Virginia. He immediately put his finger into his mouth and sucked the wound. His underlip and tongue were presently swelled to a great degree; he faltered in his speech, and in some measure lost his senses. He then drank a large quantity of oil (" a

7

reputed antidote ") and warm water upon it, by which he vomited
plentifully. A live pigeon was cut in two and applied to the finger.
Two hours after this the flesh about the wound was cut out and the
part burnt with a hot iron, and the arm embrocated with warm oil.
The man recovered."

The application of warm oil in cases of snake-bite appears to have
enjoyed a great reputation in England, but the physicians of the Royal
Academy of Paris, after investigating the subject, pronounced the
treatment ineffectual "any further than it might be a fomentation to
the tumefied part." Mead attaches the greatest value to the *Axungia
Viperina*, or viper's fat, which was said to have been the remedy used
by the English viper-catchers, from whom, after a great deal of trouble,
Mead obtained the "secret." He gives two experiments with a view of
proving its efficacy, but both are vague and unsatisfactory. He indulges
in a very wild theory to account for the efficacy of the treatment. The
"cordial remedies" recommended are "Confect Ralegh and the salt of
vipers, or, in want of this, ammonia." It is believed by many, even
in the present day, that the viper has about it the antidote to its own
poison, and it was suggested to Dr. Fayrer, by an American who found
" that crushed centipede and spirit when applied to the part always
cured the injury done by a centipede," that a tincture of spirit and
cobra should be tried in cobra-bite. The flesh of viper dressed as eels,
was strongly recommended by Galen as a remedy for elephantiasis*
(leprosy), and, it is said, that the flesh of the cobra was prescribed in
Bengal for wasting diseases, and the physicians of Italy and France
very commonly prescribed the broth and jelly of viper's flesh for the
same uses. It appears also to have been given in England, for Mead
observes " the patient ought to eat frequently of viper jelly, or rather
as the ancient manner was to boil vipers and eat them like fish; or if
the food will not go down (though really very good and delicious fare) to
make use, at least, of wine in which dried vipers have been digested six
or seven days in a gentle heat." This was actually an acknowledged
preparation of the London Pharmacopoeia. About the middle of the
seventeenth century, physicians were in the habit of prescribing
compounds which would scarcely be relished by patients in the present

* Since writing the above the following has come under our observation : " It is a common
belief in many parts of South America—a country so besotted in superstitious observances and
customs as Spain is—that the bite of the rattlesnake acts as a cure for elephantiasis. In one
sense it may be said to be a specific for the disease, as all who have tried the remedy have died
within a few hours of the experiment. The following case appears to have acted as a rude shock
to the believers in the efficacy of the poison of the crotalus horridus. Jose Machada, aged fifty
years, originally a fine athletic man, had been laid up in the hospital of Rio de Janeiro for four
years with elephantiasis in a form which obstinately resisted all treatment. The disease extended
all over his body, producing such loathsome disfigurement that the unfortunate man eventually
resolved to embrace the alternative of subjecting his hand to the fang of the deadly snake.
Accompanied by his medical attendants (a circumstance that will strike European practitioners
with profound surprise), who had taken the precaution to secure a declaration in which the
patient affirmed that he acted entirely of his own free will, and against their advice—the unfortunate man proceeded to a house in which a rattlesnake was kept caged. He put his hand to it
and grasped the animal firmly, which immediately buried its fangs in his fingers, without, however, causing him any sensation of pain ; a result no doubt due to the disorganized condition of
his tissues. This occurred at 11-50 a.m. In less than an hour the hand had swollen, and his
sight had become dim, while the pulse increased in frequency. Soon there supervened acute
pains, and the respiration became labored, with hæmorrhages and excessive evacuation of urine.
During the progress of the symptoms little medical interference was attempted on the first day.
He was given aqua ardente, the common spirit of the country, and made from the fermented
juice of the sugarcane. He died next day at 11-30."—( *Lancet*, April 16th 1876 )

day. Charles II.'s physician in ordinary, Dr. Thomas Sherley, recommended, what he termed "Balsam of Bats," as a remedy for hypochondria; it was composed of "adders, bats, sucking-whelps, earth-worms, hog's grease, the marrow of a stag, and the thigh-bone of an ox." One would scarcely have thought that such a mixture was calculated to give one an appetite. The Santhals, Dhangars, Burmese, and many natives of India partake of snakes as food.

For more than half a century the subject of snake-poisoning appears to have received little attention, but in 1776, Felix Fontana,[*] naturalist to his Royal Highness the Grand Duke of Tuscany, and a very able man, published his researches. While it is true that Francesco, Redi, and Richard Mead were the pioneers of the subject, the value of their researches was nothing as compared with that of Fontana's. He wrote a most elaborate work setting forth the results of his numerous experiments. He performed " more than 6,000 experiments, employed upwards of 3,000 vipers, and had bit more than 4,000 animals."

After entering into some anatomical questions regarding the fangs and the situation of the poison-gland, he informs us that Mead, and after him, Dr. James, asserted that the true reservoir of the poison was the sheath which covered the fangs, but he very clearly shows the position of the poison "vesicle" which is found above and behind the fang. He asserts that the poison of the viper is not a poison to itself, and in this statement he is confirmed by more recent authorities. Arguing from the fact "that certain substances are known to be poisonous to certain animals, whilst far from being hurtful to some others," he thought that the venom of the viper may not be a poison to all animals. "He made several experiments with a view of determining the point, and came to the conclusion that the poison was perfectly harmless to such cold-blooded animals as leeches, slugs, snails, and three kinds of innocent snakes. "Regarding the effects of the poison on warm-blooded animals he remarks, "I am not afraid to advance, that the venom of the viper is a poison to all warm-blooded animals." "There is not," he says, "a warm-blooded animal in all Italy that can withstand the effects of the poison."

In the latter assertion recent authorities will concur, but certainly not in the former. An innocent snake succumbs to the poison of a venomous one as certainly as does a dog, though not so rapidly by reason of its anatomical conformation.

A curious tale is told by Fontana when discussing the taste of the venom. It appears that Redi had a viper-catcher named Jacques, who boasted that he could swallow spoonfuls of the venom of the viper,

---

* "Felix Fontana, a distinguished physiologist and experimental philosopher, born at Pomarolo, a little town in the Tyrol, on the 5th of April, 1730. He began his studies at the neighbouring city of Roveredo, and continued them in the schools of Verona and Parma, and afterwards in the universities of Padua and Bologna. He then visited Rome, and went to Florence, where he obtained from the Emperor Francis I., who was at that time Grand Duke of Tuscany, the appointment of professor of philosophy at Pisa; but the Grand Duke Leopold, who was also afterwards Emperor, invited him to settle at Florence, and gave him an establishment connected with his household as fisico, or naturalist, and as director of the cabinet of natural history, which was afterwards rendered by his exertions one of the principal ornaments of the city of Florence. Fontana wrote works on physiology, natural philosophy, and chemistry.

Fontana died March 9th, 1805, and was buried in the church of the Holy Cross, not far from the tomb of Galileo." (Cuvier in *Biographie Universelle*, vol. XV., 1816.)

and Rodi declared that he had been seen to do so; he does not, however, assert that he was ever a witness to the fact. With all due deference to the memory of the late M. Jacques, one cannot place implicit confidence in his statements, since he belonged to a class as celebrated for their tricks as the snake-charmers of Bengal. Very few people in India have not heard of an instance in which a snake-charmer has offered to let himself be bitten by one of his snakes, in order to demonstrate the value of a certain antidote he possesses; the snakes in all such cases have had the poison-gland removed previously, so that although wounds are caused if the animal bites, no poison can be injected. The old viper-catchers of Europe were in the habit of stopping up the passage and hole in the poison fang with wax, from a similar motive. Some such deception was, no doubt, practised by the Psylli and Marsi, to whom we have previously alluded.

Fontana did not believe that the poison was absorbed by mucous membranes. Schlegel in his " Essai sur La Physionomie des Serpens " refers to the question. It has almost universally been held that the poison of snakes may be taken internally without any ill effects following, but Dr. Fayrer's experiments prove beyond doubt that the poison is not only absorbed, but sometimes proves fatal. We have made several experiments with a view to clearing up this point. We found that the poison kills if taken in large doses on an empty stomach.[*] Schlegel says :—*Appliqué sur la langue il produit des sensations semblables à celles produites par la graisse ; on peut même, suivant Fontana le prendre l'intérieur, sans que se déclarent les moindres conséquences fâcheuses ; cette observation cependant à été récemment contredite par les expériences que le Docteur Hering a faites à Surinam sur la nature du venin d'un crotale muel. Ce voyageur, prenant à différentes reprises des doses diverses de ce poison mêlé avec de l'eau, en ressentait les effets pendant huit jours et plus ; ils se manifestaient par des douleurs dans le larynx et dans d'autres parties du corps, par une sécrétion multipliée de mucus dans les membranes du nez et de l'œsophage, par une diarrhée fréquente accompagnée de douleurs dans le rectum, etc.; à ces symptomes s'en joignaient plusieurs autres assez curieux, dûs à l'influence que ce poison aurait, selon M. Hering, sur les facultés morales.* Mead maintained, on perfectly insufficient grounds, that the poison would not kill if taken internally; firstly, because human saliva was an antidote ; secondly, that if it should pass into the stomach and intestines, " the balsam of the bile will be an antidote there, powerful enough to overcome its force." Dr. Mead quotes Galen in support of his statement that the poison is inert when taken into the stomach, and further refers to Lucan, who introduces Cato when marching the remains of Pompey's army through Africa, very wisely telling the soldiers almost choked with thirst, yet afraid to drink of a spring they came to, because full of serpents—

" Noxia serpentum est admisto sanguine pestis.
    Morsu virus habent, et fatum dente minantur.
    Pocula morte carent."

Fontana's criticisms of the different theories then advocated are instructive, and occasionally amusing. The first reviewed is the

---

[*] For an example vide Appendix, p. liii.

spontaneous-coagulation-of-the-blood theory, which he disposes of by
asserting that the blood is sometimes found fluid, which was a sufficient
bar to the acceptation of the theory. Strangely enough, however, this
appears to be the theory which he attempted to establish in after years,
though the objection which he here advanced still held good and was
a sufficient refutation of it.* He next deals with the hypothesis that
the poison causes death by universal inflammation. He contended that
*post mortem* appearances did not indicate anything of the kind. With
reference to Mead's theory he denies that any salts are to be found in
snake-poison, and holds that what Mead saw under the microscope
must have been a "kind of skin from the mouth of the snake"
(*epithelium*) which he himself "occasionally observed." The celebrated
De Buffon, on the other hand, maintained that the "salts" observed by
Mead were "animalcules," on which the activity of the venom, as well
as other active poisons, depends. This looks like something approxi-
mating to a belief in the germ theory of disease. Fontana, of course,
flatly contradicts De Buffon and insists that nothing of the kind exists,
a fact of which he satisfied himself by frequent and repeated experiments.
He appeals to posterity in the following strong and forcible terms :—
"How many are there who judge after others! We may include in this
number all those who are not capable of immediately consulting nature ;
who prefer hypothesis to fact, and eloquence to truth ; a severe and
candid posterity will, without doubt, be astonished to find that there
have been philosophers and naturalists in the eighteenth century, who,
even in the most important particulars, have ventured to substitute
conjecture to experiment, notwithstanding that the latter would have
been made with as much ease as it would have been decisive." Fontana,
if alive, would be grieved to find that the world has not yet improved
so much as he expected. What was a grievance in his day is equally a
disgrace in the nineteenth century.

Fontana at first originated the theory that death was caused by
the direct destruction of the irritability of the muscles ; his reasons for
abandoning this theory will be referred to subsequently. He was of
opinion that opium acted in a similar manner. He disputed the fact
that snake-poison in any way acted on the nervous system, but even,
supposing him " to be of another opinion, his discovery of the proximate
cause of death would lose no part of its importance, for whether the
poison operates immediately on the nervous fluid, or on the muscular

* Fontana is not singular in having advanced a theory that was incompatible with facts
which he had previously demonstrated by experiments. Melloni, in his latter days, advocated a
theory entirely opposed to results he obtained practically in former years. Miller says, " A
consideration of the preceding facts led Melloni to expect that by a combination of screens which
allow light of a given colour to pass, radiant heat may be arrested ; and, in fact, he thus effected an
apparent separation of light from heat. By transmitting the solar rays, first through a glass vessel
filled with water which arrests the less refrangible rays, and then through a plate of a peculiar
green glass tinged by means of oxide of copper, which stops the more refrangible rays, a greenish
beam was obtained, which was concentrated by lenses, and furnished a greenish light of great
intensity, but yet produced no perceptible heating action when it was allowed to fall upon the face
of a sensitive thermoscope. A similar separation of light and heat seems to be effected in nature,
in the light reflected by the moon. Melloni concentrated the rays of the moon by means of an
excellent lens of a metre in diameter, and obtained a brilliant focus of light of one centimetre in
diameter, the intensity of which consequently was nearly 10,000 times greater than that of the
diffused light of the moon ; upon directing this focus of light upon the face of a very sensitive
thermomultiplier, only an extremely feeble indication of heat was obtained." Miller adds in a foot-
note, " Notwithstanding these results, Melloni maintained during the latter days of his life the
identity of the agent which produces light and heat."

fibres, it is not less true that it kills by depriving the animal of all motion, and the muscles of the power of contracting." He maintained that the irritability of the muscular fibres was destroyed, not only during life, but after death.

In the year 1777, M. Sage of the Academy of Sciences at Paris, published a pamphlet on the advantages of the volatile alkali (ammonia) as an antidote in cases of snake-poisoning which was first recommended to the faculty by Jussieu. This mode of treatment appears to have been founded on Mead's theory that the active principle of the venom was an acid salt. Fontana had already condemned the treatment, but he again performed a number of experiments before Dr. Troja, Member of the Royal Academy of Naples, and M. Jean Fabroni, of Florence, and attached to the Cabinet of Natural History of the Grand Duke of Tuscany. After performing numerous experiments he again condemned the ammonia as useless, if not positively hurtful.* The sentiments he then expressed may safely be repeated here. He observes : " I place the greatest importance on repeated experiments, for I know of what weight the prejudice for a favourite hypothesis, and the authority of a celebrated writer, are." It is more difficult to uproot error, than to establish truth, especially when the scientific reputation of an "authority" is at stake ; every man may err, but more especially he who has some pet theory either to defend or to establish.

Fontana was under the impression that the skin was the principal agent in the absortion of the poison, that is to say, the cut edges of the skin. This is, however, erroneous ; the poison is absorbed while lying in the areolar tissue, and frequently, as in the bite of the *daboia*, the poison is injected into the muscles. Fontana declares, not withstanding his former theory, that in the event of the poison being injected directly into a muscle, it is never fatal. The experiments he cites to prove this are full of fallacies. Fontana made several experiments on various parts of the body, and came to the mistaken opinion that the conjunctiva does not absorb the poison. Dr. Fayrer has demonstrated, and we have also observed, that the poison is not only absorbed, but is frequently fatal. He took a great deal of trouble to prove that the venom of the viper was neutral. Mead first, and Dr. James, Cantor, Laidlay, and Dr. Harlan subsequently asserted that the poison was acid ; Fontana, Russell, and Schlegel, on the contrary, declared it was neutral. The fact is, as we have found by numerous experiments, that the fresh poison is acid, and that which has been kept for a few hours is neutral.

Although the measures taken by Fontana to ascertain the quantity of posion that must be injected to kill, were clumsy, owing to the want of appliances, the results obtained by him pretty nearly correspond with those we recently obtained. Fontana's deductions are somewhat wide of the mark. He found that the thousandth part of a grain of viper's venom would kill a sparrow, and, taking this as a basis of calculation, he concluded that not less than twelve grains would kill an ox, and two and a half grains a man. As a fact, however, three grains are fatal to an ox. And one grain to one grain and a half would, we believe, be sufficient to kill a man, though six grains are sometimes

* *Vide report*, page 10.

shed at one bite of a cobra.* And we do not believe the poison of the larger vipers and that of the Colubrine snakes, differ much in strength quantity for quantity. The difference, if any, would, of course, be in favour of that of the Colubrine snakes.

While the average amount of poison possessed by a cobra is about two and a half to three grains, though it may be either more or less, the average amount possessed by many other snakes is not more than half a grain, sufficient to prove fatal to a child, and to give rise to serious, though, perhaps, not-fatal, symptoms in a man. Here, then, we have one of the reasons of the favorable reputation of so many useless remedies.

It must now be acknowledged that the only fair test of any antidote to snake-poisoning in the lower animals is the employment of the dried poison in the smallest fatal dose, whereby plenty of time is afforded the remedy to manifest its effects.

The following are Fontana's deductions regarding the physiological action of the poison, and they are well worthy of notice.

First, he asserts, that the poison has no direct action upon the nerves—that they neither are affected, nor are they the vehicle by which any change is wrought in the animal. On the other hand, it is proved that the blood is the medium by which the body is affected. He, however, considered that the changes were on the blood alone, and that death was the result of its spontaneous coagulation. This theory is opposed to facts, as he himself states in the first part of his work. The heart, he says, is the last affected. This is certainly true when the smaller doses are injected, but in the larger, death occurs from the heart's being suddenly tetanized.†

He modifies his theory regarding the effect of the poison on muscular irritability, and states: "I did not know when I wrote the first part of this work that the venom of the viper has no action on the nerves, and that, when it is introduced into the blood, it kills an animal in a few instants. It is not that in effect the irritability is not diminished in the animal that has been bit, and that it is not even destroyed in a little time, but this is rather an effect than a cause, and is a consequence of the change caused in the blood by the venom rather than an effect of the venom on the muscular fibres."

There is an undoubted change in the blood (if only mechanical by the presence of the venom), but this change is certainly not spontaneous coagulation. On the contrary, the blood is generally found fluid. And although the venom may not act on an exposed sciatic nerve, because it is not capable of absorbing the poison, still it is quite different when the fluid on which this nerve depends for its vitality is radically altered.

The subject of snake-poisoning attracted the attention of Dr. Patrick Russell in 1796. His book, which was published by the Court of Directors of the East India Company, contains drawings and descriptions of several snakes, venomous and non-venomous, but principally of the latter. Dr. Russell performed a number of experiments with

* Vide Report.
† Vide Appendix.

kraits, cobras, daboias, and the Trimeresurus virid, but there is little of importance to notice. He brought the famous Tanjore pill very prominently before the public, but it does not appear that he placed much faith in its efficacy. He does not seem to have been very favourably impressed by the knowledge of the subject possessed by the members of his profession. He says: " It was a matter of surprise as well as of regret, to find so little known on the medical history of serpents in a country where much might have been reasonably expected; numbers of stories, it is true, were to be met with of the fatal effects, as well as of singular cures of venomous bites. But such were in general related from memory; the progress of the disease and succession of symptoms, had either not been attended to or were indistinctly recollected; the same story told at different times, was found to vary in material circumstances, and the marvellous too often found place in the narrative. It is, therefore, to be wished that the medical gentlemen in India would in future bestow more attention on this subject than appears to have been done hitherto. Besides the Tanjore pill Dr. Russell recommends either immediate amputation or the ligature.

An impression prevails that the mangoose is proof against the poison of the cobra, but Dr. Fayrer has shown that this animal succumbs to the bite of a cobra as certainly as does any other animal. The mangoose, if left to itself to attack a snake, will invariably come off the victor, but if pushed on to the snake to make them fight, will probably be fatally bitten, as is recorded in a case by Russell.

A mangoose was made to approach a "; katuka rekula poda "—daboia—and was accidently forced too near when the snake bit it on the shoulder, upon which, " it seized the snake by the neck and held fast for fifteen seconds, the snake all the while wreathing round the mangoose's limbs. The instant they were separated, the mangoose fell down on its side as if dead." It died in two hours and a quarter, and the snake in eight hours.

We have not seen it recorded that the mangoose gnaws out the fangs of the snake, but it is a fact, and has been witnessed by several gentlemen.

A mangoose was let loose in a room with a cobra. The latter was gliding about the room, when the mangoose went cautiously up to it and slightly touched it with its nose; the snake hissed gently, lifted its head, but still went gliding on. The mangoose again followed as if determined to make the snake lift its head, for the mangoose is far too wise to attack the snake while its head is on the ground. The snake at once turned round, balanced itself to strike and began hissing; it darted two or three times, the little mangoose just stepping on one side to avoid the blow, its eyes fixed intently on the enemy, its nose pointed and nostrils expanded and hair bristling, watching for an opportunity to make a rush and seize the snake. This skirmishing went on for some time; the snake at last made a dart, but before it could recover itself was seized by the back of the neck by the mangoose, which immediately proceeded to *gnaw out the fangs on both sides*. It then gave the snake two or three shakes and let it go, again returning to the attack when the snake lifted its head, and so on until the snake was nearly killed. As we have before observed this was witnessed by several gentlemen to whom we afterwards showed the wounds caused by the gnawing out of the fangs. This was witnessed twice afterwards.

Russell is in error in stating that all cobra-poison is exactly alike in appearance. The spectacled cobra which lives in dry places has viscid amber-coloured poison, while the keuntiah cobra, which is generally found in paddy-fields, has a light-coloured watery poison.

In the year 1799, we find Mr. Boag not only advocating the Abbé Fontana's treatment of snake-poisoning by the administration of nitrate of silver and nitric acid baths, but attempting to establish a theory whereby to account for the efficacy of the treatment. After telling us it would be an endless and unprofitable task to enumerate all the remedies that have from time to time been recommended, he details several which he considers the most worthy of notice. Amongst these he mentions human saliva which, "as we are informed by Seneca and the elder Pliny," enjoyed considerable reputation as a remedy in viper-bite. He also refers to the snake-root recommended in both India and America. Ammonia which had been in great repute had apparently lost ground, as it was then pretty generally acknowledged that it possessed no specific power, its only action being to stimulate the heart and vascular system to a more vigorous action, and, moreover, this stimulation was only temporary. These views thoroughly coincide with those of more recent authorities who have had experience in the matter. Arsenic is condemned as producing very violent results, and therefore being liable to cause death. The only cases in which Mr. Boag considered it might be employed were the more desperate ones. Mercury is spoken of as deserving of trial, as "much good might be anticipated from its use," though it should be given in a more convenient form than was then prescribed.

Mr. Boag's theory was that the venom subtracted the oxygen of the blood, so leading to death, and he founds this theory on four arguments as he terms them; in some of which, however, we cannot concur. These four arguments are :—

1st.—"Man, and other warm-blooded animals, exposed to an atmosphere deprived of oxygen, quickly expire. The poison of a serpent when introduced into the blood also causes death, but carried into circulation by a wound, and in very small quantity, its operation is comparatively slow and gradual."

2nd.—"The appearances on dissection in both cases are very similar, the blood becomes of a darker colour, and coagulates about the heart and large vessels, the irritability of the fibres is nearly in the same degree destroyed, and the body has a strong tendency, in both instances, to putrescency."

3rd.—"Dr. Mead mixed the venom of the viper, and healthy blood together out of the body, and he did not perceive that it produced any change in its appearance; this arose from his mixing a small quantity of the venom with a large quantity of the blood, but if two or three drops of venom be mixed with forty or fifty drops of blood, it immediately loses its vermilion colour, becomes black and incapable of coagulation."

4th.—"It is a very remarkable circumstance that the poison of the serpent has most power over those animals whose blood is the warmest, and the action of whose heart is the most lively; while, on the contrary,

8

( 58 )

it is not a poison to the snake itself, nor in general to cold-blooded animals. The reason appears to be this: cold-blooded animals do not require a large quantity of oxygen to preserve them in health; this is evident from the conformation of their heart and respiratory organs, as already mentioned."

Therefore, as we have before pointed out, Mr. Boag concludes that death from snake-bite simply arises from the abstraction of oxygen from the blood.

The first argument requires no special notice, but the second contains inaccuracies; the blood may or may not coagulate in cases of snake-poisoning, and it certainly does not generally coagulate about the heart and larger vessels. It is true that blood remains fluid if mixed with a large quantity of snake-poison, but it must be remembered that in the human body the relative dilution is not 3 to 50, but perhaps 2 to 9,600. The question of the condition of the blood as regards fluidity is not, however, of much importance except from a medico-legal point of view. It is a remarkable fact that while the blood of a dog poisoned by venom coagulates after death, that of a human being remains permanently fluid.

The fourth argument is most remarkable. Mr. Boag observes that a poisonous snake is protected from the effects of its own poison by its physical conformation, which enables the animal to live with a very small amount of oxygen. Unfortunately for this argument, however, venomous and non-venomous snakes do not differ anatomically, and yet the venom of the former will kill the latter. Mr. Boag is also in error in stating that the poison is not generally fatal to cold-blooded animals. Although its action is, of course, somewhat slower, it is none the less fatal. We would not be understood to mean that de-oxidation of the blood to some extent is not a result of snake-poisoning; we believe it is, but that it is not the cause of death.

The treatment Mr. Boag recommends is interesting. The principle is the speedy oxygenation of the system, and the means to this end are the following :—

" External treatment," which may be divided into local and general; first, suction of the wound as recommended by Celsus. This measure should not be omitted, though Mr. Boag does not think it is very successful. Mr. Boag evidently believed with Celsus that this proceeding can be adopted with perfect safety to the operator, but that it is not so, has been proved by Dr. Fayrer and others; undoubtedly, the risk is slight, but still it exists.

The next measures are the ligature and scarification of the wound, which should then be washed with a weak solution of lunar caustic and water, a warm bath acidulated with nitric acid just sufficiently to irritate the skin. This bath should be continued at intervals; and lastly, the administration of nitrate of silver in half-grain doses, and " a more highly oxygenated atmosphere might be breathed by means of a pneumatic apparatus adopted for the purpose as recommended by Dr. Beddoes."*

Curiously enough, after recommending the above, Mr. Boag made some experiments, every one unsuccessful. And yet we find him stating

---

* Something of the kind has been recommended by Drs. Fayrer and Brunton.

that "I am of opinion that the method of cure mentioned in the foregoing essay is most rational, and the most likely to succeed in preventing death as well as the other bad consequences which sometimes follow the bite of a serpent that is not mortal."

It is difficult to understand on what grounds Mr. Boag comes to a conclusion so directly opposed to the result of his experiments.

In 1801, the ammonia treatment again found an advocate in Mr. John Williams. He evidently was a staunch believer in its efficacy, as he observes : "The following statement of facts relative to the cure of persons bitten by snakes selected from a number of cases which have come within my own knowledge, requires no prefatory introduction ; as it points out the means of obtaining the greatest self-gratification the human mind is capable of experiencing, that of the preservation of the life of a fellow creature, and snatching him from the jaws of death, by a method which every person is capable of availing himself of." As no system of treatment is complete without a theory, Mr. Williams stirs one up from the depths of his imagination, which, though somewhat weak and obscure, is still a theory. He observes that, "as the poison diffuses itself over the body by the returning venous blood, as proved by the effects of a ligature placed between the wound and heart, destroying the irritability and rendering the system paralytic, it is probable that volatile caustic alkali in resisting the disease of the poison, does not act so much as a specific in destroying its quality, as by counteracting the effect on the system by stimulating the fibres, and preserving that irritability which it tends to destroy."

In other words, the ammonia does not act chemically upon the poison, but it counteracts its effects physiologically. What these effects are and how the ammonia counteracts them, Mr. Williams does not inform us.

He then gives seven cases, of which only one terminated fatally.

The first case was only a supposed case of snake-bite. The second was that of "an old woman of the Brahmin caste, who was bitten between the thumb and finger, by a cobra." She became "speechless and convulsed, with locked-jaws, and a profuse discharge of saliva running from the mouth." Mr. Williams gave her two drachms of "volatile caustic alkali spirit, when she evidently got better," and "perfectly recovered in about half an hour. The Brahman of the house would not allow the snake to be killed."

The third case is not deserving of notice.

The fourth case is the following :—"In July 1784, the wife of a servant of mine was bitten by a cobra di capello on the outside of the little toe of her right foot. In a few minutes she became convulsed, particularly about the jaws and throat, with continued gnashing of the teeth. She at first complained of a numbness extending from the wound upwards, but no ligature was applied to the limb. About sixty drops of the volatile caustic alkali spirit were given to her in water by forcing open her mouth which was strongly convulsed ; in about seven minutes the dose was repeated, when the convulsions left her and in three more she became sensible and spoke to those who attended her. A few drops of spirit had also been applied to the wound. The snake was killed and brought to me, which proved to be a cobra di capello."

The other cases are equally wonderful, except the last which terminated fatally!

The administration of ammonia was again advocated in 1809 by Dr. Macrae, who was himself bitten by a cobra; he took "thirteen spoonfuls of the ammonia."

In 1825, Mr. Breton performed a series of experiments with the cobra, daboia, and bungarus faciatus, and arrived at the following conclusions :—

*Firstly.*—"Although the effect of the venom of a serpent may be for several hours very evident, an animal is capable, without any remedy whatever, of surviving its action; for the day after being bitten, the dog remained several hours apparently in a dying state, but in the course of the following day recovered perfectly."

*Secondly.*—"After the first or second emission of the poison it becomes too weak to destroy even a whelp three parts grown."

Here Mr. Breton has mistaken the quantity for the quality; it is not that the poison is too *weak*, but the quantity too *small*. But we have instances on record in which several dogs have been killed in succession by one cobra, and a case is cited by Dr. Chevers, in which three men died, and one became much affected by the bites of one krait.

*Thirdly.*—"An innoxious snake can be killed by the venom of a poisonous snake."

*Fourthly.*—"Rabbits and pigeons are killed in two or three minutes and full-grown dogs in fifteen or twenty."

*Fifthly.*—"A poisonous snake is unsusceptible of the poison of another snake." Mr. Breton was evidently a very careful observer.

Vol. II of the "Medical and Physical Transactions of the Calcutta Society," contains an article "on the treatment of persons bitten by venomous snakes, by Donald Butter, Esq., M.D." The author has such faith in his mode of treatment that he has, we believe, recently reprinted his paper and circulated it gratis. After referring briefly to the essays by Messrs. Williams and Boag, he says: "As I thought it probable that some of my professional brethren, who have had opportunities of seeing such cases, might have been in the habit of employing a more active treatment, I endeavoured, in a letter printed in the Calcutta *John Bull* of the 20th October 1823, to draw their attention to the general advantage which would arise from a publication of the results of their practice." To this letter there appears to have been little response by the medical profession. Dr. Butter recommends the administration of opium, brandy, and sulphuric æther, and this treatment is founded on the hyphothesis that the heart and arterial system are principally affected. In this theory, however, we cannot concur, as it is in overwhelming doses only—when no remedy would be of the slightest avail—that the poison acts principally on the heart, "causing its action to cease in a systole" (Fayrer and Brunton). This plan of treatment appears to have been advocated by Mr. Latta. Dr. Butter, besides recommending extreme caution, also speaks favourably of the use of the ligature, dry cupping, and suction of the wound. We have tested the efficacy of this treatment on the lower animals, but found it as unsuccessful as Fontana did nearly a hundred years ago. Dr. Butter admits that the species of snake "was ascertained in one or two instances only," but *supposes* they were cobras. The following case quoted by Dr. Butter is interesting, but some of the symptoms, so far as they are described, appear to be more the result of the treatment than the effects of snake-poisoning.

The case is as follows :—

"*April 22nd*, 1825.—Soobhan Khan, *Sipahee*, 6th Company, Goruckhporo Light Infantry, aged about 18 years. About 55 minutes after midnight bitten in the left instep and shin by a snake *supposed* (the italics are mine), from its size, to be a cobra di capello, at one o'clock five minutes A.M., and when brought to me, was speechless and insensible, but had the power of moving his legs. Ligature instantly applied, and R. Opii. drachm 1 with brandy ounce 1, and spirit menth, рip 10 minims, administered; pulse hardly perceptible either in the heart or arteries; surface cold, made to walk about between two men. At 1-10 minutes, heat and circulation returning. At 1-15 minutes, syncope. Gave a second dose as above, soon after which circulation again returned, and at 1-20 minutes he was perfectly well and described very clearly the manner in which the accident happened. He now walked about unassisted; and at 1-35 minutes, half an hour after he took the first dose, I removed the ligature as I had been in the habit of doing when the patients had completely recovered. At 1-40 minutes he suddenly fainted; ligature was instantly re-applied, and a third dose, as above, given, and the wounds well washed with hot water. Circulation still continuing very weak, with foaming at the mouth, occasional syncope, and convulsive twitches of the arms; at 1-45 minutes a fourth, and at 2 A.M. a fifth dose, all in the above proportions, were given; after which he rapidly recovered from all symtoms of collapse, but still complained of giddiness, which I now ascribed to the medicines, as his pulse was full and regular" (evidently the man was becoming intoxicated). "His wounds were again well washed with hot water, and at about 3 A.M. he became slightly delirious" (? intoxicated), "his imagination being haunted with the idea of a snake coming to attack him." This youth took 500 minims of tincture of opium. Dr. Butter concludes by stating that he gave the man three ounces of Epsom salts. Dr. Butter, after trial, condemns Mr. Williams's treatment—the administration of ammonia—which was said by him never to fail, as being sound in principle, but unsuccessful in practice; while it is true that the natives of India suppose that opium-eaters are more proof against snake-poison than other people, there can be no doubt from recent experiments carried on in the most systematic manner that the drug is useless in cases of snake-poisoning.

A curious effect is said sometimes to follow the bite of a snake :— "In 1855 Mr. Souberran published the case of a gentleman who having been bitten by a viper in the year 1849, asserted that he still experienced *attacks of rather severe pain in the arm bitten*, with sensations of lassitude and malaise; these *symptoms recurring every year in the month of April* and lasting a month.

Dr. Demeurat relates the following instance of a similar occurrence :—" A woman was bitten by a viper in the right forearm on the

28th May 1824. She suffered at the time from nausea and vomiting, headache and chilliness. The arm also became swollen and a dark red patch, covered by a large bleb, formed at the spot which was bitten. This affection extended across the forearm, and a large quantity of serosity exuded daily from the furrows between the bullæ. Beneath the raised epidermis was a thick false membrane. After eighteen months this membrane became black and dry, and the woman tore it off in one piece. The skin beneath was red, but soon recovered its healthy appearance. This was in November 1826. The next year on May the 28th the eruption returned, and continued till November. These *phenomena repeat themselves each year, commencing about the same day.*" Dr. Demourat does not say that he has witnessed the phenomena. ("Year Book of Medicine and Surgery," 1863.)

This annual recurrence of symptoms does not appear to be confined to cases of snake-bite, as Livingstone ("Missionary Travels and Researches in South Africa") mentions a case of the bite of a lion, in which it occurred. Livingstone says, after describing a fight with a lion, in which he took the most prominent part, " a wound from this animal's teeth resembles a gunshot wound; it is generally followed by a great deal of sloughing and discharge, and pains are felt in the part periodically ever afterwards. I had on a tartan jacket on the occasion, and I believe that it wiped off all the virus from the teeth that pierced the flesh, for my two companions in this affray have both suffered from the peculiar pains, while I have escaped with only the inconvenience of a false joint in my limb. The man whose shoulder was wounded, showed me *his wound actually burst forth afresh on the same month of the following year.* This curious point deserves the attention of enquirers."

The famous snake-stone has long been in repute in Asia, but it was never credited with any efficacy in cases of viper-bite in Europe. In 1662, some specimens were taken from India by three Franciscan friars and deposited in the musuem of the Grand Duke of Tuscany, where they came under the notice of Redi. It was believed that the stone was found in the head of a snake. Taverini and Kempfer, however, considered it to be an artificial fabrication. Dr. Alexander Stuart stated (1749-50) that it was made of the burnt bones of the small buffalo. Captain Herbert says, he obtained one from the people of Jowalins, who said it was found in the detritus in the valley of the Satlej. Calculi taken from the stomach and intestines of different animals are sometimes used as snake-stones. There are, no doubt, many kinds, all equally useless.*

Dr. Davy, in 1839, published an account of some experiments he performed with some of the poisonous snakes of Ceylon (*Physiological*

---

* Dr. Davy truly says :—"Too often, medicines have got into repute as antidotes from being given in slight cases, in which recovery would have taken place without medical treatment,—beneficial changes that were due merely to the preservative powers of the constitution. The reputation that many Indian medicines, and especially that snake-stones have acquired, affords striking proof of the preceding remarks. Of three different kinds of these stones which I have examined, one consisted of partially burnt bone, another of chalk, and the third principally of vegetable matter; this last resembled a bezoar. All of them (excepting the first, possessed of a slight absorbent power) were quite inert, and incapable of having any effect, exclusive of that which they might produce as superstitious medicines on the imagination of a patient." The first kind of stone referred to by Dr. Davy was manufactured by the Monks of Manilla, who carried on a lucrative trade in them with Indian merchants.

and *Anatomical Researches*), and in his "conclusions and general remarks" points out that "the principle seat of the diseased action are the lungs," but he appeared to think that this action is confined to cases of viper snake-bite. He believed that the virus of colubrine snakes acts primarily and principally on the blood and muscles, tending to coagulate the former, and convulse and paralyze the latter. He was erroneously of opinion that the bite of the daboia is generally more dangerous than that of the cobra.

At no period has the subject of snake-poisoning received so much attention as it has during the past eight or ten years. Drs. Fayrer and Shortt in India, Dr. Weir Mitchell, in America, Dr. Halford, in Australia, and Dr. Brunton—in conjunction with Dr. Fayrer—in England, have all been laboring in the hope of finding that which has baffled the ingenuity of ages, and which, if found, would be an inestimable boon to mankind. Although no antidote has been discovered, much good work has lately been done as regards the physiological action of the poison, and if there be in existence a remedy, the more intimately we become acquainted with the *modus operandi* of snake-poison, the more likely are our efforts to be crowned with success.

It is much to be regretted that some experimenters have so unwisely advocated, and in the strongest terms, a certain treatment which has not stood the test of an impartial investigation; and it seems difficult to understand, granting them honesty of purpose and common sense, how they could have arrived at conclusions so diametrically opposed to facts.

(Sd.)     VINCENT RICHARDS.

# Drs. Fayrer and Lauder Brunton on the Physiological Action of Indian Snake-poison.

*Summary of a paper read before the Royal Society.*

DRS. FAYRER AND LAUDER BRUNTON, recently read a paper before the Royal Society on "the poison of Indian snakes," in which they deal with the physiological action of snake-poison. Their experiments in London were carried on simultaneously with ours in Calcutta, but while they dealt exclusively with the physiological action of the poison, we had more particularly to determine the value of artificial respiration and the intravenous injection of ammonia in snake-poisoning. We have, nevertheless, by a careful consideration of the facts disclosed to us in the course of our experiments, been enabled to determine, in a measure, the physiological action of the poison. Our views on the subject are set forth in our report, and it will be seen on perusing the following summary of the paper above referred to, that they pretty nearly correspond with those of Drs. Fayrer and Brunton.

One is frequently asked, "Which is the most deadly snake in India?" or "Is not the krait more deadly than the cobra?" What is meant by "more deadly" is, more generally fatal by its bite. There is not much difference in the fatal power of the poison of the cobra and that of the krait; what renders the cobra so much more formidable than the krait is, its larger store of poison, and the greater rapidity with which it secretes it. With reference to the relative effects of the poison of different snakes Drs. Fayrer and Brunton observe :—

*Paper read before the Royal Society.*

*Relative effects of the poison of different snakes.*

"The effects of the poison of *Naja tripudians* are probably the same as those of *Ophiophagus elaps*, *Bungarus*, *Hydrophidæ*, and other poisonous colubrine snakes, whilst that of *Daboia Russellii* is similar to that of *Echis carinata*, and also of the *Trimeresuri*, which represent the viperine snakes in India.

"Just as the *Naja* may be regarded as among the most virulent of the colubrine, the *Daboia* is probably as venomous as any of the viperine snakes, it being very deadly; whilst the *Crotalidæ* are but feebly represented in India by the *Trimeresuri*.

"The venomous colubrine snakes in India are represented by the *Naja tripudians*, *Ophiophagus elaps*, *Bungarus fasciatus*, *B. cæruleus*, *Xenurelaps bungaroides*, and the various species of *Callophis* and *Hydrophidæ*; whilst among the viperine snakes the *Viperidæ*, or vipers, are represented in India by only two genera, each with a single species, *Daboia Russellii*, *Echis carinata*; the *Crotalidæ*, or pit-vipers, by the various *Trimeresuri*, *Peltopelor*, *Halys*, *Hypnale*, though these are much less active than their American congeners.

"The *Daboia*, however, may be considered as virulent as the most deadly form of the *Viperidæ* of Africa, or probably as the *Crotalus* or *Craspedocephalus* of the pit-vipers of America and the West Indies."

The constitutional symptoms arising from the bite of the daboia
differ little from those produced by the bite of a cobra, but the local injury is much more severe in the former. On this head our authors observe :—

*The Constitutional symptoms in daboia-poisoning and cobra-poisoning differ but little.*

"In a previous communication we have described the effect of the poison of *Naja tripudians* upon warm-blooded animals, and have illustrated it by experiments on the dog, rabbit, guineapig, and fowl.

"We purpose in the present paper to compare its action with that of the poison of the *Daboia Russellii*, a viperine snake, to describe its effects upon cold-blooded animals and invertebrata, and to examine in detail its action upon the various organs of the body.

"In our former paper we stated that the general symptoms of poisoning by cobra-venom are depression, faintness, hurried respiration and exhaustion, lethargy, unconsciousness, nausea, and vomiting. In dogs, guineapigs, and rabbits peculiar twitching movements occur, which seem to represent vomiting in them; occasionally, in fact, dogs and guineapigs do vomit, and the dogs are profusely salivated. As the poisoning proceeds, paralysis appears, sometimes affecting the hind legs first and seeming to creep up the body, and sometimes affecting the whole animal nearly at the same time. There is loss of co-ordinating power of the muscles of locomotion.

"Hæmorrhage, relaxation of the sphincters, and involuntary evacuations, not unfrequently of a sanguineous or muco-sanguineous character, often precede death, and are generally accompanied by convulsions.

"In fowls the appearance is one of extreme drowsiness; the head falls forward, rests on the beak; and gradually the bird, no longer able to support itself, crouches, then rolls over on its side. There are frequent startings, as if of sudden awaking from the drowsy state.

"The following experiments upon pigeons and guineapigs show that the general symptoms produced by the poison of the *Daboia* are nearly the same as by that of the *Naja.* The local symptoms are greater extravasation of blood and effusion into areolar tissue."

We have shown in our "review" that, Fontana believed that certain innocuous snakes, snails, and leeches, were proof against the venom of a snake. He, moreover, stated that, "there are several kinds of animals very distinct from each other to which the venom of the viper is not a poison; or if it be so, it is very rarely, and that with the least possible energy." The supposed power of the mongoose to resist the fatal effects of snake-poison is familiar to every one, and yet this animal succumbs to the bite of a cobra as readily as any other warm-blooded animal.*

*Action of cobra-poison on different animals.*

Of the action of the poison on different animals, our authors observe :—

*Action on frogs.*

First, as regards its action on frogs—"After the injection of the poison a gradually increasing torpor then comes over the animal, sometimes beginning some time after the injection, and then proceeding uninterruptedly; at other times being interrupted by occasional movements.

---

* For an account of a fight between a mongoose and a cobra, *vide* "Review."

The limbs are drawn close up to the body, and the head gradually sinks down between the hands in most instances; but sometimes the head is held at first much more erect than usual. The power of motion is lost before that of sensation; for the movements caused by painful stimuli become weaker and weaker, although they may still follow each application of the irritant. The progressive weakness is well shown in the movements of the hind legs. After the frog has sunk down and is lying flat upon the table, pinching the toes causes it to kick vigorously; but by-and-by, instead of kicking, it merely draws away the foot from the irritant with a slow wriggling motion. If it is then lifted up from the table, so as to remove the resistance occasioned by friction, the wriggling entirely disappears, and the foot is promptly and easily drawn up to the body when pinched. This weakness seems to depend on the nervous system rather than on the muscles; for, even in this state of apparent paralysis, the animal occasionally displays considerable muscular power, and is able to spring to a considerable height, as in the following experiment. A similar condition is sometimes observed in warm-blooded animals. The motor paralysis increases, no motion follows the application of any irritant, however powerful; but even then sensation exists. The heart continues to beat after all motion in the body has ceased; but its pulsations become gradually slower, and at last cease altogether."

The action of the poison on lizards and innocuous snakes is similar to that on frogs, viz. :—" a progressive paralysis."

*Action of the poison on lizards and innocuous snakes.*

Fontana found that fish were poisoned by viper poison, and Drs. Fayrer and Brunton believe that cobra-poison causes death by paralysis.

*Action on fish.*

Cobra-poison seems to destroy the irritability of snails. It first causes them to shrink within their shells and finally lessens their movements, when stimulated. Fontana failed to produce any effect on snails with the venom of the viper.

*Action on snails.*

" The activity of the poison is not destroyed, and scarcely impaired, by drying. We have made no comparative experiments with perfectly fresh poison and the dried residue of a similar quantity; but there are few, if any, instances on record of death from the fresh poison in less than half a minute, the time in which the dried poison killed a guineapig.

*The effects of re-agents, &c., on the action of the poison.*

" The local action of the poison, however, seems to be altered by drying; for extravasation of blood around the part where a snake has inserted its fangs, or venom has been injected, is one of the most prominent effects produced by the fresh poison, whereas it is very slight, or absent altogether," when the dried venom has been employed, except in occasional instances.

Dilution seems also to have no effect in lessening the activity of the venom, except so far as it retards absorption; for it is evident that a drop of pure poison, injected subcutaneously, is likely to find its way into the circulation more quickly than the same quantity diluted with a hundred times its bulk of water.

"Coagulation of the venom by alcohol does not destroy its activity, as we have shown in our former communication. The coagulum thrown down by the alcohol is innocuous, or nearly so; but the poisonous principle remains in solution, and the alcoholic extract possesses similar properties to the poison itself. A specimen of poison was received from India in a coagulated state; but we are uncertain whether this occurred spontaneously or was produced by the action of reagents. It is probable, however, that it was due to its having been mixed, in order to preserve it, with alcohol, which had evaporated before we received it.* It was active, as experiment XI shows. Coagulation by boiling does not destroy the activity of the poison; but a portion which was boiled for more than half an hour under pressure corresponding to a tempera- ture of 102° C., had no effect when injected under the thigh of a lark. The notes of this experiment have unfortunately been lost. Admixture with liquor ammoniæ and liquor potassæ does not alter the effects of the poison."

The sample of poison, which had been subjected to a temperature of 100° C, forwarded to us by Mr. Pedler, killed a dog, but the fatal effects were retarded.

Cobra-poison has the effect of interfering with germination, in
Action on germination. which fact, it agrees with rattlesnake-poison (Weir Mitchell).

The action of the poison is most rapid when it is introduced
Effects of the poison when introduced through different channels. directly into the circulation, as by injection into the jugular vein; and in such instances death may occur in less than a minute. When injected into the thoracic cavity, death occurred almost as quickly; but this may have been due to puncture of the lung and introduction of the poison directly into some of the pulmonary vessels.

Injection into the peritoneal cavity comes next in order of rapidity, but a good deal behind the last; and it is followed by subcutaneous injection.

Whatever may be the effect of the venom of the viper or crotalus, the cobra virus produces its poisonous effects tolerably rapidly when swallowed, both in the frog and in warm-blooded animals.

It is also absorbed from the conjunctiva, and produces the characteristic symptoms of poisoning. In one experiment the animal, though affected by the poison, recovered; but in several experiments made by Dr. Fayrer death rapidly occurred after the application of the fresh poison to the conjunctiva.

Regarding the local action of the poison; it acts as a local irritant
The local action of the poison. to the conjunctiva, and occasionally causes congestion of the peritoneal vessels when injected into the abdominal cavity.

"It paralyzes the ends of the motor nerves, and also the muscles of the part into which it has been injected. The muscles are not only deprived of their irritability, but become prone to putrefy. The fresh cobra-poison produces great extravasation of blood around the wound

---

* It was sent by us, and was mixed with alcohol.

through which it has been introduced; but this is not so marked when dried poison is used."

This may possibly be due to the loss of acidity in the poison, and its greater dilution.

The blood of animals killed by cobra-poison generally presents a dark colour, as death is due to failure of the respiration and not of the circulation; but it readily assumes a florid colour when exposed to air. The same is the case with the blood of animals poisoned by daboia-venom.

Action of cobra-poison on the blood.

"Coagulation usually occurs readily and firmly in the blood of animals killed by cobra-poison,* while it is frequently absent from the blood of those killed by that of the daboia. In experiments made in India, this occurred almost invariably; and it is illustrated by experiments II and IV. In experiments I, V, and VI, however, coagulation occurred in the blood of a pigeon and guineapig poisoned by daboia-venom; and a similar occurrence has been sometimes observed by one of us (Dr. Fayrer) in fowls bitten by this snake in India.

"In numerous instances we have been unable to detect any alteration in the blood-corpuscles after death from cobra-poison; but in experiments XXI and XXII we observed a most distinct cremation in the corpuscles of rats poisoned by it. This was probably due in some degree to evaporation, as in experiment XXI it was to a great extent prevented by surrounding the preparation with oil; but it indicates a change in the blood, as the corpuscles did not present this appearance before the injection of the poison—although they were prepared for observation in exactly the same way, and were as much exposed to evaporation in the one case as in the other."

Fontana erroneously insisted that snake-poison had no direct influence on muscle; indeed, that the poison was not even absorbed when applied to it. He arrived at these conclusions by experiments which are evidently fallacious. Our authors, on the contrary, found that "cobra-poison has the power of destroying the irritability of voluntary muscular fibre when applied directly to it, either in a concentrated or diluted condition. It does not produce any quivering of the fibres; and in this particular it differs from the poison of the rattlesnake as described by Dr. Weir Mitchell."

Action on muscle.

The following examples are given :—

## "Experiment.

"*A frog was decapitated, and the skin removed from both hind legs. A longitudinal cut was then made in the muscle of both thighs. A strong solution of the dried cobra-poison in distilled water, of such a strength as to resemble the fresh poison closely in appearance, was then applied to the cut in one thigh, while the other was moistened with distilled water. Immediately after the application an almost imperceptible trembling in the muscles occurred equally in both thighs; but it ceased after a few seconds, and did not reappear. On testing the muscles soon afterwards, by an*

---

* We believe, however, that the state of the blood as regards coagulability is of little importance since it is sometimes found fluid and sometimes coagulated. But in man killed by cobra-poison the blood is almost invariably fluid.

*induced current applied directly to them, those of the poisoned leg contracted feebly, but those of the non-poisoned leg forcibly.*

*"In this experiment, the quivering occurred equally in both thighs, and was therefore obviously due to the water in which the poison was dissolved, and not to the poison itself.*

*"As Weir Mitchell found that the quivering produced by the poison of the rattlesnake was not prevented by paralysis of the motor nerves by curare, the previous experiment was repeated on a curarized frog.*

### " EXPERIMENT.

*"The motor nerves having been tested and found to be completely paralyzed, a strong solution of the cobra-poison was applied to a cut in the back of the right thigh. No quivering of the muscles could be observed after its application. The poison was only applied to the middle of the back of the right thigh. After a few minutes, those muscles with which it had come into contact did not contract when irritated by the direct application of an induced current. Distance of secondary from the primary coil 0. The muscles of the sides and front of the poisoned thigh, as well as those of the other thigh, contracted well when irritated in the same way, with the coil at 13 centimetres.*

"The power of cobra-poison to paralyze muscles when applied to them, even in a diluted condition, is shown by the following experiment :—

### " EXPERIMENT.

*"The legs of a large frog were cut off close to the body, and the skin removed. Each was then placed in a glass, and sufficient quantity of fresh ox-blood serum poured over it. In one glass the serum contained about 5 centigrams of cobra-poison dissolved in about 20 cubic centims. of serum, but, with this exception, all the conditions under which the two legs were placed were exactly alike.*

*"About 19 hours after the immersion of the legs in serum their irritability was examined.*

*"The muscles of the legs in the pure serum did not contract at all when the strongest irritation was applied to the sciatic nerve, but contracted very rigorously when irritated directly. The muscles of the leg in the poisoned serum were whiter than those of the other one. They had a faint yellowish tinge, and were somewhat stiff. They did not contract in the least when the strongest irritation by a Du-Bois coil was applied either to them or the sciatic nerve.*

*"When poison was injected directly in the circulation, or is very rapidly absorbed, so that the quantity circulating in the blood is large, it destroys the irritability of the voluntary muscles rapidly, and, occasionally at least, hastens in a most remarkable manner the occurrence of rigor mortis."*

It is important to remember that all muscles do not lose their irritability with the same rapidity ; the intercostal muscles, serati, and abdominal muscles seem to lose their irritability first. When the poison is slowly absorbed so that a comparatively small quantity circulates in the blood, its action on the muscles is much less marked. This is particularly exemplified in our experiments with artificial respiration.

Weir Mitchell found that snake-poison had a peculiar disorgan-
izing action upon the muscular tissue.
Drs. Fayrer and Brunton, however,
failed to observe it, though they believe
that cobra-poison causes decomposition within the body.

Secondary action of the poison on muscles.

Action on the nervous system.

The following is of such importance
that we give it *in extenso* :—

"The most prominent symptoms of an affection of the nervous
system after the bite of a cobra or other venomous snake, in animals or
man, are depression, faintness, lethargy, and in some cases, somnolence.
There is loss of co-ordinating power, and paralysis, sometimes affecting the
hind legs first and creeping over the body, sometimes affecting the whole
body at once. Death occurs by failure of the respiration, and is preceded
by convulsions.

"These symptoms clearly point to paralysis either of the nervous
centres or of the peripheral nerves. It may be supposed that the
mention of the latter alternative is superfluous, and that paralysis of the
peripheral nerves cannot produce such symptoms, which must therefore,
by exclusion, be due to an affection of the central ganglia. More
especially may the occurrence of convulsions be thought to exclude the
possibility of death being due to paralysis of the peripheral terminations
of motor nerves ; for if their function is abolished here, how, it may be
said, can general convulsions, which have their origin in the nervous
centres, occur ?

"The answer to this is, that although the ends of the motor nerves
are so far deadened that they no longer transmit to the muscles any
ordinary stimulus proceeding from the nerve centres, their function is
not so thoroughly abolished that they cannot transmit those which are
stronger than usual. This is shown by the fact that when an animal
is slowly poisoned by curare (as for example when that poison is introduced into the stomach after ligature of the renal vessels), convulsions
occur just as in death from cobra-poison. Although the motor nerves
have their function so much impaired that they no longer transmit to
the muscles of respiration the ordinary stimuli from the medulla, which
usually keep up the movements of breathing, they can still transmit those
stronger impulses which proceed from it when greatly stimulated by the
increasing venosity of the blood, and which cause the respiratory as well
as the other muscles of the body to participate in the general convulsions.
The loss of co-ordination which occurs in poisoning by cobra-venom,
has also been noticed by Voisin and Liouville in poisoning by curare.

"That the peripheral terminations of the motor nerves are actually
paralyzed by cobra-venom is shown by experiment XXXVI, in which
the animal was able to move the leg which had been protected from the
action of the poison for some time after the rest of the body was
perfectly motionless, as well as by experiment XXXVII, and those
succeeding it. Its occurrence in man is indicated by the symptoms of a
case described by Dr. Hilson (*vide* Report, page 36).

"But paralysis of motor nerves is not the only effect of cobra-poison
on the nervous system. The spinal cord is also paralyzed, as is seen from
experiment XLI, where motion ceased in the frog's leg which remained
free from poison, although it answered with great readiness to a very

weak stimulus applied to its nerve. In some instances paralysis of the spinal cord appeared to cause death when little or no affection of the motor nerves could be observed; but in others the peripheral paralysis was strongly marked. In no case was it more obvious, and in few was it so distinct, as in experiment XXXVI, made with the virus itself, which had neither become coagulated nor dried. In experiments made with the coagulated poison, death seemed invariably to be caused by paralysis of the spinal cord, the motor nerves being little affected; while, in those made with the dried venom, sometimes the action on the cord predominated, and sometimes that on the nerves. In this respect, as well as in some of the symptoms it produces, cobra-poison agrees very closely with conia. This alkaloid, as Crum-Brown and Fraser have shown, often contains a mixture of true conia and methylconia. Conia alone paralyzes the motor nerves without affecting the spinal cord; but when mixed with methylconia, sometimes the one is affected first, and sometimes the other. When the dose is small, the motor nerves are usually paralyzed before the reflex function of the cord; but when the dose is large, the cord is paralyzed before the nerves. Methylconia also affects both; but a small dose of it paralyzes the cord before the nerves, while a large one paralyzes them first. The paralysis of the hind legs, often observed in snake-poisoning, is probably partly due to the local action of the poison in the nerves and muscles of the bitten member, and partly to its action on the cord. This paralysis is noticed in Genesis xlix., 17, where Jacob says, 'Dan is an adder in the path, biting the horse-heels, so that the rider falleth backward.' In this point cobra-venom, when dried, appears to resemble methylconia rather than its admixture with conia; but it exercises numerous other actions upon the blood, muscles, &c., which neither of these substances has been shown to do. It is doubtful whether the cerebrum is directly affected by cobra-poison, as the intelligence both in man and animals often remains almost unimpaired to the last, and the stupor and drowsiness which are sometimes noticed may be caused indirectly, by the action of the venom on the motor and vaso-motor nerves and on the functions of the cord. The reflex centres through which irritation of the fifth nerve acts, remain unaffected after the reflex function of the cord is nearly gone; and even then the power of voluntary motion still exists.

" The effect of the poison upon the respiratory and vaso-motor nerves will be considered under the heads of respiration and circulation.

" As the contraction of a muscle, on irritation of the motor nerve supplying it, is the index by which we judge of the irritability of the nerve itself, the paralyzing effect of cobra-poison upon muscle renders the exact determination of its action upon motor nerves much more difficult than in the case of such a poison as curare, which leaves the muscular irritability intact. For the failure of a muscle to contract on irritation of its motor nerve, can be due only to paralysis of the motor nerve in the case of curare; but in poisoning by cobra-venom it may be due to enfeeblement of the muscles, as well as paralysis of the nerve. But if we find instances in which the muscles still retain their irritability almost unaltered, and respond readily to direct stimulation after they have

*Action on motor nerves.*

ceased to contract on irritation of their motor nerve, we are justified in saying that the nerve is paralyzed; and such is sometimes the case.

"In experiment XXV this action on the ends of motor nerves is all the more evident from the paralysis being most complete in the part where the poison was introduced. At this part, it was brought, in a concentrated state, into contact with the ends of the motor nerves, while the other parts of the body received it after dilution with the blood; and in them the paralysis was much less marked.

"The paralysis of the hind legs, so often noticed in experiments, appears to be due, at least in considerable measure, to the local action of the poison on the ends of the motor nerves of the legs, as the injection or bite is often made on the flank or thigh."

The following experiment proves conclusively that paralysis of the motor nerves is caused by snake-poison.

### Experiment.

*In order to test the action of cobra-poison on the ends of the motor nerves, without disturbing the experiment by ligaturing one leg, two frogs were taken of as nearly as possible the same size. Both were very small; but No. 1 was somewhat larger and stronger than No. 2. The sciatic nerve was exposed in one thigh of each frog and placed on the hook electrodes used by Marey for his myograph. By means of a Pohl's commutator, with the cross pieces taken out, an interrupted current could be sent at will through either nerve. The distance of the secondary from the primary coil at which the first faint contraction took place in the muscles of either nerve was noted.*

|  | Time. | Frog 1. | Frog 2. |  |
|---|---|---|---|---|
| *About* | 1·25 | 17·7 | 22 | |
| | 1·40 | 26·3 | 12·3 | |
| | 1·46 | 26 | 18 | *Injected a solution of dried cobra-poison in water into dorsal lymph-sac of frog No. 1.* |
| | 2·7 | 31·2 | 24 | |
| | 2·27 | 31 | 18·5 | |
| | 2·50 | 24 | 17·8 | |
| | 3·10 | 17·5 | 19·2 | *Frog 1 moved the fore legs when the coil was at such a distance (19 f) that no movement occurred in leg when nerve was irritated.* |
| | 3·30 | 12 | 17·5 | |
| | 3·40 | 10·5 | 15·5 | |
| | 4 | 10 | 33 | |
| | 4·17 | 9 | 37 | |
| | 4·30 | 11 | 18 | *At 37 voluntary movements occurred in legs of frog 2.* |
| | 4·50 | 8 | 37 | |
| | 4·55 | ... | ... | *The brains of both frogs destroyed.* |
| | 4·58 | 7·5 | 16·5 | |

*May 21st.—The sciatics of the other legs were exposed and irritated.*

Distance of primary from secondary coil.

| Time. | Frog 1. | Frog 2. | |
|---|---|---|---|
| ... | 0 | 11·5 | *Frog 1, no contraction. Frog 2, slight contraction. The irritability of the muscles was now tested by single induced shocks applied to them.* |
| ... | 0 | 7·5 | *Frog 1, no contraction. Frog 2, slight contraction.* |

The sensory are little, if at all, affected by cobra-poison; they retain their power after the motor nerves are paralyzed.

As to the action of the poison on the spinal cord, Drs. Fayrer and Brunton think they are justified

*Action of the poison on the spinal cord.*

in concluding that the grey matter of spinal cord, through which painful impressions are transmitted, is paralyzed by cobra-poison; but the white sensory columns are little, if at all, affected. "The power of the cord to conduct motor impressions from the encephalic ganglia appears to be little, if at all, affected, until the apparent death of the animal; for in experiment LX we find that, very shortly before respiration ceased, and when ordinary reflex action from the cord was nearly gone, purposive or voluntary movements were still made. The absence of movements in experiment L, when the cord was irritated by a needle, as well as the rapid loss of its power to produce movement in the limbs when irritated by a Faradic current, is, we think, to be attributed to paralysis of its function as an originator, and not as a conductor, of motor impressions."

One of the most noticeable, constant and distressing symptoms of snake-poisoning is vomiting. Particu-

*Action on the stomach and intestines.*

larly is it the case in Australian snake-poisoning. Drs. Fayrer and Brunton believe that as the nervous centre by which the act of vomiting is originated is closely connected with the respiratory centre, it may be caused by an impression conveyed to it by the branches of the vagus. The vomiting is in all probability due, partly to irritation of the gastric or abdominal branches of the vagus, though not entirely since they found that attempts were made to vomit after the vagus had been divided at the neck.

"The action of cobra-poison upon respiration," observe Drs. Fayrer and Brunton, "is, perhaps, the most

*Effects upon respiration.*

important of those which it exerts upon the organism; for it is through this action that death is generally caused. The respiratory movements, besides being frequently altered in form, are generally quickened after the introduction of the poison; then the number sinks to the normal or even below it; they become weaker and, finally, cease altogether. The blood being no longer aërated, becomes more and more venous, and, by irritating either the respiratory centre itself, or some nervous centre closely associated with it, occasions general convulsions. These disappear whenever artificial respiration is begun and the blood again aërated; while they reappear when the respiration is discontinued and the blood regains its venous character."

10

If reference be made to our experiments, with artificial respiration, this condition will be observed to have been of frequent occurrence. We have seen an animal struggling most violently, become perfectly still immediately on the commencement of artificial respiration.

"After they have continued a short while the convulsions cease; for the venous blood does not maintain the vitality of the nervous centres sufficiently to keep them in action; but if artificial respiration be recommenced, the first effect of aërating the blood is to renew the convulsions, by increasing the vitality of the nervous centres, and rendering them again susceptible to the action of a stimulus, though the convulsions disappear as soon as the arterialization has proceeded sufficiently far.

"Increased rapidity of the respiratory movements may depend either upon greater excitability of the respiratory centre in the medulla, or upon stimulation of some of the afferent nerves which have the power to accelerate it. The chiefs of these are the pulmonary branches of the vagus, though there are probably others proceeding from the cerebrum, through which the emotions influence the breathing, and others from the general surface of the body.

"In order to ascertain the cause of the acceleration of respiration several experiments were made. Experiment LXIII shows that it is not due to the action of the poison on the cerebrum, for it occurs after the cerebral lobes have been removed. The ultimate arrest of respiration is probably due, in part, to paralysis of the medulla, and, in part, to paralysis of the motor nerves distributed to the respiratory muscles. The complete insensibility of the phrenic nerve to the strongest stimuli while the sciatics and vagus still retained a considerable amount of irritability, in experiments XLIV and LXVI, is very remarkable. The want of co-ordination between the diaphragm and the thoracic muscles in experiment IX is not improbably due to paralysis of the phrenic nerve, though it may be attributed to some alteration in the respiratory centre. Brown-Séquard states that the diaphragm contains ganglia which will keep up rhythmical movements in it after the central nervous system has been destroyed; if this statement is correct, it seems probable that paralysis of the phrenic, by interrupting the connexion between the respiratory centres in the medulla and those in the diaphragm, may allow the movements of the thoracic respiratory muscles and of the diaphragm to occur one after the other instead of simultaneously."

It will be observed, therefore, that the stoppage of respiration results from paralysis of the medulla and motor nerves of the muscles of respiration; but to what extent it depends on either in each case, it is impossible to say. We are inclined, however, to the belief that the *cessation* of respiration depends *generally* on the former.

Action on the circulation. The action of the poison on the circulatory apparatus is thus given :—

"In most cases of death from cobra-poison, the fatal issue is not to be attributed to any failure of the circulatory apparatus; for the heart continues to pulsate vigorously, long after all motions have ceased in the voluntary muscles, and the strongest irritation applied to the spinal cord and motor nerves fails to produce the slightest effect. But this only occurs when the dose of poison is not excessive ; and when a large quantity of it is introduced, at once, into the circulation, the heart is not exempted from its action, but is, on the contrary, most seriously affected. This is seen in experiments LXVIII and XXVIII where the poison having been either injected into the circulation, or absorbed with extreme rapidity, the action of the heart was at once arrested. But it is to be noted that it is not paralysis, but tetanic contraction of the heart, which is produced, the poison, in fact, seeming to act as an excessive stimulus ; and this being the case, we feel less surprise on finding that, in ordinary cases of poisoning, the cardiac action may be maintained by the use of artificial respiration for more than thirty hours, as Mr. Richards has succeeded in doing in India."

We believe that instances of death from tetanus of the heart, in cases of snake-bite in human beings, are comparatively rare. In fact, they are quite the exception. Should snake-poison be directly injected into the circulation, death may occur in this manner, but even then, unless the quantity is large, we are inclined to the opinion that, death would result rather from a combination of the lethal effects of the poison upon the respiratory centre, and ganglia of the heart.

"The action of cobra-poison being exerted on the heart of the frog after its excision, shows that it acts on the heart itself ; and its effect being very much the same without the body as within it renders it probable that the central nervous system is little concerned in the arrest of circulation by the poison, at least in the frog.

" The stoppage of the excised heart may be due (1) to irritation of the inhibitory centres contained within it, or (2) to paralysis of its motor ganglia, or (3) to excessive stimulation of them producing tetanus, or (4) to the action of the poison on the muscular fibre of the organ. It is not due to the first of these causes ; for atropia, which paralyzes the inhibitory ganglia, does not restore the movements. The second is improbable, as the heart does not stop in diastole but in systole, and resists distention by fluid within it. The third seems the most probable cause, as one does not see why the poison should arrest the cardiac pulsations at once when applied, to the interior of the organ, and not do so when placed on the outside, if it acted on the muscular fibre, whereas it may readily be supposed that the poison may reach the ganglia more readily from the inner side of the heart—though we do not venture to assert that this is the true explanation of the facts we have observed.

" The inhibitory branches of the vagus are not always paralyzed ; but sometimes the cobra-poison appears to affect them as well as the motor nerves ; and in this it resembles curare, which in small doses does not impair the inhibitory action of the vagus, but in large doses completely destroys it.

" The capillary circulation is not unaffected by the poison. In experiment IV of our former paper, the rhythmical contractions and dilatations, altogether independent of the cardiac pulsations, which Schiff first observed in the rabbit's ear, and which were noticed by Ludwig and Brunton in the vessels of many parts of the body, were greatly increased by the injection of the poison."

*The following experiment is particularly interesting as demonstrating the direct effect on the heart.*

### EXPERIMENT.

A canula was placed in the aorta, and another in the vena cava of a frog. All branches were tied, the heart excised, and placed in connexion with H. P. Bowditch's apparatus for keeping a stream of serum circulating through the heart and recording its pulsation by means of a manometer on a revolving cylinder. When fed with pure serum, the heart's contractions were regular and strong; but whenever serum containing dried cobra-poison in solution (in the proportion of about two grains in three fluid drachms) was introduced into the apparatus, the heart stopped almost immediately. As will be seen from the accompanying tracing, it became partially contracted and gave one or two feeble beats; but did not dilate, and then remained still, the contraction, however, very slowly and gradually increasing.

These tracings were obtained from a frog's heart by means of a small mercurial manometer connected by the aorta. The tracings all read from right to left.

1. Tracing obtained from the heart supplied with pure serum by means of a tube in the vena cava.
2. Tracing of the same kind, with the addition of the line A, which indicates the zero of the mercury. The tracing B, given by the heart, sinks down to zero during each diastole.
3. Tracing given by the heart after it had been supplied with serum containing a small quantity of cobra-poison in solution. The heart makes a few ineffectual attempts, but can neither contract nor relax, and remains still, in a condition midway between complete systole and complete diastole. The line A is the zero to which B would sink if the heart relaxed completely during diastole.

Drs. Fayrer and Brunton believe that the poison " is excreted by the kidneys and mammary glands, and probably also by the salivary glands and mucous membrane of the stomach. A case reported by Mr. Shircore, of Calcutta, in which an infant, suckled by its mother after

Excretion of the poison.

she had been bitten by a snake (species unknown), died in two hours after it had partaken of the milk, shows that the poison is excreted by the mammary glands, and with considerable rapidity; for the child took the breast before any marked symptoms had occurred in the mother. Its excretion by the kidneys appears from an experiment of Mr. Richards, of Balasoro, who found that some urine from a dog poisoned by the bite of a sea-snake (*Enhydrina Bengalensis*) killed a pigeon in 22 hours after being hypodermically injected. Some saliva, which we obtained from the sub-maxillary gland of a dog poisoned by cobra-venom, had no effect when injected under the skin of the thigh of a lark; but the Snake-poison Commission found that one drachm of the greenish liquid which flowed from the mouth of a dog poisoned by cobra-venom killed a pigeon in two hours. As this fluid flowed constantly from the mouth, and the animal was paralyzed and motionless, it seems probable that, notwithstanding its colour, it was saliva and not bile."

Although that desirable object, the discovery of an antidote, has not yet been attained, much good work

The different ways in which snake-poison has lately been done in elucidating the may cause death. physiological action of the poison. We have shown, in our "review" that until very recently absolute ignorance prevailed, and it is mainly due to the ability and untiring zeal of Drs. Fayrer and Brunton, that so much light has been thrown on the subject. The more we know of the action of the poison, the more likely are we to discover its antidote; and it is only by the most patient and impartial investigation that we can ever hope to succeed.

*Snake-poison causes death in either of the following ways:—*

*Firstly.*—By tetanising the heart, and so stopping the circulation of the blood.

*Secondly.*—By paralyzing the muscles of respiration, and so giving rise to asphyxia. (This is by far the most common cause of death.)

*Thirdly.*—By a combination of the above two causes.

*Lastly.*—By septicæmia. (This latter occurs but seldom, and only when small doses of the poison have been injected.

(Sd.) JOSEPH EWART, M.D., .. *President.*

VINCENT RICHARDS, M.R.C.S., } *Members.*

S. CQULL MACKENZIE, M.D., }

# INDEX TO APPENDIX NO. I.

|  |  | PAGE. |
|---|---|---|
| Artificial respiration in cobra-bite ... ... ... ... ... | | i—viii |
| Ditto | with half the poison of a cobra... ... ... | viii |
| Ditto | with 2½ grains of cobra-poison ... ... ... | x—xiii |
| Ditto | with 2 grains of poison ... ... ... | x |
| Ditto | with 1 grain of poison ... ... ... | xiii—xvi |
| Ditto | with ½ grain of poison ... ... ... | xvii—xix |
| Ditto | with ¼ grain of poison ... ... ... | xx |
| Artificial respiration in snake-poisoning and the exhibition of— | | |
| Acid, Acetic ... ... ... ... ... ... | | xxviii |
| Do., Phosphoric ... ... ... ... ... | | xxviii |
| Do., Sulphuric ... ... ... ... ... | | xxvi |
| Ammonia ... ... ... ... ... ... | | xxi—xxiii |
| Ditto and Transfusion... ... ... ... ... | | xxiii |
| Atropine ... ... ... ... ... ... | | xxx |
| Chloral Hydrate ... ... ... ... ... | | xxvii |
| Emetine ... ... ... ... ... ... | | xxix |
| Morphia ... ... ... ... ... ... | | xxiii |
| Podophyllin ... ... ... ... ... ... | | xxix & xxxi |
| Strychnine ... ... ... ... ... ... | | xxv—xxvii |
| Transfusion ... ... ... ... ... ... | | xxiv & xxxi |
| Tr. Cannabis Indica ... ... ... ... ... | | xxviii |
| Tr. of Iodine ... ... ... ... ... | | xxxii |
| Antidotes—Experiments with ... ... ... ... | | xliii—lii |
| Acid, Acetic ... ... ... ... ... ... | | l |
| Do., Hydrochloric ... ... ... ... ... | | l |
| Do., Nitric ... ... ... ... ... | | xlix & l |
| Do., Phosphoric ... ... ... ... ... | | l |
| Do., Sulphuric ... ... ... ... ... | | xlix |
| Ammonia—Intravenous injection of ... ... ... ... | | liii—lvii |
| Baptisin ... ... ... ... ... ... | | xlvii |
| Bichloride of Mercury ... ... ... ... ... | | xlviii |
| Brandy and Opium ... ... ... ... ... | | xliii & xlv |
| Cannabis Indica ... ... ... ... ... | | xlviii |
| Chloral Hydrate ... ... ... ... ... | | xlvii |
| Iridin ... ... ... ... ... ... | | xlvii |
| Leptandrin ... ... ... ... ... ... | | xlviii |
| Liquor Arsenicalis ... ... ... ... ... | | xlvii |
| Magnesia, Sulphate of ... ... ... ... ... | | xlv |
| Morphia ... ... ... ... ... ... | | xlv |
| Nicotin ... ... ... ... ... ... | | xlviii |
| Opium ... ... ... ... ... ... | | xliii—xlv |
| Strychnine ... ... ... ... ... ... | | xlv & xlvi |
| Miscellaneous experiments ... ... ... ... | | li—liii |
| Snake-bite ... ... ... ... ... ... | | xxxiii |
| Snake-poison—Administration of ... ... ... ... | | liii |
| Ditto | Hypodermic injection of ... ... ... ... | xxx—xlii & lii |
| Ditto | Injection of—into the peritoneal cavity ... ... | xlii & xliii |
| Ditto | Intravenous injection of ... ... ... ... | xliii |

# INDEX TO APPENDIX NO. II.

|  |  |  |  |  |  |  | PAGES |
|---|---|---|---|---|---|---|---|
| Snake-bite with ammonia injection— | | | | | | | |
| Ditto | ditto | death in | | | ... | ... | lxiii |
| Ditto | ditto | ,, | | | ... | ... | lxiii |
| Ditto | ditto | ,, | | | ... | ... | lxiv |
| Ditto | ditto | ,, | | | ... | ... | lxv |
| Ditto | ditto | ,, | | | ... | ... | lxvi |
| Ditto | ditto | recovery in | | | ... | ... | lxiv |
| Ditto | without ammonia— | | | | | | |
| Ditto | ditto | death in | ... | ... | ... | ... | lxiii |
| Ditto | ditto | ,, | ... | ... | ... | ... | lxvi |
| Ditto | ditto | recovery in | ... | ... | ... | ... | lxvi |
| Ditto | ditto | ,, ,, | ... | ... | ... | ... | lxvii |
| Snake-poison, hypodermic injection of, with ammonia— | | | | | | | |
| Ditto | ditto | death in | ... | ... | | | lx |
| Ditto | ditto | ,, | ... | ... | | | lxi |
| Ditto | ditto | ,, | ... | ... | | | lxii |
| Ditto | ditto | without ammonia— | | | | | |
| Ditto | ditto | death in | ... | ... | ... | ... | lix |
| Ditto | ditto | ,, | ... | ... | ... | ... | lxi |
| Ditto | ditto | recovery in | ... | ... | ... | ... | lxii |

# APPENDIX No. I.

## FIRST SERIES.

### Artificial respiration with varying doses of snake-poison.

#### No. 1.

A DOG was bitten by a cobra, at 7-30 A.M. The bite not being considered satisfactory, another cobra was made to bite the dog, at 7-40 A.M.

7-59 A.M.—The animal is extremely restless; passed water.

8-10 A.M.—The respiration is hurried, and there are spasmodic twitchings about the mouth.

8-12.—Universal convulsions.

8-15.—The dog to all appearances is dead; the heart's action was at first regular, but afterwards irregular. Commenced artificial respiration.

9-15 A.M.—The heart is beating rapidly but, without force; lachrymation; no response to galvanism.

9-40 A.M.—The heart is beating well; temperature 101° 2′.

11-15 A.M.—The bellows slipped out of the trachea owing to the carelessness of the man manipulating it.

1 P.M.—The heart is beating well; passed fœces after having had two enemas of hot water. Pupils dilate by galvanism.

2-30 P.M.—Passed water in a good stream after the application of galvanism. Dilatation of pupils by galvanism.

6-30 P.M.—The heart is beating well.

8-10 P.M.—In the same state.

10 P.M.—The lungs were not being properly inflated; the nozzle of the bellows was found to be occluded with inspissated mucus; the heart was at first beating very feebly, but on the removal of the impediment to free respiration it began to beat vigorously again.

11-30 P.M.—Heart beating well.

MIDNIGHT.—Heart beating feebly; lungs not properly inflated; cleared the tube of the bellows.

12-30 A.M.—Heart's action very weak; body cold.

1-5 A.M.—Heart ceased to beat, 16 hours and 50 minutes after the commencement of artificial respiration.

*N.B.*—This experiment can scarcely be called a test, as not only had we no intention, at first, of performing artificial respiration, but the appliances at our command were of the most primitive nature.

## No. 2.

A dog was bitten by a cobra, at 8-16 A.M.; normal temperature 101° 8′.

8-35 A.M.—Temperature 101° 8′.

8-45 A.M.—Commenced artificial respiration (29 minutes after the bite).

9 A.M.—Temperature 101° 1 .

10 A.M.—Temperature 101°; respirations 44 ; pulse beating very quickly and forcibly; dilatation of the pupils in response to galvanism.

11-55 A.M.—Heart ceased to, beat, 3 hours and 10 minutes after the commencement of artificial respiration.

*N.B.*—The dog was small, and the cobra a large vigorous one.

## No. 3.

A dog was bitten by a cobra at 8 A.M.

8-14 A.M.—The animal is very restless.

8-20 A.M.—Respiration laborious ; is whining and is greatly distressed.

8-40 A.M.—Convulsed.

8-45 A.M.—Commenced artificial respiration ; the pupils, which were fully dilated, became normal and the convulsions ceased; the animal then appeared sensible.

9 A.M.—Heart beating 68 per minute; occasional universal convulsions; lachrymation and blinking of the eye-lids.

9-30 A.M.—Heart beating forcibly, 136 ; respirations 40 ; temperature 101° 8′; universal convulsions ; irides act; lachrymation ; applied heat.

10-15 A.M.—Respirations 40 ; heart beating so rapidly as to render it impossible to count the beats ; tremor of the hind quarters ; irides act by galvanism ; temperature 101° 8′; salivation has been going on since the commencement of artificial respiration.

11-5 A.M.—Respirations 44 ; heart beating 180, not very strongly ; temperature 102°; no response to galvanism.

12-5 P.M.—Respirations 40 ; heart beating 160, not very strongly ; temperature 103° 1′; the only response to galvanism is micturition ; this occurred again at 12-30 P.M. ; pupils have been dilated since the irides ceased to act.

12-50 P.M.—Respirations 46 ; pupils are now contracted and the irides respond to galvanism ; heart beating regularly and pretty strongly, 168 ; temperature 103° 6′; the mucous membrane of the mouth, and the tongue have somewhat recovered their natural colour.

1-30 P.M.—Irides act by galvanism ; turned the dog over on to its right side ; the animal passed water in a pretty good stream ; respirations 44 ; heart beating extremely rapidly ; temperature 104° 5′.

2-15 P.M.—Respirations 44 ; temperature 105° 1′; heart beating very rapidly ; the only response to galvanism is micturition.

3-15 P.M.—Respirations 44 ; heart beating too rapidly to count ; pupils normal, but dilate by galvanism ; temperature 106° 4′; the tube had become twisted, and so artificial respiration was not complete;

changed the bellows at 4 P.M., as the air was escaping, but the air escapes from the present one also.

4-15 P.M.—Heart beating feebly and rapidly; irides act, but very slightly; respirations 36; temperature 106° 3'.

5-12 P.M.—Heart ceased to beat, 7 hours and 27 minutes after the commencement of artificial respiration; temperature when the heart ceased to beat 107° 8'.

---

## No. 4.

A large dog was bitten by a cobra, at 7-15 A.M.

7-30 A.M.—Respirations much hurried, sometimes 100 or more; pulse slow (80); temperature 103°.

7-45 A.M.—Respirations not so hurried (80); pulse slower (60); temperature falling, 102° 3'.

7-50 A.M.—Appears much distressed, and is salivated.

7-58 A.M.—Convulsed.

7-59 A.M.—Commenced artificial respiration; the convulsions at once ceased, but returned immediately on interruption of the artificial respiration; the pupils from being widely dilated became contracted; the animal appears to be sensible.

8-7 A.M.—Pulse 160; respirations 40; pupils natural; blinking of the lids; temperature 102°; applied heat.

8-24 A.M.—Convulsive movements of the hind quarters.

8-47 A.M.—In the same state.

9 A.M.—Pulse beating rapidly, 176; respirations 32; pupils normal; temperature 101° 4' (has been gradually falling from the commencement); dilatation of the pupils only in response to galvanism.

10 A.M.—Pulse 140; respirations 40; temperature now rising, 102° 6'; dilatation of the pupils and micturition in response to galvanism; lachrymation and salivation going on continually.

10-30 A.M.—Respirations 32; pulse (femoral) 176; temperature 103°; dilatation of the pupils and micturition in response to galvanism.

11 A.M.—Respirations 32; temperature 103° 2'; pulse, very rapid, about 200; dilatation of the pupils in response to galvanism.

NOON.—Pulse 160; respirations 32; dilatation of the pupils and micturition in response to galvanism; temperature 103° 4'.

1 P.M.—Pulse (femoral) good, 160; respirations 44; temperature 103° 2'; urine passed, and pupils dilated in response to galvanism.

2 P.M.—Pulse (femoral) pretty strong, 176; respirations 40; temperature the same, 103° 2'. The same response to galvanism.

3 P.M.—Pulse regular but quick, about 200; respirations 36; temperature 103° 4'. The same response to galvanism.

4 P.M.—Pulse 160, regular, but weaker. Very slight action of the irides, and micturition in response to galvanism; temperature 105°.

5 P.M.—Pulse 176, very weak; respirations 36; temperature 104° 2'.

6 P.M.—Pulse 166, very weak; respirations 42; temperature 104°.

7 P.M.—Pulse 160, stronger; respirations 39, temperature 103° 5'.

8 P.M.—Pulse 176, pretty strong; respirations 42; temperature 103° 7'.

9 P.M.—Respirations 32; temperature 103° 7′; pulse too quick to count; irides act by galvanism.

10-10 P.M.—Pulse good, 128; respirations 32; temperature 104° 5′; micturition and dilatation of the pupils on the application of galvanism.

11 P.M.—Pulse pretty good, 160; respirations 36; temperature 104°; pupils dilate by galvanism.

MIDNIGHT.—Pulse pretty good, 160; respirations 36; temperature 105°; micturition only in response to galvanism.

1-5 A.M.—Heart ceased to beat, 17 hours and 6 minutes after the commencement of artificial respiration; temperature 105° 2′.

---

## No. 5.

A dog was bitten by a cobra, at 6-50 A.M; temperature 103°; (rectum full).

7 A.M.—Temperature 103° 8′; (rectum now empty).

7-10 A.M.—Temperature 103° 6′.

7-55 A.M.—Convulsed; temperature 105°.

8 A.M.—Commenced artificial respiration.

8-3 A.M.—Temperature 100° 1′.

8-5 A.M.—Slight convulsive movements.

8-12 A.M.—Respirations 36; pulse over 200, pretty regular; temperature 103°.

8-42 A.M.—Universal convulsions in response to galvanism.

9-12 A.M.—Temperature 103° 8′; respirations 36; heart beating very quickly, but without force.

10 A.M.—Temperature 101° 8′; respirations 40; pulse 160, not very strong. Action of the irides, and micturition in response to galvanism.

11 A.M.—Temperature 10° 28′; respirations 36; pulse 176, pretty strong. Slight action of the irides, and micturition in response to galvanism.

NOON.—Temperature 104° 4′; respirations 40; pulse 180, weak. Irides do not act, but there is micturition by galvanism.

1 P.M.—Temperature 103° 6′; respirations 36; pulse 140, weak; pupils dilate, and water is passed in response to galvanism.

2 P.M.—Had passed fœces; temperature 105° 2′; respirations 36; no reflex action of any kind; heart beating too quickly to count.

3 P.M.—Had passed a stool; temperature 105° 4′; femoral could not be felt, and the heart was beating very feebly.

3-20 P.M.—Heart ceased to beat, 7 hours and 20 minutes after the commencement of artificial respiration.

NOTE.—Artificial respiration was not complete, as we found the lungs much congested.

---

## No. 6.

A dog was bitten by a cobra, at 7-17 A.M.; temperature 102° 4′.

7-25 A.M.—Temperature 102° 2′.

7-34 A.M.—Temperature 101° 8′; extremely restless.

7-40 A.M.—Temperature 101° 6′; convulsed.

7-43 A.M.—Commenced artificial respiration. The pupils were dilated and the animal was much convulsed. The pupils gradually assumed their natural appearance and convulsions ceased. The dog shakes its ear when a fly settles on it.

8-8 A.M.—Temperature 101° 4′.

8-30 A.M.—Temperature 101° 3′; the heart is beating steadily and well, 100; respirations 36.

9-30 A.M.—Temperature 101° 2′; respirations 28, much too slow; pulse 200, strong and regular; the usual response to galvanism.

10-30 A.M.—Temperature 100° 2′; respirations 36; pulse good, 144.

11-30 A.M.—Temperature the same, 100° 2′; respirations 32; pulse 112, very strong; same response to galvanism.

12-30 P.M.—Temperature 98°; respirations 32.

1-20 P.M.—Heart ceased to beat, 5 hours and 37 minutes after the commencement of artificial respiration.

---

## No. 7.

A dog was bitten by a cobra, at 8-25 A.M.; temperature 103° 2′.

8-35 A.M.—Temperature 103° 4′.

8-44 A.M.—Temperature 103°; convulsed.

8-50 A.M.—Commenced artificial respiration; the pupils were at first dilated, but afterwards became natural.

9-5 A.M.—Temperature 103°; applied heat; pulse 36; respirations 60.

10 A.M.—Temperature 101° 6′; respirations 40; pulse beating very rapidly; no response to galvanism.

11 A.M.—Temperature 103° 8′; respirations 40; pulse 200; urine passed, and pupils dilated by galvanism.

NOON.—Pulse 190; temperature 103° 5′; respirations 42; pupils dilate by galvanism.

1 P.M.—Respirations 44; pulse 180; one pupil only dilates when galvanism is applied; temperature 105°.

2 P.M.—Respirations 42; pulse 172; temperature 104°; no dilatation of the pupils in response to galvanism.

3 P.M.—Respirations 44; pulse 190; femoral artery's pulsations cannot be felt; temperature 103° 8′.

4 P.M.—Temperature 104° 4′; respirations 40; pulse (femoral) beating very rapidly; no response to galvanism.

5 P.M.—Temperature 104° 7′; respirations 36; pulse 200; no response to galvanism.

5 P.M.—Temperature 104° 2′; respirations 36; pulse about 200, and pretty strong.

7-30 P.M.—The heart is beating quickly, but pretty strongly; respirations 44; temperature 104° 2′; tears are being secreted; no response to galvanism.

9-30 P.M.—Heart ceased to beat, 12 hours and 40 minutes after the commencement of artificial respiration.

## No. 8.

A dog was bitten by a cobra, at 8 A.M.; temperature 101° 6'.

8-15 A.M.—Temperature has risen to 102°.

8-20 A.M.—Temperature 102° 4'.

8-30 A.M.—Temperature 102°.

8-52 A.M—Again bitten by another cobra.

8-58 A.M.—Temperature 102° 5'; convulsed.

9-5 A.M.—Commenced artificial respiration; temperature 102° 5'.

9-20 A.M.—Temperature 101° 6'; the heart did not begin to beat either so forcibly or well as usual; respirations 44; applied heat.

10-20 A.M.—Temperature 101° 1'; pulse 100, pretty strong; respirations 40.

11 A.M.—Temperature 101° 6'; pulse very quick, and weak respirations, 56; irides and bladder act by galvanism.

Noon.—Temperature 103° 2'; pulse 160, but very irregular; respirations 44; bladder act by galvanism.

1 P.M.—Respirations 36; temperature 104° 2'; pulse very quick and weak; a few drops of urine were passed on applying galvanism.

2 P.M.—Temperature 104° 2'; respirations 36; pulse beating very rapidly, and without force; no response to the galvanic current.

3 P.M.—Temperature 104° 2'; respirations 44; pulse beating rapidly; no response to the galvanic current.

4 P.M.—Temperature 103°; respirations 36; heart beating very rapidly, and is extremely weak.

4-20 P.M.—Heart ceased to beat, 7 hours and 15 minutes after the commencement of artificial respiration.

N.B.—In this instance the blood only imperfectly coagulated.

---

## No. 9.

A middling-sized dog was bitten by a cobra, at 8-20 A.M.; temperature 103°.

8-28 A.M.—Passed a stool.

8-30 A.M.—Temperature 104° 2'.

8-45 A.M.—Fell over; temperature 104° 8'; pulse 132; respirations 36.

8-55 A.M.—Commenced artificial respiration. This dog was scarcely convulsed at all at the time, though it appeared perfectly dead soon after it fell over.

9-5 A.M.—Temperature 105°; respirations 44; pulse 134, pretty strong; slight convulsions have occurred since the commencement of artificial respiration; the pupils are normal.

10 A.M.—Temperature 103°; respirations 44; heart beating very rapidly and with but litle force.

Noon.—Respirations 40; heart beating extremely rapidly and without force; temperature 105°; passes water in response to the galvanic current.

1 P.M.—The heart can scarcely be felt beating; temperature 104°.

1-10 P.M.—Heart ceased to beat, 4 hours and 15 minutes after the commencement of artificial respiration.

*N.B.*—This dog was the smallest yet operated on.

## No. 10.

A dog was bitten by a cobra, at 7-52 A.M.; temperature 103°; had first given an enema to the dog as the temperature varies considerably according to the state of the rectum as regards contents.

8-10 A.M.—The temperature has fallen to 102° 8′; the animal is much purged.

8-20 A.M.—Convulsed.

8-23 A.M.—Commenced artificial respiration; the pupils from being widely dilated become perfectly natural; convulsions ceased and sensibility returned; sensibility lasted for an unusually long time, viz., from 8-23 A.M. until 9-12 A.M. when it was lost; temperature 102°.

10 A.M.—Heart beating quickly and very forcibly, respirations 50; temperature 100° 8′.

11 A.M.—Heart, respirations, and temperature, the same; irides act by galvanism.

11-30 A.M.—Belly, all at once, became tympanitic; the bases of the lungs are evidently congested; heart has been beating very irregularly.

Noon.—Temperature 104°; heart beating very strongly, though slowly; respirations 46; heart, irides, and bladder respond to galvanism, especially the heart.

1 P.M.—Exactly the same in all respects.

2 P.M.—Temperature 104°; respirations 44.

3 P.M.—Respirations 46; pulse very rapid and weak; temperature 105°.

4 P.M.—Respirations 44; temperature 103° 8′; heart 190.

5 P.M.—Temperature 103° 3′; respirations 48; heart strong, 200; irides act very slightly indeed in response to galvanism.

6 P.M.—Temperature 102° 9′; respirations 48, heart strong, 200; irides respond but slightly to galvanism.

8 P.M.—Temperature 103°; heart beating very rapidly and tolerably strongly, over 200; respirations 48.

10 P.M.—Temperature 103°; heart beating 160; respirations 48; no response to galvanism.

11 P.M.—In the same state.

Midnight.—Temperature 103°; respirations 48; heart beating very rapidly.

1 A.M.—Heart beating very feebly; respirations 44; temperature 105°.

1-25 A.M.—Heart ceased to beat, 17 hours and 2 minutes after the commencement of artificial respiration.

## No. 11.

First gave the dog an enema; temperature 103°. It was bitten at 7-50 A.M.

8 A.M.—Temperature 104°.

8-20 A.M.—Temperature 104°.

8-37 A.M.—Is much affected.

8-38 A.M.—Is convulsed.

8-40 A.M.—Commenced artificial respiration.

9-10 A.M.—Temperature 101° 1'; had a sharp convulsive movement; is now perfectly senseless; heart beating slowly and irregularly; passes water, and the pupils dilate in response to galvanism.

10 A.M.—Temperature 101°; respirations 40; pulse 176; the usual response to galvanism.

11 A.M.—Temperature 102° 7'; pulse 152; respirations 52; the same response to galvanism.

1 P.M.—Respirations 44; pulse 160; temperature 102° 5'; galvanism causes the urine to pass.

3 P.M.—Temperature 103° 2'; respirations 44; pulse 120; galvanism causes the urine to pass.

5 P.M.—Temperature 103°; pulse 200, small and weak; respirations 44; the same response to galvanism.

6-30 P.M.—Temperature 106° 2'.

8 P.M.—Heart beating very rapidly; respirations 44; temperature 103°. From this time the heart's action gradually became weaker until it ceased at 11-30 P.M., 14 hours and 50 minutes after the commencement of artificial respiration.

---

## No. 12.

A dog was bitten by a cobra, at 7-50 A.M.

8 A.M.—Temperature 103° 4'.

8-23 A.M.—The animal was bitten again by another snake.

8-30 A.M.—Affected; commenced artificial respiration.

9 A.M.—Respirations 36; temperature 102° 5'; applied heat; pulse weak and irregular, 64.

11 A.M.—Respirations 36; temperature 102° 8'; pulse 200; there is response to galvanism.

1 P.M.—Pulse 180; temperature 103°; respirations 38.

3 P.M.—Pulse 140; temperature 103° 2'; respirations 36; dilatation of the pupils by galvanism.

5 P.M.—Pulse 160; temperature 102° 8'; respirations 36; the same response to galvanism.

6 P.M.—Pulse 200; temperature 102° 6'; respirations 32.

8 P.M.—Pulse 136; respirations 36; temperature 100° 2'.

10 P.M.—Temperature 103° 2'; pulse 160, pretty good; respirations 28; had passed water; no response to galvanism.

11-20 P.M.—Heart ceased to beat, 14 hours and 50 minutes after the commencement of artificial respiration.

---

## No. 13.

Hypodermically injected half of the poison extracted from a vigorous cobra, into a dog, at 7-30 A.M.

7-40 A.M.—Temperature 102° 2'.

8 A.M.—Temperature 102° 4′.

8-18 A.M.—Temperature 103°.

8-40 A.M.—Temperature 102° 8′; pulse 160.

8-50 A.M.—Commenced artificial respiration. There were very few convulsive movements in this instance, and the tongue did not at first appear to be paralyzed, but afterwards became so.

9-10 A.M.—Eyes apparently sensible; convulsive tremor all over the body.

10 A.M.—Response to galvanism. Convulsive movement of the extremities, and dilatation of the pupils. Heart beating very fast, over 200; lachrymation and salivation. Respirations 48; temperature 101° 6′; applied heat.

11 A.M.—Pulse 140—good; respirations 48; temperature 102° 3′; dilatation of the pupils, and micturition in response to galvanism; lachrymation and salivation still going on.

NOON.—Pulse 180—good; respirations 44; temperature 104° 6′; dilatation of the pupils and micturition in response to galvanism.

1 P.M.—Pulse 186; respirations 42; temperature 103°; slight dilatation of the pupils in response to galvanism.

2 P.M.—Pulse about 200; respirations 44; temperature 102° 5′; dilatation of the pupils only in response to galvanism.

3 P.M.—Temperature 100° 9′; respirations 40; pulse 200; a few drops of urine passed, and dilatation of the pupils in response to galvanism; lachrymation and salivation still going on; applied more heat.

4 P.M.—Pulse 200; respirations 44; temperature 102° 9′; no response to galvanism.

5 P.M.—Pulse 200; respirations 44; temperature 102° 5′; a very small quantity of urine was passed in response to galvanism; lachrymation and salivation is still going on; applied more heat.

6 P.M.—Pulse 200; respirations 48; temperature 103°.

7 P.M.—Pulse 200; respirations 44; temperature 103°.

9-30 P.M.—Pulse very quick, much over 200; respirations 44; temperature 102°.

11 P.M.—Pulse still very quick; respirations 44; temperature 102°.

MIDNIGHT.—Temperature 102° 2′; respirations 36; pulse too quick to count.

1 A.M.—Pulse beating too quickly to count; respirations 44; temperature 102°.

2 A.M.—Pulse the same; respirations 36; temperature 102°.

3 A.M.—Pulse too quick to count; respirations 36; temperature 101° 6′.

4 A.M.—Pulse still beating too rapidly to count; respirations 40; temperature 101° 2′; applied more heat; past a very small quantity of urine in response to galvanism; lachrymation and salivation going on.

5 A.M.—Pulse beating about the same; respirations 40; temperature 102° 2′; applied more heat.

6 A.M.—Pulse the same; respirations 40; temperature 102° 6′; lachrymation and salivation still going on.

7 A.M.—Heart beating very rapidly, but is very weak; respirations 40; temperature 102° 1′; passed a small quantity of urine in response to galvanism.

8 A.M.—Heart beating very quickly, but with more force; respirations 36; temperature 103° 6'; partially removed the heat; passed a very large quantity of urine in response to galvanism.

9 A.M.—Heart beating very feebly; temperature 102° 1'; respirations 44; applied heat to the body; no response to galvanism.

10 A.M.—Heart beating feebly; temperature 103° 9'.

11-5 A.M.—Heart ceased to beat, 26 hours and 15 minutes after the commencement of artificial respiration; temperature at the time the heart ceased to beat, 104° 1'.

---

## No. 14.

Hypodermically injected 2 grains of cobra-poison into a small dog, at 6-24 A.M.

6-35 A.M.—Temperature 102° 4'.

7 A.M.—Temperature 102° 8'.

7-13 A.M.—Convulsed; the heart was at this time beating at long intervals, and with but little force. Commenced artificial respiration.

7-26 A.M.—Temperature 102° 5'.

8 A.M.—Temperature 100° 8'; respirations 52; pulse very weak and quick; no response to galvanism, not even dilatation of the pupils.

9 A.M.—Temperature 102° 5'; pulse, weak, 200; respirations 56 (much too quick); no reflex action.

10 A.M.—Temperature 102° 8'; heart beating very rapidly; respirations 44; slight dilatation of the pupils in response to galvanism.

11 A.M.—Heart beating very rapidly; temperature 103° 1'; respirations 44.

NOON.—Heart beating feebly and quickly; temperature 102° 9'; respirations 48; no reflex action.

1 P.M.—Heart beating as before; temperature 102° 8'; respirations 44.

2 P.M.—Temperature 101° 6'; respirations 36; heart beating as before; one or two drops of urine passed in response to galvanism.

3 P.M.—Respirations 44; temperature 103° 8'; heart beating as before.

4 P.M.—Respirations 48; heart as before.

5 P.M.—Respirations 44; temperature 102° 6'; heart beating as before, too quickly to count.

6 P.M.—Respirations 48; temperature 103° 2'; heart beating very rapidly, but without force; no reflex action.

7 P.M.—Temperature 101° 8'; heart beating very feebly.

8-15 P.M.—Temperature 103° 9'; heart beating very feebly.

10 P.M.—The heart ceased to beat, 14 hours and 47 minutes after the commencement of artificial respiration.

N.B.—There was very little response to galvanism throughout the above experiment.

---

## No. 15.

Hypodermically injected into a dog 2½ grains of cobra-poison, at 8-30 A.M.; temperature before the injection, 102° 2'.

8-38 A.M.—Temperature 102° 2'.

8-50 A.M.—Temperature 102° 9'.

9 A.M.—Temperature 102° 6'.

9-15 A.M.—Temperature 102° 5'.

9-20 A.M.—Convulsed; commenced artificial respiration; the pupils were widely dilated and the heart was beating very slowly; the pupils became natural, convulsions ceased, and the heart began to beat somewhat more regularly.

9-30 A.M.—Temperature 101° 4'; still apparently sensible.

9-37 A.M.—Starts on a noise being made, and becomes universally convulsed.

9-42 A.M.—The eyes ceased to be sensitive.

10 A.M.—Pulse over 200, not very strong; temperature 100° 9'; respirations 48; dilatation of the pupils in response to galvanism.

NOON.—Temperature 103°; respirations 56 (much too quick); pulse better, 160; the irides act by galvanism.

2 P.M.—Temperature 108° 1'; heart beating very rapidly and somewhat feebly; irides still act by galvanism; respirations 56; lachrymation and salivation have been going on, but not very profusely.

4 P.M.—Pulse 200; respirations 40; temperature 101° 9'; no reflex action; applied heat.

6 P.M.—Respirations 48; pulse beating very feebly, 200; temperature 103° 1'; no reflex action.

7-30 P.M.—Temperature 103° 5'; pulse 200; pretty strong; respirations 48; very slight action of the irides by galvanism.

MIDNIGHT.—Pulse 200; respirations 44; temperature 101° 6'.

2 A.M.—Respirations 48; pulse 200; temperature 100° 9'; no reflex action.

4 A.M.—Temperature 99° 8'; heart beating pretty steadily, 168; respirations 44; no reflex action; applied heat.

5-45 A.M.—Heart ceased to beat, 20 hours and 25 minutes after the commencement of artificial respiration.

----

## No. 16.

Hypodermically injected into a dog 2½ grains of cobra-poison, at 7-40 A.M.; temperature 102°.

7-50 A.M.—Temperature 102° 1'.

8-5 A.M.—Temperature 102° 2'.

8-15 A.M.—Temperature 102°.

8-30 A.M.—Temperature 102° 2'; defœcation; convulsions; commenced artificial respiration.

8-40 A.M.—Temperature 101° 8'.

8-50 A.M.—Reflex action in response to galvanism.

10 A.M.—Temperature 100° 2'; respirations 56; heart beating rapidly; slight tremor, micturition and dilatation of the pupils in response to galvanism.

11 A.M.—Pulse 180; temperature 101° 9'; respirations 44; micturition and dilatation of the pupils by galvanism.

NOON.—Pulse 140; respirations 48; temperature 101° 5'; pupils dilate with a weak shock of galvanism.

1 p.m.—Pulse 180; temperature 104°; respirations 48; slight dilatation of the pupils in response to galvanism; removed the heat.

2 p.m.—Respirations 44; pulse 194; temperature 102° 5'; dilatation of the pupils and micturition in response to galvanism.

4 p.m.—Respirations 44; pulse 200; temperature 101° 8'; micturition by galvanism; applied heat.

6 p.m.—Respirations 48; pulse over 200; temperature 104° 6'; no reflex action; removed the heat.

7 p.m.—Respirations 44; pulse over 200; temperature 104° 3', it had been 104° 8'; irides act, and there is micturition by galvanism.

9 p.m.—Pulse 200; temperature 101° 2'; respirations 40; micturition in response to galvanism.

11 p.m.—Respirations 44; pulse over 200; temperature 102° 8'; dilatation of pupils and micturition in response to galvanism.

1 a.m.—Respirations 44; pulse over 200; temperature 104°; no response to galvanism, and there is a gradual failure in the heart's action.

2-30 a.m.—The heart was beating very feebly indeed; artificial respiration was stopped, there being no light in the operating room; heart ceased to beat, 18 hours since artificial respiration was commenced.

----

## No. 17.

Hypodermically injected 2½ grains of cobra-poison into a dog, at 7-25 a.m.; temperature 102° 4'.

7-35 a.m.—Temperature 102° 4'.

7-50 a.m.—Temperature 102°.

8-30 a.m.—Temperature 102° 2'.

8-40 a.m.—Commenced artificial respiration; temperature 103°; convulsive movements continued for a longer period than is usual, and the galvanic current gave rise to violent reflex movements, one of which, viz.—an attempt to bark, was of an abnormal character.

9-30 a.m.—Temperature 104°; respirations 44; pulse 160; dilatation of the pupils; slight convulsive movement of the lower jaw, and micturition in response to galvanism.

11-30 a.m.—Pulse 200; respirations 40; temperature 102° 3'; dilatation of the pupils and micturition in response to galvanism.

1-30 p.m.—Pulse 216; temperature 105° 3'; respirations 42; micturition by galvanism.

3-30 p.m.—Pulse 200—strong; respirations 56; temperature 104° 4'; micturition by galvanism.

5-30 p.m.—Pulse very rapid, over 200; temperature 103° 7'; respirations 46; no response to galvansim.

7-30 p.m.—Respirations 44; pulse very rapid and feeble; temperature 102° 2'; the same response to galvanism.

9-30 p.m.—The heart ceased to beat, 12 hours and 50 minutes after the commencement of artificial respiration; temperature 104° 5'.

## No. 18.

Hypodermically injected into a dog suffering from dysentery 2¼ grains of cobra-poison, at 7-55 A.M.; temperature 103° 8′.

8-2 A.M.—Temperature 103° 4′.

8-27 A.M.—Temperature 103° 2′.

8-35 A.M.—Temperature 103° 1′.

8-45 A.M.—Temperature 103° 1′.

9 A.M.—Temperature 103° 1′.

9-10 A.M.—Temperature 103′.

9-30 A.M.—Temperature 102° 8′.

9-40 A.M.—Respirations 40; pulse about 80; convulsed slightly, but is just able to stand.

9-50 A.M.—Temperature 103°.

9-55 A.M.—Commenced artificial respiration.

10-30 A.M.—Respirations 44; temperature 101° 6′.

Violent contraction of the muscles in response to galvanism; tremor and spasmodic contractions of the lower jaw and legs are produced by the application of cold water to the head.

12-30 P.M.—Temperature 101° 8′; pulse 158, irregular; respirations 44; slight twitching of the muscles of the thighs; micturition, defæcation, and dilatation of the pupils in response to galvanism.

2-30 P.M.—Temperature 100° 6′; respirations 36; pulse 140; micturition and dilatation of the pupils in response to galvanism.

4-30 P.M.—Respirations 40; temperature 100° 6′; pulse over 200; micturition by galvanism.

6-30 P.M.—Respirations 44; pulse very rapid; temperature 101° 2′; micturition by galvanism.

8 P.M.—Temperature 100° 5′; pulse very rapid and feeble; respirations 44; micturition by galvanism.

10-30 P.M.—Temperature 102° 8′; pulse rapid and feeble; respirations 36; very small quantity of urine past by galvanism; the heart is evidently failing.

11-30 P.M.—The heart is beating very feebly.

MIDNIGHT.—The heart ceased to beat, 14 hours and 5 minutes after the commencement of artificial respiration.

---

## No. 19.

Hypodermically injected into a dog 1 grain of cobra-poison, at 7-40 A.M.; temperature 102° 2′.

7-50 A.M.—Temperature 103°.

8-15 A.M.—Convulsed; commenced artificial respiration.

8-30 A.M.—Is still convulsed.

8-40 A.M.—Temperature 102° 1′.

9 A.M.—Temperature 101° 6′; pulse 180; respirations 46; universal response to galvanism.

11 A.M.—Temperature 100° 1′; respirations 44; pulse over 200, somewhat weak; micturition and dilatation of the pupils in response to galvanism.

1-30 P.M.—Heart's action weak and irregular (190); respirations 44; temperature 101°; micturition by galvanism.

3 P.M.—Temperature 100° 8′; respirations 44; pulse over 200, weak; micturition and dilatation of the pupils by galvanism.

5 P.M.—Heart beating very feebly; respirations 40; temperature 104°; no response to galvanism.

8 P.M.—Respirations 48; pulse very rapid and somewhat weak; temperature 103° 2′; micturition only in response to galvanism.

10 P.M.—Heart ceased to beat, 9 hours and 45 minutes after the commencement of artificial respiration.

*N.B.*—This dog was a small one.

---

## No. 20.

Hypodermically injected into a middling-sized dog 1 grain of cobra-poison, at 7-35 A.M. In this instance the injected leg was decidedly paralyzed, the toes being dragged along the ground.

7-45 A.M.—Temperature 103°.

8 A.M.—Temperature 102° 3′.

8-30 A.M.—Temperature 101° 9′.

9 A.M.—Temperature 102° 1′.

9-20 A.M.—Temperature 102°; convulsed. Commenced artificial respiration, 1 hour and 45 minutes since the injection of the poison.

10 A.M.—Respirations 42; pulse 100, strong but intermitting; temperature 101° 5′; convulsions are continuing for an unusually long time; there is now tremor of the hind quarters and occasional universal convulsions.

NOON.—Heart beating very forcibly and quickly (over 200); respirations 44; temperature 101° 3′; micturition and dilatation of the pupils in response to galvanism; applied heat.

2 P.M.—Heart beating very rapidly (over 200); respirations 44; temperature 103°; micturition and dilatation of the pupils by galvanism.

4 P.M.—Temperature 104°; respirations 48; pulse very rapid indeed; micturition in response to galvanism; removed the heat.

6 P.M.—Temperature 102° 8′; respirations 56; pulse very rapid; no reflex action.

MIDNIGHT.—Temperature 102° 1′; respirations 40; pulse over 200; micturition by galvanism.

2-30 A.M.—Heart ceased to beat, 17 hours and 10 minutes after the commencement of artificial respiration.

---

## No. 21.

Hypodermically injected into a dog 1 grain of cobra-poison, at 8-10 A.M.

8-27 A.M.—Temperature 103°.

8-45 A.M.—Temperature 102° 8′.

9 A.M.—Temperature 102° 2′.

9-15 A.M.—Temperature 102° 2′.

9-30 A.M.—Temperature 102  4'.

9-41 A.M.—Begins to stagger about.

9-45 A.M.—Temperature 102° 6'.

9-55 A.M.—Convulsed; commenced artificial respiration (105 minutes since the poison was injected); natural respiration had not quite ceased, though the animal was much convulsed.

This animal presented more signs of being really sensible than any other dog we have operated on. We opened a vein for the purpose of taking some blood and the animal betrayed evident signs of feeling, such as an attempt to whine and withdrawal of the leg. Violent convulsions in response both to galvanism and the application of cold water to the head.

11 A.M.—Temperature 102°; pulse intermitting but strong, 176; respirations 44; dilatation of pupils and micturition in response to galvanism.

1 P.M.—Pulse beating strongly, 176; temperature 101° 2'; respirations 44; slight tremor of the hind quarters; micturition and dilatation of the pupils in response to galvanism.

3 P.M.—Temperature 101° 9'; pulse 180; respirations 44; dilatation of the pupils and micturition in response to galvanism.

5 P.M.—Pulse 180, strong; temperature 102° 4'; respirations 44; slight dilatation of pupils and micturition in response to galvanism.

7-45 P.M.—The heart ceased to beat, 9 hours and 50 minutes after the commencement of artificial respiration. The dog was a very small one.

---

## No. 22.

Hypodermically injected into a middling-sized dog 1 grain of cobra-poison, at 7-53 A.M.; temperature 102° 1'.

8-5 A.M.—Temperature 102° 2'; the breathing is becoming affected, and the dog is uneasy.

8-15 A.M.—Temperature 102° 4'.

8-30 A.M.—Temperature 101° 5'.

8-45 A.M.—Temperature 101° 6'.

9 A.M.—Temperature 101° 8'.

9-35 A.M.—Temperature 101° 6'.

10 A.M.—Temperature 101° 5'.

10-20 A.M—Temperature 101° 4'.

10-45 A.M.—Heart beating 132; pupils natural; respirations 40; first convulsive movement; pupils have become quite widely dilated, and the conjunctivæ pitted, as it were; temperature 101° 7'.

10-50 A.M.—Pupils widely dilated; convulsions very strong; commenced artificial respiration (2 hours and 57 minutes since the injection of the poison); the convulsions at once ceased.

11 A.M.—Temperature 101° 5'; pulse 200, strong and regular; respirations 44; universal convulsions in response to galvanism.

1 P.M.—Temperature 101° 2'; respirations 40; pulse 200; galvanism causes universal convulsions, micturition, and defœcation; universal convulsions on the application of water to the head. It is remarkable that there are still convulsive movements even when the battery is not applied.

2·35 P.M.—Slight convulsive movements, the tongue is protruded and retracted very rapidly in response to voltaic electricity.

4 P.M.—Temperature 101° 2′; pulse over 200; respirations 44; the same response to voltaic electricity; at first, however, there was no response to negative electricity, but afterwards there was much more response to negative electricity than to positive. Response also to galvanism, the convulsions being much more violent from this than from voltaic electricity.

6 P.M.—Temperature 102°; pulse 200; respirations 44.

8 P.M.—Temperature 101° 2′.

8·10 P.M.—Heart ceased to beat, 9 hours and 20 minutes after the commencement of artificial respiration.

---

## No. 23.

Hypodermically injected into a dog 1 grain of cobra-poison, at 8·45 A.M.

9 A.M.—Temperature 101° 5′.

9·10 A.M.—Temperature 101° 2′.

10 A.M.—Temperature 101°; slightly convulsed.

10·5 A.M.—Commenced artificial respiration (1 hour and 10 minutes since the injection).

10·20 A.M.—No response to voltaic electricity, but response to galvanism.

10·30 A.M.—Temperature 101°.

11 A.M.—Temperature 101°; pulse over 200; respirations 42; response to galvanism, but none to voltaic electricity.

1 P.M.—Temperature 101°; pulse 200, weak; respirations 36; no response to voltaic electricity, and the only response to galvanism is micturition.

2·30 P.M.—Temperature 101° 6′; pulse very weak indeed, appears to be rapidly failing; respirations 48; lungs are being well inflated; the only response to galvanism is micturition.

4·30 P.M.—Temperature 102°; pulse weak, about 200; respirations 44; no response to voltaic electricity, but micturition by galvanism.

6 P.M.—Temperature 102° 1′; pulse very feeble; respirations 44; no response to galvanism.

7·30 P.M.—Heart ceased to beat, 9 hours and 25 minutes after the commencement of artificial respiration.

---

## No. 24.

Hypodermically injected into a dog 1 grain of cobra-poison, at 7·30 A.M.; temperature 101° 8′.

7·45 A.M.—Temperature 102° 5′.

8·5 A.M.—Temperature 102°.

8·20 A.M.—Temperature 101° 8′.

8·30 A.M.—Commenced artificial respiration (one hour after the injection); temperature 99° 9′.

9-30 A.M.—Slight convulsive movements in response to galvanism ; there is also micturition ; the pupils are widely dilated ; pulse beating very hard, nearly 200 ; respirations steadily kept up at 44 ; temperature 98°.

11-30 A.M.—Micturition and dilitation of one pupil in response to galvanism ; pulse strong, 192 ; respirations 44 ; temperature 96° 2′.

12-30 P.M.—Temperature 95° 8′ ; respirations 36 ; pulse 200 ; micturition by galvanism.

1-30 P.M.—Pulse 200 ; respirations 44 ; temperature 94° 3′ ; micturition and dilatation of the pupils in response to galvanism ; eyes look more natural.

2-30 P.M.—Temperature 93° 9′ ; pulse the same.

4 P.M.—Temperature 93° 8′ ; pulse and respirations the same.

5 P.M.—Temperature 97° 9′ ; respirations 48 ; pulse very rapid and weak ; micturition by galvanism.

6-30 P.M.—Temperature 94° ; respirations 44 ; pulse very rapid, over 200 ; micturition and dilatation of the pupils by galvanism ; the dog feels cold ; applied heat.

7-30 P.M.—Temperature 94° 9′ ; pulse 200, strong ; respirations 44.

9-30 P.M.—Temperature 98° 5′ ; pulse not very strong ; respirations 44.

10-30 P.M.—No response to galvanism ; pulse very weak ; respirations 44 ; temperature 106°.

11 P.M.—Heart ceased to beat, 14½ hours after the commencement of artificial respiration.

*N.B.*—The dogs used in the last six experiments were very much smaller than those used in the other experiments.

---

## No. 25.

Hypodermically injected ¼ grain of cobra-poison into a dog, at 8-55 A.M. ; temperature 101° 8′.

9-15 A.M.—Temperature 102° 3′.

9-50 A.M.—Temperature 102° 1′.

10-30 A.M.—Temperature 102° 2′.

11 A.M.—Temperature 102° 2′ ; vomiting now for the first time ; it begins to show decided symptoms of snake-poisoning ; is continually retching, and extremely restless ; it jumps about as if mad, and is violently convulsed.

11-5 P.M.—Commenced artificial respiration (2 hours and 10 minutes since the injection of the poison) ; temperature 101° 7′. This dog presented the usual symptoms on the commencement of artificial respiration, viz., from being violently convulsed it became perfectly quiet, and the pupils became natural.

2 P.M.—Temperature 101° 4′ ; pulse 200 ; respirations 44 ; no response to galvanism except micturition and dilatation of the pupils.

4 P.M.—Temperature 101° 8′ ; pulse beating strongly, over 200 ; respirations 44 ; no response to galvanism.

6 P.M.—Temperature 102° ; pulse 200 ; respirations 38 ; no response to galvanism.

9-50 P.M.—Temperature 102°; pulse 200; respirations 44.

12-45 A.M.—Temperature 101° 5′; respirations 44; pulse over 200; very slight response to galvanism.

2-30 A.M.—Temperature 102° 1′.

6 A.M.—Temperature 101° 4′; pulse very rapid; respirations 44; dilatation of the pupils, and micturition in response to galvanism.

8 A.M.—Temperature 101° 8′; pulse very rapid and weak; respirations 48; the same response to galvanism.

9-10 A.M.—Temperature 10° 1′.

10 A.M.—Temperature 100° 2′.

11 A.M.—Temperature 99° 5′; respirations 44; pulse very weak and quick; had passed two stools; micturition in response to galvanism; applied heat.

12-30 P.M.—Temperature 102°.

1-30 P.M.—Temperature 102° 4′.

3 P.M.—Temperature 102° 2′; pulse beating very rapidly and feebly; respirations 50; dilatation of the pupils by galvanism.

4-30 P.M.—Temperature 102° 1′.

5-20 P.M.—Heart ceased to beat, 30 hours and 25 minutes after the commencement of artificial respiration.

------

## No. 26.

Hypodermically injected into a dog ⅓ grain of cobra-poison, at 8-30 A.M.

8-40 A.M.—Temperature 101° 9′.

9-20 A.M.—Temperature 101° 9′.

9-50 A.M.—Temperature 101° 9′.

10-14 A.M.—Convulsed; the heart's action nearly ceased; commenced artificial respiration (1 hour and 44 minutes after the injection).

1 P.M.—Micturition and dilatation of the pupils in response to galvanism; respirations 44; pulse 176, not very strong; temperature 100° 3′; applied heat.

2 P.M.—Temperature 101° 2′; heart beating very fast; respirations 44.

3 P.M.—Temperature 102°.

4 P.M.—Temperature 102°; heart beating very fast; respirations 42.

5 P.M.—Heart beating strongly, 100; respirations 44; temperature 102° 2′; scarcely any reflex action.

6 P.M.—Temperature 102°.

8 P.M.—Temperature 101°; heart beating as before; respirations 44; slight micturition by galvanism.

10 P.M.—Temperature 102° 8′; heart beating as before.

MIDNIGHT.—Temperature 102° 8′; heart slower, about 190; very slight micturition in response to galvanism.

2 A.M.—Temperature 102° 1′.

4 A.M.—Temperature 101° 6′.

6 A.M.—Temperature 102° 4.

6-40 A.M.—Heart ceased to beat, 22 hours and 10 minutes after the commencement of artificial respiration.

## No. 27.

Hypodermically injected into a middling-sized dog, ¼ grain of cobra-poison, at 7-40 A.M.; temperature 102° 6'.

8-5 A.M.—Temperature 102° 8'.

8-55 A.M.—Temperature 102° 6'.

9-5 A.M.—Temperature 101° 2'.

9-26 A.M.—Temperature 102° 1'.

9-58 A.M.—Temperature 102° 1'.

10-20 A.M.—Temperature 102° 2'.

10-50 A.M.—Temperature 102° 1'.

11-15 A.M.—Temperature 102° 2'.

11-20 A.M.—Temperature 102° 2'; first symptoms of snake-poisoning appeared; the animal began to be restless and endeavoured to get away.

11-28 A.M.—Passed a stool; staggers about backwards, and runs about with its head down, and neck much arched; is wagging its tail the whole time; pupils natural.

11-36 A.M.—Temperature 102° 7'; passed a quantity of hard fœces; dyspnœa.

11-40 A.M.—The pupils are now somewhat dilated, but they soon become natural again; temperature 102° 7'. There is not so much salivation as usual. The animal is perfectly sensible as proved by the fact of its wagging its tail when spoken to; the heart is beating rather feebly and slowly.

11-46 A.M.—Beginning to retch, but vomits nothing.

11-55 A.M.—Fell over on its side, and immediately became very convulsed.

Noon.—Commenced artificial respiration (4 hours and 20 minutes after the injection). The dog was convulsed; its pupils dilated, and it was insensible. The effects of artificial respiration in this instance were remarkable: the animal immediately became conscious, took notice when called, began to wag its tail, and endeavoured to get up from the table. It was, however, occasionally convulsed.

12-30 P.M.—In the same state; is perfectly sensible; there is a great deal of tremor, especially of the hind quarters; the heart is beating steadily and well, 160. A little water thrown on the head makes the animal struggle violently.

12-42 P.M.—Temperature 101° 8'; still continues sensible; there is a great quantity of saliva running out of its mouth.

1-30 P.M.—In the same state.

1-55 P.M.—Beginning to lose consciousness very fast, but is still sensible.

2 P.M.—The heart is beating pretty strongly.

2-50 P.M.—No longer sensible; temperature 99° 8'; respirations 40; universal convulsions in response to galvanism; pulse 168; applied heat.

4-30 P.M.—Temperature 101° 4'; heart beating very strongly, about 160; respirations 44; marked response to the galvanic current, especially of the hind-legs, the fore-legs little affected; there is also response on pouring water on to the head; passed some bloody urine.

6 P.M.—Heart beating steadily and well; the same response to galvanism; urine as before; respirations 41; temperature 101°.

8·10 P.M.—Heart beating very forcibly and regularly, 200 ; respirations 44 ; temperature 100° 1′ ; same reflex action both by galvanism and the application of water.

10·30 P.M.—Temperature 99° 2′.

1 A.M.—Temperature 98° ; respirations 50 ; pulse 180, very regularly and strongly ; slight convulsive movements and micturition of bloody urine in response to galvanism ; there is also slight convulsive movements about the mouth when water is poured on the head.

3·45 A.M.—Temperature 102°.

6 A.M.—Temperature 103° ; heart beating pretty steadily and well, 180 ; respirations 44 ; contractions about the mouth, hind and fore extremities in response to galvanism, also on the application of cold water to the head ; passed a large quantity of urine and fæces.

8 A.M.—Temperature 100° 1′ ; pulse 160, rather weaker but still regular ; respirations 44 ; slight twitchings of the legs by galvanism, as also by the application of cold water to the head ; applied heat.

10 A.M.—Temperature 102° ; in the same state ; the temperature had been so high as 104° 1′.

NOON.—Temperature 103° 2′ ; heart beating less forcibly though regularly, about 200 ; respirations 48 ; slight movement of the legs, and micturition by galvanism.

2·20 P.M.—Heart ceased to beat, 26 hours and 20 minutes after the commencement of artificial respiration.

----

## No. 28.

Hypodermically injected into a dog weighing 37lbs, ¼ grain of cobra-poison, at 8·53 A. M. ; temperature 101° 2′.

9·3 A.M.—Temperature 101°.

9·15 A.M.—Temperature 101° 9′.

9·30 A.M.—Temperature 101° 8′.

9·40 A.M.—Temperature 101° 7′.

10 A.M.—Temperature 101° 6′.

10·8 A.M.—Is rather restless, and is suffering from dyspnœa.

10·20 A.M.—Temperature 101° 6′.

10·50 A.M.—Temperature 101° 8′ ; is apparently easy again.

11·15 A.M.—Temperature 101° 8′ ; is again uneasy.

11·35 A.M.—Temperature 101° 9′.

11·40 A.M.—Vomited and is continually retching ; passed water ; is very restless, and is going about with its head down and neck arched ; pupils dilated.

11·53 A.M.—Is constantly vomiting and making water, and occasionally passes flatus ; it can hear.

NOON.—Temperature 102° 7′ ; in the same state ; is now jumping about in a most violent manner.

12·15 P.M.—In the same state ; temperature 102° 9′.

12·55 P.M.—Commenced artificial respiration ; the animal was breathing very slightly ; the usual effects followed on the commencement of artificial respiration.

1 P.M.—Temperature 102° 7′.

2 P.M.—Convulsed so violently as to require holding down to the table; heart beating forcibly and well; temperature 101° 4'.

3 P.M.—Respirations 44; pulse 80, rather forcibly; temperature 101° 1'; universal convulsions in response both to galvanism and the application of cold water to the head.

5-30 P.M.—Temperature 102° 6'; respirations 40; pulse about 200. The same response to galvanism.

8 P.M.—Temperature 102° 4'; pulse 128; respirations 40; slight movement of the leg and dilatation of the pupils in response to galvanism.

11 P.M.—Temperature 101° 1'; respirations 36; pulse 132; slight convulsive movements of the hind quarters; micturition and dilatation of the pupils in response to galvanism. The urine passed is alkaline, and contains no albumen.

MIDNIGHT.—Temperature 101° 3'.

7 A.M.—Temperature 101° 2'.

4 A.M.—Temperature 101° 2'.

6 A.M.—Temperature 101° 8'; pulse irregular, 160; respirations 40; no response to galvanism.

8 A.M.—Temperature 102° 1'; respirations 40; pulse over 200; micturition, in a very large stream, in response to galvanism.

10. A.M.—Temperature 102° 9'; respirations 44; pulse 188; slight contraction of the fore-paws and micturitition by galvanism.

NOON.—Temperature 102° 8', very nearly the same as it was 24 hours since.

2 P.M.—Temperature 103° 2'.

5 P.M.—Temperature 103° 5'; no reflex action.

7 P.M.—Temperature 103° 1'; no reflex action.

9 P.M.—Temperature 102° 2'; no reflex action.

11 P.M.—Temperature 101° 1'; heart beating very quickly and feebly; respirations 50; no reflex action. The head presented all the appearance of death, the muscles being shrunken, and the eyes disorganized.

6 A.M.—Temperature 101° 8'; respirations 26; pulse beating very feebly indeed; no reflex action; the head and the neck are perfectly stiff, and the legs are also somewhat stiffened.

2-55 A.M.—Heart ceased to beat, 37 hours and 50 minutes after the commencement of artificial respiration.

---

## SECOND SERIES.

---

### Artificial Respiration and the exhibition of various Drugs in Snake-poisoning.

---

#### No. 1.

*Liq. Ammoniæ Fort.*

A dog, weighing 26lbs, was bitten by a cobra, at 8-20 A.M.; normal temperature 101° 5'.

8-37 A.M.—Temperature 103° 2'.

9-6 A.M.—It being more than doubtful whether the bite is an effectual one, another snake is made to bite the dog; temperature 103° 2'.

9-18 A.M.—Began to be effected; convulsed; salivation; dilitation of the pupils, and paralysis of the tongue.

9-25 A.M.—Heart beating slowly; commenced artificial respiration.

9-30 A.M.—Injected Liq. Ammoniæ Fort. 15 minims, diluted with water, into a vein; at first there was no preceptible increase in the heart's action, but in the course of a minute or so, the dog was slightly convulsed; and the heart began to beat strongly and more regularly.

9-36 A.M.—The heart's action again becoming weak, injected another 15 minims of Liq. Ammoniæ; the same spasm and increased action of the heart followed. The heart, however, soon began to flag and was beating very slowly at 9-40 A.M.; temperature 100° 7'.

9-45 A.M.—Injected 15 minims more of the Liq. Ammoniæ; twenty seconds after the injection the spasm and acceleration of the heart's action commenced.

9-53 A.M.—Temperature 101° 6'.

10-30 A.M.—Pulse 128, strong and regular; respirations 42; temperature 99° 1'; no reflex action; the pupils are widely dilated.

11-30 A.M.—Injected Liq. Ammoniæ 10 minims; the heart's action became strengthened. There was very slight response to galvanism by the iris.

12-30 P.M.—Temperature 96° 2'; heart beating irregularly though forcibly, 120; respirations 38; has passed water many times; applied heat.

1-25 P.M.—Heart ceased to beat, 4 hours after the commencement of artificial respiration.

---

## No. 2.

A dog, weighing 40lbs, was bitten by a cobra, at 8-35 A.M., normal temperature 103° 7'.

9-7 A.M.—Affected.

9-24 A.M.—Commenced artificial respiration.

9-27 A.M.—Injected Liq. Ammoniæ 10 minims (diluted) into a vein; in twenty-five seconds spasm of the hind quarters occurred, but there was no marked acceleration of the heart's action.

9-37 A.M.—Injected Liq. Ammoniæ mxv (diluted); the heart's action was at first accelerated, but afterwards considerably lowered.

9-49 A.M.—Temperature 101° 5'.

11-12 A.M.—Injected Liq. Ammoniæ mxv; the same effects followed the injection; the pupils are dilated, but dilate still more by galvanism; micturition; temperature 101° 2'; pulse 96, weak; respirations 44; applied heat.

12-40 P.M.—Injected 15 minims more ammonia; the same effects followed; temperature 102° 5; respirations 46.

2 P.M.—Temperature 102° 4'; injected 15 minims of Liq. Ammoniæ, with the usual results.

3-45 P.M.—Heart ceased to beat, 6 hours and 21 minutes after the commencement of artificial respiration.

## No. 3.

A dog, weighing 33½lbs, was bitten by a cobra, at 8-10 A.M.

8-35 A.M.—Affected; convulsed.

8-40 A.M.—Commenced artificial respiration.

9 A.M—Injected Liquor Ammoniæ 1 dram diluted with water 1 oz.; the animal was bled slightly; the heart gradually ceased to beat, and finally ceased at 9-15 A.M., 35 minutes after the commencement of artificial respiration.

---

## No. 4.

### Transfusion and Ammonia.

A dog, weighing 42 lbs, was hypodermically injected with 3 grains of cobra-poison, at 11-20 A.M.

11-45 A.M.—Is now sluggish, but had been affected for some time.

12-15 P.M.—Is now very much affected.

12-20 P.M.—Convulsed.

12-25 P.M—Commenced artificial respiration.

1 P.M.—Bled the animal from the femoral artery, to the extent of 4 oz., while 4 oz. of fresh blood, 2 oz of water, and 1 dram of Liq. Ammoniæ were injected into a vein; applied heat; the heart is very weak and fluttering.

2-15 P.M.—First gave an enema of warm water and then of brandy, ammonia and turpentine; the heart continues to beat feebly.

4 P.M.—The heart is beating more forcibly and better; the respirations have been kept up pretty steadily at 44.

6 P.M.—In the same state; no response to galvanism.

8 P.M.—The heart's action is stronger and there is response to galvanism.

11 P.M.—In the same state.

12-30 A.M—In the same state.

2 A.M.—The heart is more feeble.

3 A.M.—Heart ceased to beat, 14 hours and 35 minutes after the commencement of artificial respiration.

---

## No. 5.

### Morphia.

A dog, weighing 36 lbs, was bitten by a cobra, at 9-31 A.M.

9-51 A.M—Considerably affected.

10 A.M.—Injected into a vein morphia ¾ of a grain, spirit 10 minims, and water 10 minims. The effects of the injection were remarkable; the breathing, which had entirely ceased, returned for a short time, and the convulsions became much slighter.

10-10 A.M.—Breathing ceased; commenced artificial respiration; the heart began to beat pretty steadily.

11-15 A.M.—Heart beating very feebly. There is a great deal of bleeding from the bitten part; stopped it by the application of strong nitric acid. Irides act by galvanism.

1-10 P.M.—Again injected ? of a grain of morphia, &c.; the heart is beating very feebly.

5 P.M.—In the same state.

7-30 P.M.—The heart ceased to beat, in 9 hours and 20 minutes.

---

## No. 6.

### *Transfusion.*

A dog, weighing 26lbs, was bitten by a cobra, at 8-40 A.M.

8-57 A.M.—Is affected.

9-5 A.M.—Salivated and is vomiting.

9-7 A.M.—Convulsed.

9-10 A.M.—Fell over and almost immediately appeared to be dead; artificial respiration was commenced, but the heart was beating very feebly.

9-12 A.M.—Transfused 3 oz. of blood and two drams of sulphate of magnesia.

9-15 A.M.—The heart ceased to beat five minutes after the commencement of artificial respiration.

---

## No. 7.

### *Strychnine.*

A dog, weighing 30lbs, was bitten by a cobra, at 8-33 A.M.

8-58 A.M.—Fell over, and at once became convulsed.

9 A.M.—Artificial respiration was commenced; the heart had almost ceased to beat. [The snakes appear to be much more vigorous now (October).] The usual symptoms presented themselves.

9-25 A.M.—The heart is beating very feebly indeed; injected ¼ of a grain of strychnia into the vein; the heart's action was strengthened considerably, and there was spasm of the whole body.

9-40 A.M.—No response to galvanism.

10 A.M.—The heart is beating feebly.

11 A.M.—Injected ½ of a grain more strychnia; the heart did not appear to be much affected.

NOON.—The heart ceased to beat, 3 hours after the commencement of artificial respiration.

---

## No. 8.

A dog, weighing 38lbs, was bitten by a cobra, at 8-30 A.M.; normal temperature 101° 6'.

8-44 A.M.—Micturition considerable.

8-50 A.M.—Temperature 101° 6'.

8-55 A.M.—Convulsed.

8-57 A.M.—Commenced artificial respiration.

9-10 A.M.—Injected into a vein one-fourth of a grain of strychnia.

10 A.M.—Temperature 99° 3′; heart almost stopped.

10-16 A.M.—Ceased to beat, 1 hour and 19 minutes after the commencement of artificial respiration.

———

### No. 9.

A dog weighing 32lbs, was hypodermically injected with 3 grains of cobra-poison and half a grain of strychnia, at 12-10 P.M.; temperature 101°.

12-35 P.M.—Is unable to stand.

12-37 P.M.—Commenced artificial respiration.

12-40 P.M.—Strychnia, quarter of a grain, injected into a vein.

12-48 P.M.—Injected strychnia, quarter of a grain, into the right jugular vein; action of the heart accelerated.

2 P.M.—In the same state.

5 P.M.—Dead, in 4 hours and 23 minutes.

———

### No. 10.

A dog, weighing 31lbs, was injected with strychnia and cobra-poison, at 1-40 P.M. It is impossible to say how much was injected as the syringe leaked considerably.

This animal did not at first exhibit any symptoms of snake-poisoning; but during the night it was taken ill, and when we saw it at 8-30 A.M. was nearly dead. Respiration had ceased and the beating of the heart was almost imperceptible. At once commenced artificial respiration. The effects were very remarkable, complete reaction having occurred; the heart, however, did not beat with any degree of force.

8-55 A.M.—Injected the one-eighth of a grain of strychnia into the femoral vein; the animal became convulsed at intervals, sometimes very violently.

10-10 A.M.—Heat has been constantly applied; galvanism causes violent convulsions; the eye is still slightly sensitive; occasional convulsions.

11 A.M.—On touching the table on which the animal is placed, there are violent convulsions; the occasional convulsions have continued up to the present time.

11-35 A.M.—In the same state, though the heart is beating somewhat feebly.

1 P.M.—In the same state.

2-30 P.M.—The heart is beating as before, and occasional convulsions occur, though the head has the appearance of death.

5 P.M.—The pulse is much weaker, though there is the same response to galvanism.

8 P.M.—In the same state.

MIDNIGHT.—The heart is very much weaker.

3 A.M.—Heart very weak indeed.

6 A.M.—Heart ceased to beat, 21 hours and 30 minutes after the commencement of artificial respiration.

xxvi

## No. 11.

*Sulphuric Acid.*

A dog was hypodermically injected with half a grain of cobra-poison and 15 minims of decinormal sulphuric acid (1 cc. = ·0017 grammes of ammonia) at 9-5 A.M.; temperature 102°.

10-30 A.M.—Is very much convulsed.

10-35 A.M.—Commenced artificial respiration.

10-45 A.M.—Injected 20 minims of the same acid into a vein.

12-30 P.M.—The heart is beating very feebly.

12-45 P.M.—Injected 20 minims more acid into a vein.

4-30 P.M.—Very slight response to galvanism; temperature 96° 9'; heart beating feebly.

8 P.M.—In the same state.

1 A.M.—Temperature 101° 9'; no reaction; heart beating fairly well.

6 A.M.—In the same state.

8 A.M.—Spasm and micturition (in a full stream) in response to galvanism; the heart is beating quite strongly, about 88; temperature 102° 5'.

10-15 A.M.—In the same state; temperature 102°.

Noon.—In the same state.

2 P.M.—In the same state.

5-30 P.M.—The heart is beating feebly; there is micturition, spasmodic contraction about the mouth, and defæcation in response to galvanism.

8 P.M.—Heart ceased to beat, 33 hours and 25 minutes after the commencement of artificial respiration.

---

## No. 12.

Hypodermically injected into a dog, weighing 35lbs, half a grain of cobra-poison, at 8-54 A.M.; temperature 102° 5'.

9-30 A.M.—Hypodermically injected the one-tenth of a grain of strychnia.

9-35 A.M.—Had a tetanic spasm; temperature 102° 5'; violent spasms continue.

9-40 A.M.—Both hind legs became rigid, and the respiration extremely hurried, difficult, and sometimes spasmodic.

10-20 A.M.—Temperature 103°; commenced artificial respiration.

Noon.—There is response to galvanism, and the heart is beating pretty strongly.

4 P.M.—In the same state.

5 P.M.—Heart much weaker.

6 P.M.—Heart stronger again.

Midnight.—In the same state.

2 A.M.—The heart is beating very feebly, and the head has the appearance of death.

6 A.M.—Heart ceased to beat, 19 hours and 40 minutes after the commencement of artificial respiration.

## No. 13.
### *Chloral Hydrate.*

Hypodermically injected into a dog, weighing 28lbs, $\frac{6}{10}$ths of a grain of cobra-poison, at 11-45 A.M.; temperature 101° 9′.

11-51 A.M.—Hypodermically injected 10 grains of chloral hydrate.

12-25 P.M.—Left hind-leg is paralyzed.

12-35 P.M.—Injected 5 grains more chloral hydrate.

12-4 P.M.—Is vomiting.

12-55 P.M.—Is convulsed.

1-5 P.M.—Commenced artificial respiration; the heart was beating pretty forcibly though respiration had entirely ceased.

1-7 P.M.—Injected 5 grains of chloral hydrate into a vein; the heart's action was considerably reduced; temperature 101° 3′.

1-20 P.M.—There is violent response to galvanism.

3-40 P.M.—Temperature 98° 5′.

6 P.M.—The heart is beating very slowly and the body is cold; applied external warmth.

8 P.M.—In the same state, except that there is now no response to galvanism.

12-30 A.M.—In the same state.

6 A.M.—The heart's action is now much weaker.

9 A.M.—The heart is beating very feebly, and the head has the appearance of death.

11-30 A.M.—Heart ceased to beat, 22 hours and 25 minutes after the commencement of artificial respiration.

---

## No. 14.
### *Strychnine.*

Hypodermically injected into a dog, weighing 31lbs, $\frac{1}{2}$ a grain of cobra-poison, at 11 A.M.

11-10 A.M.—Hypodermically injected $\frac{1}{12}$th of a grain of strychnia.

12-40 P.M.—Hypodermically injected $\frac{1}{17}$ of a grain of strychnia.

1-15 P.M.—Has been suffering occasionally from tetanic spasms.

1-55 P.M.—Became convulsed.

2-10 P.M.—Commenced artificial respiration.

2-20 P.M.—Injected $\frac{1}{3}$ grain a of strychnia into a vein; there was the usual spasm, and then acceleration of the heart's action; several tetanic spasms also followed.

4 P.M.—In the same state; response to galvanism.

6 P.M.—In the same state.

MIDNIGHT.—The heart is beating pretty steadily.

6 A.M.—In the same state.

8 A.M.—Temperature 95° 9′; applied heat to the heart; is beating very feebly, and the animal feels cold; there is still slight response to galvanism.

10 A.M.—In the same state.

1 P.M.—Temperature 95° 9′; heart still beating, but feebly.

3 P.M.—Heart ceased to beat, 28 hours after the commencement of artificial respiration.

## No. 15.

### *Phosphoric Acid.*

Hypodermically injected into a dog, weighing 42℔s, 3 grains of cobra-poison and decinormal phosphoric acid (1cc.=·0017 grammes of ammonia) ¼ dram, at 2·35 P.M.; temperature 100° 2′.

2·45 P.M.—Appears affected, and is whining a great deal.

3 P.M.—Temperature 100° 5′; is becoming restless; micturition, the water is very high coloured.

3·1 P.M.—Cannot stand.

3·4 P.M.—Convulsed.

3·10 P.M.—Commenced artificial respiration.

3·15 P.M.—Injected 15 minims of phosphoric acid into a vein.

5·30 P.M.—Micturition and defœcation; heart beating fairly well.

8 P.M.—In the same state, except that the heart is beating more feebly.

12·30 A.M.—Heart ceased to beat, 9 hours and 20 minutes after the commencement of artificial respiration.

------

## No. 16.

### *Acetic Acid.*

Hypodermically injected 30 minims of decinormal acetic acid (1 cc=·0017 grammes of ammonia), and 2 grains of cobra-poison, at 8·48 A.M.; temperature 101°.

9·5 A.M.—Convulsed.

9·10 A.M.—Commenced artificial respiration.

9·20 A.M.—Injected 15 minims of acetic acid into a vein; it had not the slightest influence on the heart's action.

9·30 A.M.—Temperature 98° 8′; applied heat.

12·30 P.M.—Temperature 96° 7′; the heart is now beating with much more force.

4 P.M.—In the same state.

8 P.M.—The heart is beating feebly and the animal feels cold; applied heat.

MIDNIGHT.—In the same state.

6 A.M.—The heart is beating feebly.

9 A.M.—Heart's action very feeble and intermittent; temperature 85° 7′; applied heat.

10 A.M.—Heart ceased to beat, 24 hours and 50 minutes after the commencement of artificial respiration.

------

## No. 17.

### *Tr. Cannabis Indica.*

Hypodermically injected into a dog ⅓rd of a grain of snake-poison, at 1 P.M., and immediately afterwards 40 minims of Tr. Cannabis Indica.

3·15 P.M.—Became affected.

3·20 P.M.—Convulsed.

3-30 P.M.—Commenced artificial respiration.

3-35 P.M.—Injected 30 minims more Tr. Cannabis Indica into a vein. The effects after about three minutes were remarkable; the eye, which was before perfectly devoid of sense, became sensitive, and the leg which had been without feeling was drawn up when pricked with the scalpel.

4-40 P.M.—The eye is not sensitive; injected 30 minims more Tr. Cannabis Indica into a vein. At first there was no difference, but gradually the animal began to open its mouth and struggle, and the eye became very slightly sensitive; temperature 98° 4'.

4-55 P.M.—It is now struggling somewhat violently, and the heart is beating steadily and well.

5-30 P.M.—Violent struggling still going on; heart beating forcibly and well.

8 P.M.—The heart is not beating so forcibly; no convulsive movements.

MIDNIGHT.—In the same state.

5 A.M.—The heart is much weaker.

4 A.M.—Temperature 89° 9'; heart beating very feebly.

3 P.M.—In the same state.

4-30. P.M.—Heart ceased to beat, 25 hours after the commencement of artificial respiration.

———

## No. 18.

### Emetine.

Hypodermically injected into a dog, weighing 37lbs, ½ grain of snake-poison, and ¾ of a grain of Emetine, at 9-50 A.M.

10-15 A.M.—Convulsed.

10-20 A.M.—Commenced artificial respiration.

NOON.—Heart beating well.

12-50 P.M.—Temperature 93° 3'.

3-30 P.M.—Heart beating fairly well; temperature 94° 4'.

5 P.M.—In the same state.

8. P.M.—Heart beating well.

1 A.M.—In the same state.

6 A.M.—Heart still beating.

11-30 A.M.—The heart is now beating very feebly, and the lungs do not appear to be properly inflated; passed water.

3 P.M.—Heart ceased to beat, 28 hours and 40 minutes after the commencement of artificial respiration.

———

## No. 19.

### Podophyllin.

Hypodermically injected into a dog ½ grain of cobra-poison and one grain of Podophyllin, at 8-45 A.M.

8-52 A.M.—Passed a hard stool; is trembling a great deal.

9-8 A.M.—Seems better.

9-24 A.M.—Passed another stool.

9-43 A.M.—Staggering about.

9-52 A.M.—Is slightly convulsed; pupils widely dilated.

10 A.M.—Commenced artificial respiration.

NOON.—Heart beating well.

4 P.M.—Heart beating fairly well.

6 P.M.—In the same state.

8 P.M.—The heart is now beating less forcibly.

MIDNIGHT.—In the same state.

1-30 A.M.—The heart is now beating much more strongly.

8-30 A.M.—The heart is beating well, but the head is looking somewhat collapsed; temperature 96° 3'.

9-30 A.M.—In the same state.

NOON.—Temperature 96° 6'.

3 P.M.—The heart is beating very feebly.

5 P.M.—Heart ceased to beat, 31 hours after the commencement of artificial respiration.

---

## No. 20.

### *Atropine.*

Hypodermically injected into a dog, weighing 16lbs, ¼ grain of snake-poison and ⅒th of a grain of Atropine, at 10-15 A.M.

Temperature 101°.

11 A.M.—The animal is now restless and uneasy; seems drowsy; there is no salivation.

11-10 A.M.—Respiration laborious; micturition; convulsions; the heart's action is very feeble.

11-15 A.M.—Temperature 101°; still convulsed.

11-20 A.M.—Spasmodic micturition; breathing very difficult.

11-28 A.M.—Hypodermically injected ¼ grain of strychnine; pupils insensitive to touch.

11-30 A.M.—Commenced artificial respiration; heart's action is now very strong; pupils now sensitive to the touch; the animal constantly opens and shuts its mouth.

11-45 A.M.—Temperature 97°; heart's action not so strong, but still tolerably strong.

NOON.—Spasms about every 20 seconds.

1 P.M.—Temperature 98°; heart's action very powerful.

2 P.M.—In the same state; temperature 98°.

3 P.M.—Temperature 85°; heart beating forcibly.

3-30 P.M.—The heart's action is slower; temperature 85°.

8 P.M.—Heart is beating well.

MIDNIGHT.—In the same state.

3 A.M.—Heart still beating well.

11-15 A.M.—Temperature below 85°. The lungs do not seem to inflate well owing to the rigidity of the intercostal muscles.

NOON.—Heart still beating.

1 P.M.—Heart's action very feeble.

2 P.M.—Heart still beating, but very feebly.

2-25 P.M.—Heart ceased to beat, 27 hours and 15 minutes after the commencement of artificial respiration.

## No. 21.

### *Transfusion.*

A dog was bitten by a cobra, at 8-55 A.M.

2-20 A.M.—Staggering about.

9-25 A.M.—Convulsed.

9-27 A.M.—Commenced artificial respiration; there was some trouble at first, the apparatus being new and imperfect.

9-35 A.M.—Heart beating slowly; is apparently sensible.

9-40 A.M.—The artificial respiration is 44 to a minute, pulse 44 also.

10-3 A.M.—There had been considerable response to galvanism, but there is now little or none except of the irides, which alternately expand and contract.

10-30 A.M.—Very nearly in the same state; the irides are scarcely so active; temperature 101° 3′; heart beating 112, forcibly but irregularly; respirations 40; lachrymation has gone on continually.

11-10 A.M.—The femoral pulse is beating very steadily and well.

11-15 A.M.—Temperature 100° 8′; respirations 36; heart beating 100, strong but very irregularly; it was beating much more quickly at first; irides still act by galvanism.

11-40 A.M.—Changed the bellows as air was escaping from the one we were using.

NOON.—Irides still act; respirations 44; heart 160, strong; temperature 100° 6′; applied heat.

12-30 P.M.—Heart beating very strongly and regularly, 140; temperature 100° 7′; respirations 44; irides still act.

1-15 P.M.—Respirations 32; heart beating 184, pretty strongly; temperature 102° 3′; only one iris, the right, responds to galvanism.

1-40 P.M.—Both irides act.

2-30 P.M.—Transfused 3 ounces of blood with warm water and ammonia, into a vein. There was marked improvement in the action of the heart which had been beating feebly and irregularly. We now opened the thorax and observed the action of the heart, and inflation of the lungs; the arteries bled freely when cut, the blood spirting out in regular jets.

3-30 P.M.—The heart began to fail considerably.

Injected 3 ounces of warm water and 15 grains of chlorate of potash into the right femoral vien; the animal passed fœces and urine, and the heart almost immediately ceased, 6 hours and 3 minutes after the commencement of artificial respiration.

---

## No. 22.

### *Podophyllin.*

Hypodermically injected into a dog, weighing 37lbs, ½ grain of cobra-poison and one grain of Podophyllin, at 8-45 A.M.

8-52 A.M.—Passed a hard stool; is trembling a great deal.

9-8 A.M.—Seems better.

9-24 A.M.—Passed another hard stool.

9-43 A.M.—Is staggering about.

9-52 A.M.—Is slightly convulsed ; pupils widely dilated.

10 A.M.—Commenced artificial respiration.

Noon.—Heart beating well.

4 P.M.—Heart beating fairly well.

6 P.M.—In the same state.

8 P.M.—The heart is now beating less forcibly.

Midnight.—In the same state.

1-30 A.M.—The heart is now beating much more forcibly.

8-30 A.M.—The heart is beating well, but the head is looking as if the animal were dead ; temperature 96° 3′.

9-30 A.M.—In the same state.

Noon.—Temperature 96° 6′.

3 P.M.—The heart is beating very feebly.

5 P.M.—Heart ceased to beat, in 31 hours.

---

## No. 23.

### *Tincture of Iodine.*

Hypodermically injected into a dog, weighing 25lbs, ½ grain of cobra-poison and 30 minims of Tincture of Iodine, at 9-35 A.M.

9-55 A.M.—Vomited.

10 A.M.—Temperature 100° 7′.

10-20 A.M.—Whining, and is very restless.

Noon.—Extremely restless ; is salivated, and constantly vomiting ; temperature 100° 5′.

12-30 P.M.—Convulsed.

12-45 P.M.—Commenced artificial respiration.

12-50 P.M.—Injected 15 minims of the Tincture of Iodine and 15 minims of water into a vein ; the heart's action was at first considerably accelerated.

2-15 P.M.—Very slight response to galvanism ; temperature 96° 3′; the heart is beating very feebly.

4-30 P.M.—Temperature 94° ; applied heat ; there is little response to galvanism, but the heart is now beating steadily and well.

6 P.M.—In the same state.

8 P.M.—Heart is beating strongly ; very little response to galvanism.

12-30 A.M.—No response to galvanism, but the heart is beating forcibly and regularly, 140 ; temperature 96° 2′.

6 A.M.—In the same state.

8 A.M.—There is very slight response to galvanism ; heart beating less strongly.

10 A.M.—In the same state.

Noon.—The heart is still beating well, very slight response to galvanism.

4 P.M.—In the same state.

6 P.M.—Slight response to galvanism ; the pupils are contracted ; there is little salivation.

8 P.M.—Temperature 91°.

1 A.M.—The heart is still beating, but very feebly; the body of the animal feels cold.

2 A.M.—The heart is beating very feebly; temperature still 91°.

3-10 A.M.—Dead, 38 hours and 25 minutes since the commencement of artificial respiration.

---

## THIRD SERIES.

---

## The Hypodermic Injection of various doses of Snake-poison, &c., &c.

---

The following experiments were made to ascertain the time required to kill with various doses, also the minimum fatal dose.

---

### No. 1.

A dog, weighing 24lbs, was bitten by a cobra (which had been a long time in captivity), at 8 A.M.

8-30 A.M.—Affected; salivated, and is restless.

8-35 A.M.—Pupils dilated; breathing intermittent; heart beating irregularly.

8-40 A.M.—Very much convulsed; tongue paralyzed.

8-41 A.M.—Has ceased to breathe; applied galvanism.

8-50 A.M.—Heart ceased to beat, in 50 minutes; galvanism evidently kept the heart beating.

---

### No. 2.

A dog, weighing 36lbs, was bitten by a cobra, at 7-33 A.M.; temperature 102° 5'.

7-40 A.M.—Getting drowsy, and has some difficulty in walking.

7-50 A.M.—Panting and hurried respirations.

7-57 A.M.—Defœcation and salivation.

8 A.M.—Temperature 103°; has diarrhœa; pupils dilated.

8-4 A.M.—Getting very uneasy.

8-7 A.M.—Head drooping; appears very drowsy; pupils dilated; respiration very slow and difficult; much twitching of the muscles of the abdomen.

8-8 A.M.—Passed a quantity of limpid urine; hind legs completely paralysed.

8-12 A.M.—Muscles of the chest almost paralysed; respiration scarcely perceptible.

8-15 A.M.—Temperature 101°.

8-19 A.M.—Convulsed and gasping for breath, but appears to be conscious; pupils not sensible; breathing irregular and spasmodic; much salivation.

8-23 A.M.—Dead, in 50 minutes.

---

### No. 3.

Hypodermically injected into a dog, weighing 33lbs, 2½ grains of cobra-poison, at 7-54 A.M.

9-15 A.M.—Is very drowsy.

9-16 A.M.—Got up and staggered about with its head hanging down, and neck well arched.

9-20 A.M.—Retching, and is much convulsed.

9-25 A.M.—Tongue paralysed.

9-34 A.M.—Still convulsed; defœcation.

9-43 A.M.—Ceased to breathe.

9-49 A.M.—Heart ceased to beat, in 1 hour and 43 minutes.

---

### No. 4.

Hypodermically injected into a dog, weighing 25lbs, 2 grains of cobra-poison, at 7-46 A.M.; temperature 103°.

8-5 A.M.—Temperature 103°.

8-15 A.M.—Somewhat drowsy; pupils dilated.

8-20 A.M.—Temperature 102°.

8-31 A.M.—Is very uneasy.

8-40 A.M.—Temperature 102°.

8-55 A.M.—Getting very drowsy; defœcation and micturition.

9-10 A.M.—Temperature 101°.

9-12 A.M.—Vomited; breathing hurried; paralysis of the muscles of respiration coming on.

9-14 A.M.—Partially convulsed, and is salivated.

9-16 A.M.—Temperature 101°.

9-18 A.M.—Is getting more drowsy.

9-20 A.M.—Staggering about with its head hanging down; foaming at the mouth and micturating.

9-21 A.M.—Much convulsed.

9-29 A.M.—Dead, in 1 hour and 43 minutes.

---

### No. 5.

Hypodermically injected into a dog, weighing 39lbs, 1½ grains of cobra-poison, at 8-14 A.M.; temperature 103°.

8-23 A.M.—Getting drowsy.

8-25 A.M.—Is very drowsy.

8-30 A.M.—Temperature 101°.

8-44 A.M.—Pupils dilated.

8-45 A.M.—Temperature 100°.

8-56 A.M.—Temperature 100°.

9-4 A.M.—Temperature 102°.

9-10 A.M.—Breathing is getting laborious.

9-13 A.M.—Temperature 101°; very drowsy; tongue protruding; breathing scarcely perceptible.

9-18 A.M.—Almost dead.

9-27 A.M.—Passed a large quantity of limpid urine.

9-28 A.M.—Is convulsed.

9-31 A.M.—Respiration has ceased.

9-35 A.M.—Heart ceased to beat, in 1 hour 21 minutes; temperature at death 100°.

---

## No. 6.

Hypodermically injected into a dog, weighing 28lbs, 1 grain of cobra-poison, at 9-53 A.M.

10-5 A.M.—Temperature 102° 1'.

10-25 A.M.—Temperature 101° 8'.

10-35 A.M.—Temperature 101° 6'.

11 A.M.—Slight convulsions; it is lying down; the tongue is paralysed.

11-15 A.M.—Temperature 1° 2'.

11-35 A.M.—Heart ceased to beat, in 1 hour 42 minutes.

---

## No. 7.

Hypodermically injected into a dog, weighing 24lbs, 1 grain of cobra-poison, at 7-53 A.M.; temperature 102°.

8-5 A.M.—Salivation.

8-11 A.M.—Temperature 103°.

8-13 A.M.—Is getting very drowsy, and is slightly paralysed in the hind quarters; breathing hurried.

8-26 A.M.—Temperature 101°; breathing hurried.

8-28 A.M.—Foaming at the mouth; vomiting.

8-31 A.M.—Again vomited.

8-35 A.M.—Is much convulsed; pupils much dilated; breathing laborious.

8-38 A.M.—Temperature 102; is very drowsy; twitchings of the muscles of the hind legs.

8-45 A.M.—Is much distressed; respiration laborious

8-49 A.M.—Convulsed; breathing almost ceased; temperature 100°.

8-50 A.M.—Dead, in 57 minutes.

---

## No. 8.

Hypodermically injected into a dog, weighing 35lbs, ¾ of a grain of cobra-poison, at 8-35 A.M.; temperature 101°.

8-43 A.M.—Appears drowsy.

8-50 A.M.—Temperature 100°; the animal is panting, and the tongue protrudes.

8-58 A.M.—Breathing getting difficult.

9 A.M.—Temperature 101°; is getting drowsy.

9-8 A.M.—Paralysis of the hind legs coming on.

9-19 A.M.—Temperature 101°; appears drowsy.

9-32 A.M.—Temperature 101°; is foaming at the mouth.

9-35 A.M.—Passed a solid stool; vomiting; paralysis of extremities commencing.

9-40 A.M.—Micturition, in drops; convulsions coming on.

9-45 A.M.—Very much convulsed; temperature 100°; pupils much dilated.

9-50 A.M.—Is much convulsed, and is rolling about on the ground; respirations gasping.

9-55 A.M.—Respiration scarcely perceptible; universal convulsions.

10 A.M.—Temperature 101°.

10-5 A.M.—Temperature the same (100°).

10-7 A.M.—Dead, in 1 hour and 32 minutes.

----

## No. 9.

Hypodermically injected into a dog, weighing 24lbs, ½ grain of cobra-poison, at 10-12 A.M.

11-27 A.M.—Very slightly affected.

11-37 A.M.—Temperature 102° 2'.

12-15 P.M.—Temperature 102° 5'.

12-21 P.M.—Is very restless, and vomits violently.

12-25 P.M.—Much convulsed, and is constantly retching.

12-31 P.M.—Respiration has ceased.

12-36 P.M.—Heart ceased to beat, in 2 hours and 24 minutes.

----

## No. 10.

Hypodermically injected into a dog, weighing 19lbs, ½ grain of cobra-poison, at 8-47 A.M.; temperature 103°.

8-50 A.M.—Appears to be getting drowsy.

9 A.M.—Temperature 103°.

9-20 A.M.—Temperature 101°; very drowsy.

9-40 A.M.—Temperature 101°; pupils dilated.

9-55 A.M.—Great disinclination to move; temperature 101°.

10-3 A.M.—Tongue protruding, and head hanging down.

10-5 A.M.—Temperature 101°; respiration very slow.

10-10 A.M.—Struggling violently; is senseless.

10-12 A.M.—Convulsive twitchings of the extremities.

10-15 A.M.—Temperature 102°.

10-20 A.M.—Breathing very feebly.

10-28 A.M.—Salivation; micturition.

10-35 A.M.—Temperature 101°; breathing scarcely perceptible.

10-42 A.M.—Respiration ceased; heart beating.

10-45 A.M.—Heart ceased, in 1 hour and 58 minutes.

## No. 11.

Hypodermically injected into a dog, weighing 20lbs, ¼ of a grain of cobra-poison, at 10-19 A.M.

10-27 A.M.—Is but little affected.
11-40 A.M.—Temperature 103° 3′.
12-26 P.M.—Temperature 103°.
1-55 P.M.—Convulsed.
2-3 P.M.—Respiration ceased.
2-11 P.M.—Heart ceased to beat, in 4 hours and 20 minutes.

---

## No. 12.

A dog, weighing 41lbs, was hypodermically injected with ¼ of a grain of cobra-poison at 9-20 A.M. ; temperature 101° 5′.

10-48 A.M.—Temperature 102°.
11-15 A.M.—Temperature 102°.
NOON.—Temperature 101° 8′.
12-30 P.M.—Sleeping ; respiration regular.
1-50 P.M.—Is walking about.
2-15 P.M.—Holds the head down, and looks depressed ; temperature, 101° 5′.
3-10 P.M.—Is greatly depressed ; walks with great difficulty and with head hanging down ; pupils much dilated ; considerable swelling at the seat of injection ; salivation.
3-18 P.M.—Vomited a great deal of bile mixed with mucus ; stands with difficulty.
3-22 P.M.—Passed fæces.
3-30 P.M.—Vomited with great difficulty ; respirations 20 ; temperature 101°.
3-35 P.M.—Involuntary micturition in drops ; heart 74, irregular ; temperature 101° 2′.
3-45 P.M.—Retching.
4 P.M.—Lies with the tongue protruded ; respirations 16.
4-10 P.M.—Defœcation ; convulsed.
4-20 P.M.—Insensible.
5-20 P.M.—Dead, in 8 hours.

---

## No. 13.

At 8-50 A.M.—Hypodermically injected into a dog, weighing 44lbs, ¼th of a grain of cobra-poison ; temperature 101° 5′.

9-10 A.M.—Temperature 102°.
10-38 A.M.—Temperature 102°.
11-15 A.M.—Temperature 102° 2′.
NOON.—Temperature 101° 6′.
1-50 P.M.—Walking about, and is quite lively.
2-20 P.M.—Temperature 101° 3′.
3-50 P.M.—Temperature 105° 5′.
7-4 P.M.—Partook of food.

8-45 P.M.—Temperature 102°; vomited.

9-15 P.M.—Copious salivation.

10-30 P.M.—Temperature 102° 7'

12-50 A.M.—Temperature 103° 7'; no salivation; sleeping quietly.

1-15 A.M.—Vomited.

6-27 A.M.—The .part where the poison was injected is much swollen; the animal is very drowsy.

6-35 A.M.—Temperature 102°.

8-55 A.M.—Temperature 103° 1'.

1 P.M.—Temperature 103° 4'.

The leg became very painful and ultimately suppurated at the injected part; it recovered.

---

## No. 14.

Hypodermically injected into a dog, weighing 18½lbs, one-tenth of a grain of cobra-poison, at 12-30 P.M.

2-10 P.M.—Unaffected.

3-50 P.M.—The same.

5-30 P.M.—Is slightly restless, and is vomiting.

10-30 P.M.—Convulsed.

11 P.M.—Dead, in 11 hours and 30 minutes.

---

## No. 15.

Hypodermically injected into a dog, weighing 30lbs, one-tenth of a grain of cobra-poison, at 8-21 A.M

The animal was but slightly affected, and ultimately recovered.

---

## No. 16.

12-31 P.M.—Hypodermically injected one-sixth of a grain of cobra-poison into a dog, weighing 40lbs.

2-10 P.M.—Unaffected.

3-50 P.M.—The same.

5 P.M.—Became very restless; vomiting.

5-20 P.M.—Convulsed.

5-32 P.M.—Respiration ceased.

5-36 P.M.—Heart ceased to beat, in 5 hours and 6 minutes. The bladder is enormously distended.

---

## No. 17.

12-32 P.M.—Hypodermically injected into a dog, weighing 14lbs, one-eighth of a grain of cobra-poison.

2-8 P.M.—Is slightly affected.

3-50 P.M.—In the same state.

4-45 P.M.—Is restless; all at once it fell over, became convulsed, and died at 5 P.M., in 4 hours and 28 minutes.

---

### No. 18.

8-45 A.M.—Hypodermically injected 1 grain of cobra-poison into a dog, weighing 40℔s.

10-30 A.M.—Is very restless.

11-40 A.M.—Is lying down on its side; tongue is paralyzed, and there is a great deal of salivation.

11-50 A.M.—Convulsed.

12-30 A.M.—Dead, in 3 hours and 45 minutes.

---

### No. 19.

9 A.M.—Hypodermically injected one-twelfth of a grain of cobra-poison into a dog, weighing 41½℔s.

11-45 P.M.—Looks slightly drowsy.

2 P.M.—In the same state.

5-30 P.M.—Has been vomiting; is lying down, and seems much distressed; is salivated.

8 P.M.—In the same state.

11 P.M.—In the same state; had taken little food.

8-30 A.M.—Is lying down, occasionally vomiting, and is very drowsy; temperature 103° 1′.

10 A.M.—In the same state.

1 P.M.—Rather worse.

4 P.M.—Still very drowsy.

The injected part sloughed, and the animal ultimately recovered.

---

### No. 20.

9-5 A.M.—Hypodermically injected into a dog, weighing 17℔s, $\frac{1}{15}$th of a grain of cobra-poison.

11-45 A.M.—Appears to be a little sluggish.

2 P.M.—In the same state.

5-30 P.M.—Has been vomiting; is lying down and seems much distressed; is salivated.

8 P.M.—In the same state; had taken very little food.

8-30 A.M.—Is lying down on its side, breathing quickly but quietly; is occasionally slightly convulsed; the pupils are dilated; it is sensible, as shown by the fact of its whining and attempting to bite when it is lifted. The animal got up and staggered off with its head hanging down and its neck arched, and then fell over.

10 A.M.—In the same state.

1 P.M.—Very much worse; convulsions gradually came on, and increased, and the animal died at 4-30 P.M., in 31 hours and 25 minutes.

## No. 21.

11-55 A.M.—Hypodermically injected into a dog, weighing 44lbs, $\frac{1}{77}$ of a grain of cobra-poison.
12-55 P.M.—Appears but slightly affected.
6 P.M.—Very slightly affected.
MIDNIGHT.—Well. This animal recovered.

## No. 22.

9 A.M.—Hypodermically injected into a dog, weighing 18lbs, $\frac{1}{77}$th of a grain of cobra-poison ; was never affected.

## No. 23.

9-42 A.M.—Hypodermically injected into a dog, weighing 15lbs, $\frac{1}{17}$th of a grain of cobra-poison.
At midnight we found the dog much affected, but it ultimately recovered.

## No. 24.

8-53 A.M.—A goat, weighing 44lbs, was hypodermically injected with one grain of cobra-poison.
9-25 A.M.—Fell down, and could not again get up.
9-28 A.M.—Convulsed ; tongue paralyzed.
9-30 A.M.—Respiration ceased.
9-45 A.M.—Heart ceased to beat, in 52 minutes.

## No. 25.

9-30 A.M.—A dog, weighing 36lbs, was hypodermically injected with nearly $\frac{1}{4}$ a grain of daboia-poison.
11 A.M.—Affected.
4 P.M.—In the same state.
6 P.M.—Convulsed
7 P.M.—Dead, in 9 hours and 30 minutes.

## No. 26.

9-32 A.M.—Hypodermically injected into a dog, weighing 39lbs, $\frac{1}{4}$ of a grain of daboia-poison.
11 A.M.—Is unaffected.
4 P.M.—Is very drowsy ; there is a great deal of salivation.
6 P.M.—In the same state.
8 P.M.—Rather worse.
MIDNIGHT.—Is much worse.
7 A.M.—Dead, in 21 hours and 28 minutes.

## No. 27.

9-40 A.M.—Hypodermically injected into a dog, weighing 18tbs, $\frac{1}{75}$th of a grain of daboia-poison.

Noon.—Unaffected.

8 P.M.—Very slightly affected.

The injected part became enormously swollen, and afterwards sloughed, but the animal recovered.

---

## No. 28.

8-51 A.M.—Hypodermically injected into a dog, weighing 33tbs, $\frac{1}{18}$th of a grain of cobra-poison; temperature 101° 5'.

Was little affected, except that the injected part became swollen.

---

## No. 29.

8-43 A.M.—Hypodermically injected into a dog, weighing 28tbs, $\frac{1}{17}$th of a grain of cobra-poison; temperature 101° 7'.

Quite unaffected.

---

## No. 30.

9-10 A.M.—Hypodermically injected into a dog, weighing 38tbs, $\frac{1}{15}$th of a grain of cobra-poison; temperature 101° 8'.

9-20 A.M.—Temperature 101°.

10-13 A.M.—Temperature 102°.

Noon.—Temperature 102° 8'.

3-40 P.M.—Some swelling about the injected part; temperature 100° 2'.

9-8 P.M.—Temperature 103°.

10-30 P.M.—Temperature 102° 8'.

12-40 A.M.—Temperature 101°; is unaffected.

6-30 A.M.—Is drowsy; temperature 104°.

8-45 A.M.—Marked depression; head hanging down; difficulty in walking; great swelling at the part; temperature 103° 6'.

1-45 P.M.—Temperature 102° 7'; great depression; respirations 26.

4-15 P.M.—Temperature 102° 7'.

The part sloughed, but the animal recovered.

---

## No. 31.

Hypodermically injected into a dog, weighing 29tbs, $\frac{1}{17}$th of a grain of cobra-poison, at 10-45 A.M.; temperature 103°.

Noon.—Temperature 101°.

4 P.M.—Temperature 101°; swelling at the seat of injection.

5-30 P.M.—Vomited.

6-45 P.M.—Again vomited.

8-53 P.M.—Temperature 102°.

12-50 A.M.—Temperature 101° 5'.

1 A.M.—Slight salivation.

The animal is reported to have broken its chain and "bolted."

F

## No. 32.

Hypodermically injected into a dog, weighing 40lbs, $\frac{1}{2}$th of a grain of cobra-poison, at 9 A.M.; temperature 100°.

Noon.—Temperature 101° 7'; unaffected.

4 P.M.—Temperature 101° 6'; slightly swelling at the seat of injection.

7-50 P.M.—Partook of a hearty meal.

10-30 P.M.—Temperature 102° 1'.

6-22 A.M.—Vomited a large quantity of undigested food.

This animal continued to be slightly affected for a whole day, but ultimately recovered.

---

## No. 33.

9-30 A.M.—Hypodermically injected into a dog, weighing 26lbs, $\frac{1}{8}$th of a grain of cobra-poison; temperature 102° 2'.

11-15 A.M.—Temperature 101°.

4-10 P.M.—Temperature 101° 4'.

10-30 P.M.—Temperature 102° 1'.

12-15 P.M.—Temperature 103° 7'.

6-47 A.M.—Temperature 101°.

9 A.M.—Temperature 102°.

10 A.M.—Vomited; slightly drowsy.

4-15 P.M.—Has continued in the same drowsy state, and has vomited two or three times.

8 A.M.—Temperature 102° 1'; is better.

Noon.—Temperature 102°.

This animal recovered.

---

## No. 34.

8-49 A.M.—Hypodermically injected into a dog, weighing 29lbs, $\frac{1}{8}$th of a grain of cobra-poison; temperature 102° 5'; unaffected.

---

## No. 35.

Hypodermically injected into a dog, weighing 29lbs, $\frac{1}{8}$th of a grain of cobra-poison, at 8-45 A.M.; temperature 101° 1'; unaffected.

---

### *The Injection of Cobra-poison into the Peritoneal Cavity.*

---

## No. 36.

Injected into the peritoneal cavity of a dog, weighing 16lbs, $\frac{1}{8}$th of a grain of cobra-poison.

Dead, in 3 hours and 29 minutes.

## No. 37.

Injected into the peritoneal cavity of a dog, weighing 12lbs, $\frac{1}{16}$ of a grain of cobra-poison.

Dead, in 49 hours and 20 minutes. This animal exhibited all the symptoms of snake-poisoning.

---

## No. 38.

Injected into the peritoneal cavity of a small dog 3 grains of cobra-poison.

Dead, in 25 minutes.

---

### *The Intravenous Injection of Snake-poison.*

---

## No. 39.

Injected $\frac{1}{2}$ grain of cobra-poison into the jugular vein of a small dog, at 3 P.M.

4 P.M.—Found dead in the room in which it had been confined.

*Note.*—The blood was found *fluid* and *non-coagulable.*

---

## No. 40.

Injected 1$\frac{1}{2}$ grains of cobra-poison into a vein of a dog, at 7-45 A.M.; temperature 103° 2'.

Dead, in 75 minutes.

*Note.*—The blood only very partially coagulated after 4 hours.

---

# FOURTH SERIES.

---

The administration of various drugs without artificial respiration, and miscellaneous experiments.

---

### OPIUM AS AN ANTIDOTE.

---

## No. 1.

A large dog was bitten by a cobra, at 10-3 A.M.

10-5 A.M.—Administered 3 drams of the Tincture of Opium, and half an ounce of brandy.

11 A.M.—The animal has been foaming at the mouth and is evidently uneasy.

11-25 A.M.—Administered Tr. Opii. 1$\frac{1}{2}$ dram, and half an ounce of brandy.

11-30 A.M.—Is under the influence of snake-poison; passed stools at first hard, and then soft and slimy.

11-37 A.M.—Vomited ; the pupils are somewhat contracted ; a good deal of spasm about the œsophagus.

11-45 A.M.—Is lying down, and seems very weak and uneasy.

12-20 P.M.—Is standing up and breathing very rapidly.

12-30 P.M.—Gave another dram of the Tincture.

2 P.M.—Gave two drams of Tr. Opii.

3-30 P.M.—Tr. Opii. 1 dram, brandy 1 oz.

The dog is exceedingly weak, and is much affected ; apparently more from the opium than the snake-poison ; there is, however, one unmistakeable sympton of snake-poisoning, viz., paralysis of the tongue; the animal is very drowsy indeed.

4 P.M.—In the same state ; gave another dram of the tincture.

5 P.M.—In the same state.

6 P.M.—The animal is exceedingly weak, but is sensible.

8 P.M.—Occasional convulsions ; administered Tr. Opii. 1 dram, brandy 1 oz. ; some of this was lost.

9-30 P.M.—Dead, in 11 hours 27 minutes.

*Note.*—The opium had a good chance if it had been of any use, as the cobra was evidently very weak.

### No. 2.

8-15 A.M.—A dog was bitten by a cobra, which had had its poison removed two days previously.

8-20 A.M.—Three drams of tincture of opium.

8-27 A.M.—Is affected with symptoms of snake-poisoning ; administered half an ounce of Tr. Opii.

8-34 A.M.—Convulsed.

8-40 A.M.—Dead, in 25 minutes.

*Note.*—In this case the heart was apparently paralyzed.

### No. 3.

Hypodermically injected into a small pariah dog's thigh ⅛th of a grain of cobra-poison, at 8-50 A.M. ; temperature 103° 1′.

9-5 A.M.—Tr. Opii. two drams administered.

9-40 A.M.—Temperature 103° 6′ ; is drowsy.

10-30 A.M.—Temperature 102° 7′.

NOON.—Is lying down and is much affected ; gave Tr. Opii. 1 dram ; temperature 102° 5′.

12-30 P.M.—Dead, in 3 hours and 40 minutes.

*N.B.*—The dog was small, but the amount of poison injected was only the one-thirtieth part of what a cobra *can* shed at one bite. A smaller dog was killed in 3 hours after the injection of the same quantity of poison.

### No. 4.

Hypodermically injected into the thigh of a large dog, 1 grain of cobra-poison, at 9 A.M. ; temperature 101° 8′.

9-30 A.M.—Temperature 102° 4′. Tr. Opii. 3 drams.

9-45 A.M.—Is very much affected.  Tr. Opii. 3 drams.

10 A.M.—Convulsed.

11 A.M.—Dead, in 2 hours.

----

## No. 5.

A dog was bitten by a cobra, at 8-40 A.M.

9 A.M.—Administered opium ½ oz., brandy 1 oz.

9-10 A.M.—Is staggering about.

9-20 A.M.—Is convulsed, though not violently.

9-25 A.M.—Dead, in 25 minutes.

----

### MORPHIA AS AN ANTIDOTE.

----

## No. 6.

1-45 P.M.—Hypodermically injected into a dog a solution containing 1 grain of morphia with ½ grain of cobra-poison; temperature 102° 2′.

2 P.M.—Temperature 101° 8′.

3-30 P.M.—Is convulsed; injected one grain of morphia into the peritoneal cavity and another into a vein.

2-55 P.M.—Dead, in 1 hour and 50 minutes.

*N.B.*—The dog was middling-sized.

----

### SULPHATE OF MAGNESIA AS AN ANTIDOTE.

----

## No. 7.

A dog was bitten by a cobra, at 8-52 A.M.

8-56 A.M.—Administered Mag. Sulph. 1 oz.

9-1 A.M.—Dead, in 9 minutes.

*N.B.*—This is one of the most rapid deaths on record, considering that the snake had been kept for some time in captivity, and the dog was large and healthy.

----

### STRYCHNINE AS AN ANTIDOTE.

----

## No. 8.

A dog was bitten by a cobra, from which the poison had been taken the day previously, at 1-15 P.M.  Immediately hypodermically injected ¼th of a grain of strychnine.

1-30 P.M.—Very sluggish.

2 P.M.—Dead, in 45 minutes.

## No. 9.

A dog, weighing 21lbs, was hypodermically injected with 3 grains of snake-poison and ½ grain of strychnine, at 1 P.M.; temperature 100° 8′.

The effects of the administration of strychnine almost immediately followed.

1-30 P.M.—Administered ½ grain of strychnine by the mouth; tetanic spasm immediately came on, and chloroform was administered.

2-4 P.M.—Dead, in 1 hour and 4 minutes.

———

## No. 10.

A dog, weighing 32lbs, was hypodermically injected with ¼ grain of cobra-poison and ¼ grain of strychnine, at 1-50 P.M.

1-55 P.M.—Exhibited the tetanic spasms of strychnine poisoning.

1-59 P.M.—Had a severe spasm; the spasms are now constant; respiration is perfectly free.

2-33 P.M.—Dead, in 43 minutes.

The strychnine evidently killed this dog.

———

## No. 11.

A dog, weighing 25lbs, was hypodermically injected with ¼ grain of cobra-poison and ¼ grain of strychnine, at 1-53 P.M.

2-10 P.M.—Is very uneasy, whining constantly; the hind legs are kept widely apart, and the animal unsuccessfully endeavours to sit down.

2-17 P.M.—Had a tetanic spasm.

2-18 P.M.—Is drowsy.

2-20 P.M.—Is seized with a very strong spasm.

3 P.M.—Dead, in 1 hour and 7 minutes.

———

## No. 12.

Hypodermically injected into a dog, weighing 19lbs, ¼ grain of cobra-poison and $\frac{1}{16}$th of a grain of strychnine, at 1-55 P.M.

2-5 P.M.—Is seized with a very severe tetanic spasm; respiration perfectly free.

3 P.M.—Dead, in 1 hour and 5 minutes.

———

## No. 13.

Hypodermically injected into a dog, weighing 15lbs, ¼ grain of cobra-poison and ¼th of a grain of strychnine, at 1-58 P.M.

2-15 P.M.—Tries to sit down, but cannot; the hind legs are kept wide apart and the tail is turned between the legs.

2-21 P.M.—Muscular twitchings.

2-23 P.M.—Fell over in tetanic spasms.

3-48 P.M—Dead, in 1 hour and 50 minutes.

### Liq. Arsenicalis as an Antidote.

## No. 14.

Hypodermically injected into a dog, weighing 35lbs, ½ a grain of cobra-poison, at 8·56 A.M.; temperature 102°.

9-35 A.M.—Hypodermically injected Liq. Arsenicalis ¼ dram.

9-45 A.M.—Temperature 102°.

10-30 A.M.—Appears affected; injected 15 minims more Liq. Arsenicalis.

10-40 A.M.—Temperature 102°; became convulsed; breathing very slowly; pupils alternately contracting and dilating.

10-52 A.M.—Injected 15 minims of Liq. Arsenicalis into a vein. The heart's action was very feeble.

11-7 A.M.—Dead, in 2 hours and 11 minutes.

### Chloral Hydrate as an Antidote.

## No. 15.

Hypodermically injected into a dog, weighing 25lbs, ⁷⁄ₓths of a grain of cobra-poison, at 12-10 P.M.; temperature 101° 2′.

12-16 P.M.—Hypodermically injected 10 grains of Chloral Hydrate.

12-40 P.M.—Injected 10 grains of Chloral Hydrate.

1-15 P.M.—Is very drowsy.

1-30 P.M.—Slightly affected by the snake-poison. Injected 10 grains more Chloral Hydrate; temperature 101° 9′.

2 P.M.—Has been sleeping, and is still sleeping.

3 P.M.—Woke up and was seized with convulsions; 10 grains more Choloral Hydrate were injected.

3-38 P.M.—Temperature 101° 7′; in the same state.

3-45 P.M.—Dead, in 3 hours and 35 minutes.

### Eclectic Medicines, &c., as Antidotes.

## No. 16.

Hypodermically injected into a dog 1 grain of snake-poison and Baptisin 5 grains, at 12-5 P.M.

12-30 P.M.—Is drowsy.

12-40 P.M.—Convulsed; administered 5 grains of Baptisin.

1 P.M.—Dead, in 55 minutes.

## No. 17.

Hypodermically injected into a dog 1 grain of cobra-poison and 3 grains of Iridin, at 9-1 A.M.

9-21 A.M.—Is slightly affected.
9-59 A.M.—Occasional convulsions.
10-45 A.M.—Dead, in 1 hour and 44 minutes.

## No. 18.

Hypodermically injected into a dog, weighing 29½lbs, ½ grain of cobra-poison, at 9-20 A.M.
9-24 A.M.—Hypodermically injected 4 grains of Leptandrin (*Veronica Virginica*).
9-57 A.M.—Fell over and became very restless; there is a great deal of defœcation.
10-2 A.M.—Convulsed.
10-15 A.M.—Dead, in 55 minutes.

## No. 19.

Hypodermically injected into a dog, weighing 30lbs, ½ a grain of cobra-poison and 2 minims of nicotin, at 12-43 P.M.
The animal almost immediately became salivated, and the breathing extremely hurried. (These were the effects of an over dose of nicotin.)
12-48 P.M.—Having vomited, the animal seems relieved; is constantly vomiting.
1 P.M.—Temperature 100° 4′; is much easier.
1-5 P.M.—Again breathing rapidly, but not so violently as before.
1-10 P.M.—Temperature 103° 2′. The effects of the nicotin are passing off; the animal is much easier, but is still salivated.
1-15 P.M.—The heart is beating irregularly and slowly.
1-45 P.M.—Is convulsed.
1-55 P.M.—Dead, in 1 hour and 55 minutes.

### CANNABIS INDICA AS AN ANTIDOTE.

## No. 20.

Hypodermically injected into a dog, weighing 29lbs, ½ a grain of cobra-poison and 30 minims of Tinct Cannabis Ind., at 9-40 A.M.
10-15 A.M.—Convulsed.
10-35 P.M.—Dead, in 12 hours and 55 minutes.
*N.B.*—Life had been sustained by artificial respiration.

### BICHLORIDE OF MERCURY AS AN ANTIDOTE.

## No. 21.

Hypodermically injected into a dog, weighing 21lbs, ⅓th of a grain of the poison of an Andamanese cobra and 1 grain of bichloride of mercury, at 10-5 A.M.

11-35 A.M.—Temperature 101° 5'.

12-15 P.M.—Is extremely drowsy.

1 P.M.—Temperature 101° 5'.

1-30 P.M.—Injected ½ grain of bichloride of mercury.

3 P.M.—Temperature 101°.

3-25 P.M.—In the same drowsy state.

4-10 P.M.—Temperature 101° 9'; is extremely drowsy, and breathing spasmodically; there is no salivation.

10-30 P.M.—Respiration, abdominal and spasmodic; salivation, but not profuse.

MIDNIGHT.—Pupils dilated, and the animal is convulsed.

4 A.M.—Dead, in 17 hours and 50 minutes.

## No. 22.

Hypodermically injected into a dog, weighing 13lbs, ¼ grain of cobra-poison and ½ grain of bichloride of mercury, at 3-35 P.M.

5-20 P.M.—Dead, in 1 hour and 45 minutes.

## No. 23.

Hypodermically injected into a dog, weighing 15lbs, ¼ grain of cobra-poison and 1 grain of bichloride of mercury, at 3-45 P.M.

5-30 P.M.—Dead, in 1 hour and 45 minutes.

## THE MINERAL ACIDS AS ANTIDOTES.

## No. 24.

Hypodermically injected into a dog, weighing 19lbs, ¼ grain of cobra-poison and 15 minims of Decinormal Sulphuric Acid (1cc = ·0017 grammes of ammonia), at 9-19 A.M.; temperature 102° 2'.

10-30 A.M.—Is convulsed.

11 A.M.—Dead, in 1 hour and 41 minutes.

## No. 25.

Hypodermically injected into a dog, weighing 34lbs, ½ grain of cobra-poison and 15 minims of decinormal nitric acid (1cc = ·0017 grammes of ammonia), at 9 A.M.

10. A.M.—Temperature 101° 5'; is very restless.

10-15 A.M.—Is occasionally convulsed; defœcation, micturition, and salivation; partially paralyzed.

10-20 A.M.—Injected hypodermically 20 minims of the acid.

11-30 A.M.—Dead, in 2 hours and 30 minutes.

G

## No. 26.

Hypodermically injected into a dog, weighing 24lbs, $\frac{1}{4}$ grain of cobra-poison and 15 minims of the decinormal nitric acid, at 8-55 A.M.

10. A.M.—Temperature 101° 4'; at present the animal appears little affected.

10-15 A.M.—Is drowsy.

11 A.M.—Convulsed.

11-45 A.M.—Dead, in 2 hours and 50 minutes.

## No. 27.

Hypodermically injected into a dog $\frac{1}{4}$ grain of cobra-poison and 15 minims of decinormal hydrochloric acid, at 10-22 A.M.

11-30 A.M.—Is not yet affected.

12-5 P.M.—Is getting restless; hypodermically injected 15 minims more acid.

12-30 P.M.—Convulsed.

1 P.M.—Dead, in 2 hours and 38 minutes.

## No. 28.

Hypodermically injected into a dog, weighing 22lbs, $\frac{1}{4}$ grain of cobra-poison and 30 minims of decinormal acetic acid, (1cc= ·0017 grains of ammonia—$\frac{N H}{3}$), at 9-55 A.M.

10-12 A.M.—Temperature 101° 2'.

10-35 A.M.—Temperature 101° 5'; is whining and becoming restless.

10-45 A.M.—Seems quite exhausted; the breathing is hurried and laborious.

11 A.M.—Convulsed; temperature 101°.

11-15 A.M.—Profuse salivation; is still convulsed.

11-35 A.M.—Dead, in 1 hour and 40 minutes.

## No. 29.

Hypodermically injected into a dog, weighing 44lbs, $\frac{1}{2}$ grain of cobra-poison and 30 minims of decinormal phosphoric acid, at 9-47 A.M.

10-50 A.M.—Convulsed.

11-25 A.M.—Temperature 101°.

Noon.—Dead, in 2 hours and 13 minutes.

## No. 30.

Hypodermically injected into a dog, weighing 22lbs, $\frac{1}{2}$ grain of poison (taken from a cobra brought from the Andaman Islands) and decinormal acetic acid 1 dram, at 9-58 A.M.

10-30 A.M.—Convulsed.

10-40 A.M.—Dead, in 42 minutes.

*Note.*—Though this snake sheds much less poison than the ordinary Indian cobra, the poison appears to be more rapidly fatal. As the snake died shortly after these experiments and before we could procure any more of its poison, we were unable to settle the point definitely. It is possible that acetic acid causes more rapid absorption of the snake-poison.

## No. 31.

Hypodermically injected into a dog, weighing 18lbs, $\frac{1}{4}$ grain of cobra-poison and 30 minims of decinormal phosphoric acid (1cc = ·0017 grammes of ammonia—($N_3H$), at 3-56 P.M.

5-14 P.M.—Is convulsed.

5-30 P.M.—Dead, in 1 hour and 34 minutes.

## MISCELLANEOUS EXPERIMENTS.

## No. 32.

### *The action of Ammonia and Snake-poison on the Blood.*

Placed in three separate watch-glasses ammonia, water, and snake-poison, and mixed fresh fowl's blood with each, with the following results:—

Ammonia and blood.—Partially coagulated and became dark in colour.

Water and blood.—Coagulated, and remained the bright red colour.

Snake-poison and blood.—Remained fluid, and became very dark.

## No. 33.

Repeated experiment No. 32, with similar results.

## No. 34.

This experiment refers to No. 11, page 5.

Hypodermically injected into a pigeon $\frac{1}{4}$ a dram of the poisoned dog's saliva, at 11-30 A.M.

12-30 P.M.—Is decidedly affected.

2-30 P.M.—Has a very drowsy appearance.

4-30 P.M.—Is drooping, and has been standing in one place since 2 o'clock.

5 P.M.—Is now feeding in the centre of the room.

The next day it crouched in a corner of the room, and was much affected; it died two days after the injection.

## No. 35.

This experiment refers to the same as the above.

At 12-15 P.M. injected into the right femoral vein of a dog 10 drams of the poisoned dog's saliva, diluted with one ounce of water.

12-30 P.M.—Temperature 104° 2'.
1-30 P.M.—Temperature 104° 7'.
2-30 P.M.—Temperature 105°.
3-30 P.M.—Temperature 108° 5'.
4-30 P.M.—Temperature 106°.
5-30 P.M.—Temperature 106° 4'.
7-30 P.M.—Temperature 105°.
MIDNIGHT.—Temperature 106° 2'.

The next morning the temperature was 104° 8'. This animal became very ill and ultimately refused food; it died 63 hours after the injection of the saliva.

---

## No. 36.

Hypodermically injected into a dog ⅓th of a grain of cobra-poison, at 9 A.M.; temperature 103°.

9-45 A.M.—Temperature 102° 8'.
10-20 A.M.—Temperature 102° 4'.
11-30 A.M.—Temperature 101° 9'; is very much affected.
11-45 A.M.—Convulsed.
NOON.—Dead, in 3 hours.

---

## No. 37.

Hypodermically injected into a dog 1 grain of cobra-posion, at 9-53 A.M.—(Weight of dog 28lbs.)

10-5. A.M.—Temperature 102° 1'.
10-25 A.M.—Temperature 101° 8'.
10-35 A.M.—Temperature 101° 6'.
11 A.M.—Convulsed.
11-15 A.M.—Temperature 102°.
11-35 A.M.—Dead, in 1 hour and 42 minutes.

---

## No. 38.

A dog was bitten by a cobra, from which the poison had been taken the day previously, at 1-20 P.M.

1-35 P.M.—Convulsed.
1-41 P.M.—Dead, in 21 minutes.

---

## No. 39.

A cat was bitten by a cobra, at 12-38 P.M. The bite was a doubtful one.

12-45 P.M.—Injected hypodermically 1 grain of cobra-poison.

1 P.M.—Breathing hurried; pupils normal.

3 P.M.—Is now very much affected.

5 P.M.—Convulsed.

5-30 P.M.—Dead, in 4 hours 52 minutes from the bite, and 4 hours 45 minutes from the injection.

———

## No. 40.

One grain of cobra-poison was injected into the peritoneal cavity of a dog, at 12-9 P.M.

12-27 P.M.—Convulsed.

12-35 P.M.—Dead, in 26 minutes.

———

## No. 41.

Gave a small fowl 4 grains of cobra-poison by the mouth, at 12-22 P.M.

12-35 P.M.—Is drowsy.

12-40 P.M.—Convulsed.

12-50 P.M.—Dead, in 28 minutes.

———

## FIFTH SERIES.

———

### The intravenous injection of Liquor Ammoniæ Fort., as advocated by Professor Halford, of Melbourne.

———

### No. 1.

A large dog was bitten by a cobra, at 7-26 A.M.

7-31 A.M.—Twenty minims of Liquor Ammoniæ Fort., diluted with 20 minims of water, were injected into a vein.

7-34 A.M.—Dog permitted to move about; passed stools. Breathing very quickly.

7-41 A.M.—Passed a stool.

7-47 A.M.—Passed water and a stool.

7-48 A.M.—Is lying down, and trembling.

7-51 A.M.—Again injected 10 minims of the ammonia, diluted as before, with an equal quantity of water; the dog at once became completely paralyzed. Heart beating very strongly.

7-54 A.M.—Strongly convulsed.

7-55 A.M.—Again injected 20 minims of ammonia and an equal quantity of water.

7-56 A.M.—Ceased to breathe. Heart beating very quickly.

7-57 A.M.—The heart has almost ceased to beat.

7-58 A.M.—Again injected 20 minims of ammonia and 20 of water.

8 A.M.—Heart ceased to beat, in 34 minutes.

## No. 2.

A small dog was bitten by a cobra, which had been in our possession for some time, at 9 A.M.

9-5 A.M.—Injected into a vein 20 minims of ammonia, diluted with an equal quantity of water.

9-15 A.M.—Dead, in 15 minutes.

---

## No. 3.

Injected 30 minims of ammonia and 30 of water into a vein of a dog, at 12-50 P.M.

12-55 P.M.—The animal was now bitten by a cobra.

1-5 P.M.—Is much affected.

1-10 P.M.—Fell over and became strongly convulsed; pupils widely dilated; tongue paralyzed, and there is a great deal of foaming at the mouth.

1-15 P.M.—Respiration has ceased.

1-17 P.M.—Dead, in 22 minutes.

---

## No. 4.

Hypodermically injected into a dog, weighing 27lbs, ¼th of a grain of cobra-poison, at 9-22 A.M.

9-43 A.M.—Temperature 101° 4'.

11-24 A.M.—Appears to be slightly affected.

11-30 A.M.—Injected 15 minims of ammonia with 15 minims of water into a vein; the heart at first began to beat very rapidly.

11-40 A.M.—Is staggering about.

11-45 A.M.—Injected 20 minims of ammonia and 20 minims of water into a vein.

11-55 A.M.—When lifted up, went staggering about the place. Defœcation.

12-15 P.M.—Is trembling a great deal.

12-24 P.M.—Convulsed.

12-32 P.M.—Still convulsed.

1-15 P.M.—Dead, in 3 hours and 43 minutes.

---

## No. 5.

Hypodermically injected into a dog, weighing 29lbs, ½ grain of cobra-poison, at 9-20 A.M.

9-45 A.M.—Temperature 102° 2'.

10 A.M.—Injected 20 minims of ammonia and 20 minims of water into a vein. Temperature, 5 minutes after the injection, 102°.

10-9 A.M.—Vomited; the respiration was at first much hurried; the heart at first began to beat very rapidly.

10-12 A.M.—Appears to be intoxicated; is constantly vomiting, and is scarcely able to stand; there is constant spasm and frothing at the mouth.

11 A.M.—Dead, in 1 hour and 40 minutes.

## No. 6.

Hypodermically injected into a dog, weighing 27lbs, ½ grain of cobra-poison, at 9-35 A.M.

9-49 A.M.—Temperature 201° 2′.

10-56 A.M.—Convulsed.

11-12 A.M.—Injected 15 minims of ammonia and an equal quantity of water into a vein. The heart at first began to beat rapidly, but was soon much depressed; pupils dilated.

11-18 A.M.—Injected 20 minims of ammonia and 20 of water into a vein. The same effects on the heart.

11-21 A.M.—Dead, in 1 hour and 25 minutes.

———

## No. 7.

Hypodermically injected into a dog, weighing 30lbs, ½ grain of cobra-poison, at 8-40 A.M.

8-52 A.M.—Injected into a vein 30 minims of ammonia with 30 of water. The animal almost immediately became convulsed, and constantly vomited. The animal is extremely prostrated; defœcation.

9-30 A.M.—Is lying down and is breathing spasmodically; is much salivated.

9-55 A.M.—Dead, in 1 hour and 15 minutes.

———

## No. 8.

Hypodermically injected into a dog, weighing 32lbs, ½ a grain of cobra-poison, at 8-40 A.M.

8-46 A.M.—Defœcation.

9 A.M.—Injected 20 minims of ammonia and 20 of water into a vein.

9-45 A.M.—Can scarcely stand.

9-54 A.M.—Is very slightly convulsed; injected 10 minims more ammonia.

10 A.M.—Is convulsed considerably, and the heart is not beating with any degree of force.

10-2 A.M.—The heart is beating very slowly indeed; injected 10 minims of ammonia into the heart.

10-10 A.M.—Dead, in 1 hour and 30 minutes.

———

## No. 9.

Hypodermically injected into a dog, weighing 19lbs, ½ a grain of cobra-poison, at 8-43 A.M.

9-15 A.M.—Injected into a vein 20 minims of ammonia and 20 of water.

9-45 A.M.—Is lying down, but can just stand if lifted up.

9-53 A.M.—Vomited considerably; is very uneasy.

10 A.M.—Is convulsed.

10-30 A.M.—Dead, in 1 hour 47 minutes.

## No. 10.

Hypodermically injected into a middling-sized dog ¾ of a grain of cobra-poison, at 8-47 A.M.

8-50 A.M.—Defœcation.

9-15 A.M.—Appears to be much affected; immediately injected 10 minims of ammonia with 10 of water into a vein.

9-27 A.M.—Again injected 10 minims of ammonia and 10 of water into a vein. There were at this time convulsions, the pupils were dilated, the tongue was paralyzed, and the heart was beating slowly. The only effect of the injection was increased action of the heart for a short time.

9-35 A.M.—Dead, in 48 minutes.

## No. 11.

Hypodermically injected into a dog, weighing 25lbs, 1½ grains of cobra-poison, at 1-24 P.M.

1-40 P.M.—Rapidly injected 15 minims of ammonia and 15 of water into a vein; the animal immediately became violently convulsed.

1-46 P.M.—Dead, in 22 minutes.

## No. 12.

Hypodermically injected into a dog 1½ grains of cobra-poison, at 1-26 P.M.

1-45 P.M.—Injected 20 minims of ammonia and 20 of water into a vein.

2 P.M.—Is trembling considerably.

3 P.M.—Convulsed.

3-30 P.M.—Dead, in 2 hours 4 minutes.

## No. 13.

Hypodermically injected into a dog 1½ grains of cobra-poison, at 1-22 P.M.

1-36 P.M.—Injected 20 minims of ammonia and 20 of water into a vein.

2 P.M.—Is trembling all over, and staring vacantly; tongue protruding.

2-15 P.M.—Convulsed.

3-3 P.M.—Dead, in 1 hour and 41 minutes.

## No. 14.

Hypodermically injected into a dog 1½ grains of cobra-poison, at 1-20 P.M.

1-32 P.M.—Injected 20 minims of ammonia and 20 of water into a vein.

2-13 P.M.—Is convulsed.

3 P.M.—Dead, in 1 hour and 40 minutes.

## No. 15.

Hypodermically injected into a dog 1½ grains of daboia-poison, at 8-59 A.M.

9-11 A.M.—Injected 10 minims of ammonia and 10 of water into a vein.

9-26 A.M.—Is slightly drowsy.

2 P.M.—Convulsed.

2-30 P.M.—Dead, in 5 hours and 31 minutes.

---

## No. 16.

Hypodermically injected into a dog 1½ grains of daboia-poison, at 9-1 A.M.

9-26 A.M.—Is rather drowsy.

10-30 A.M.—Injected 10 minims of ammonia with 10 of water into a vein.

3 P.M.—Convulsed.

3-30 P.M.—Dead, in 6 hours and 29 minutes.

*Note.*—In the two last experiments the only available syringe broke.

---

## No. 17.

3-44 P.M.—Injected into the vein of a dog, weighing 42℔s, 30 minims of ammonia and 30 minims of water.

3-44½ P.M.—Convulsed.

3-45 P.M.—Passed water; the breathing became hurried; the animal was extremely salivated.

3-55 P.M.—Injected 30 minims more ammonia.

4-5 P.M.—Is a great deal salivated, and extremely restless.

4-15 P.M.—Injected hypodermically ⅓ of a grain of cobra-poison.

4-50 P.M.—Is lying down.

5-10 P.M.—Convulsed.

5-30 P.M.—Dead, in 1 hour and 15 minutes.

---

## No. 18.

4 P.M.—Injected into the vein of a dog, weighing 22℔s, 30 minims of ammonia and 30 minims of water.

4-6 P.M.—Looks much distressed.

4-20 P.M.—Injected ¼ grain of decomposing cobra-poison into the peritoneal cavity.

4-35 P.M.—Is partially paralyzed in the hind quarters.

4-56 P.M.—Cannot stand.

4-57 P.M.—Is convulsed.

5 P.M.—Dead, in 40 minutes.

(Sd.)  JOSEPH EWART, M.D.,  *President.*

VINCENT RICHARDS,

S. COULL MACKENZIE, M.D.,  } *Members.*

H.

# APPENDIX No. II.

## REPORT ON THE INTRAVENOUS INJECTION OF AMMONIA IN AUSTRALIAN SNAKE-POISONING.

### No. 1.

#### Snake-bite without Ammonia

A dog, weighing 26lbs, was bitten by a snake that had just arrived from Australia, at 11-23 A.M.

11-39 A.M.—Vomited twice.

11-43 A.M.—Is restless; vomited twice.

11-48 A.M.—Again vomited.

11-52 A.M.—Again vomited, and is purged.

11-55 A.M.—Frequently purged; vomited again; is able to jump.

Noon.—Vomited bloody mucus.

12-6 P.M.—Again vomited bloody mucus; is still purged.

12-24 P.M.—Again vomited, but it is not purged so much.

12-30 P.M.—Vomiting white, frothy, very viscid mucus.

12-37 P.M.—Vomiting as before.

1 P.M.—Is lying down; drowsy; breathing quietly; salivation.

1-21 P.M.—Tongue partially paralyzed; the animal is perfectly sensible.

1-30 P.M.—Is still perfectly sensible.

1-35 P.M.—Is slightly convulsed; still sensible; heart's action regular, but somewhat weak—52.

1-45 P.M.—Heart 48.

1-48 P.M.—Eye still sensitive; slight convulsive movements continue.

1-53 P.M.—Heart irregular—52; eye much less sensitive; pupils widely dilated.

1-56 P.M.—Eye insensitive.

1-58 P.M.—Commenced artificial respiration; eyes at once became sensitive, and the heart's action, which was before weak and slow, became strong and rapid; the heart was beating nearly 200, but on stopping artificial respiration it fell to 80, and gradually failed.

2-11 P.M.—Dead, in 2 hours and 40 minutes.

### No. 2.

#### The Injection of Ammonia in Snake-bite. Sixty-two minims of the Ammonia were injected.

A dog, weighing 16lbs, was bitten by a snake, at 11-25 A.M.

11-28 A.M.—Micturated considerably.

11-29 A.M.—Drags the hind quarters as if paralyzed, but this may be due to pain; breathing naturally; bowels moved.

11-34 A.M.—Breathing quickly; injected 45 minims of diluted ammonia. The heart was acting regularly before the injection, but afterwards it at first began to beat quickly, and then slowly.

11-40 A.M.—Was able to stand for a few moments on its fore-legs; resisted an attempt to throw it on its side.

11-46 A.M.—Injected 20 minims more of the dilute ammonia; after a few seconds the animal began to howl, and the respiration became extremely hurried. There was no appreciable effect on the heart, which continued to beat slowly as before; able to stand on the fore-legs only.

11-52 A.M.—Heart's action rapid.

11-55 A.M.—Whining, but is looking more lively; is sensible.

12-4 P.M.—Heart beating normally.

12-10 P.M.—Only just able to walk, the hind quarters being dragged along.

12-29 P.M.—Is somewhat restless, and runs about a little.

12-47 P.M.—Is getting rapidly affected by the snake-poison; beginning to lose the power of raising its head; staggers about with neck arched and head hanging down, and wagging about precisely as dogs sometimes do when bitten by an Indian cobra—the symptoms are in fact identical; pupils dilated; tongue paralyzed. Injected 35 minims of ammonia; heart beating irregularly as before; convulsed during the injection; after it the heart was slow, very irregular, but strong.

1 P.M.—Injected 35 minims of ammonia; heart at first quickened, but it soon began to beat slowly and irregularly, beating 36 in the minute; quite insensible.

1-7 P.M.—Dead, in 1 hour and 42 minutes.

The blood was fluid in the heart, and did not coagulate after half an hour.

———

## No. 3.

*The Hypodermic Injection of the Australian Snake-poison, ½ grain.*

9 A.M.—Injected ½ grain of the poison into a dog, weighing 28 lbs.

9-21 A.M.—Appears to be in pain; is whining a great deal; vomited.

9-52 A.M.—Vomited.

10-3 A.M.—Is still in pain.

10-25 A.M.—Is lying down quietly.

10-43 A.M.—In pain, and is restless.

10-45 A.M.—Vomited white frothy mucus.

Noon.—Lying quiet; no more vomiting.

12-30 P.M.—On trying to get up it fell back, as if beginning to lose its power.

1-48 P.M.—Seems drowsy.

4-15 P.M.—Dead, in 7 hours and 15 minutes.

Blood in the heart was partially coagulated.

## No. 4.

*The Hypodermic Injection of ½ grain of the Poison, and the Intravenous Injection of 80 minims of Ammonia.*

Hypodermically injected into a dog, weighing 32lbs, ½ grain of Australian snake-poison, at 9-6 A.M.

9-30 A.M.—Vomited.

9-35 A.M.—Vomited.

9-42 A.M.—Vomited.

9-45 A.M.—Injected 60 minims of the ammonia. The dog howled a good deal; heart's action became very rapid, and a few minutes after the injection it became slow and regular; micturated freely.

9-47 A.M.—Became convulsed, and appeared to be in great pain for a few seconds.

9-48 A.M.—Lying on its side; heart beating slowly; its condition seems now much worse than before the injection. It was running about before the injection, but is now quite prostrate.

9-58 A.M.—Injected 40 minims of the ammonia; the eyes were fixed, and the pupils dilated during the spasm which followed the injection.

10-5 A.M.—Heart beating slowly; breathing naturally; is able to stand on all four legs.

10-20 A.M.—Looking more lively.

11-45 A.M.—Vomited white frothy mucus, which is so viscid that the animal tries to pull it out of its mouth with its paw; beginning to droop its head; back slightly arched.

11-56 A.M.—Injected 60 minims of the ammonia. The heart's action was strong and a little irregular before the injection; it became weaker and more regular after it; tongue paralyzed; pupils widely dilated.

12-43 P.M.—Convulsed.

1-10 P.M.—Dead, in 4 hours and 4 minutes.

Blood in the heart partially coagulated.

―――

## No. 5.

*The Hypodermic Injection of $\frac{1}{10}$th of a grain of Snake-poison, and the Injection of Ammonia when the animal was comatose.*

Hypodermically injected into a strong healthy dog, weighing 34lbs, $\frac{1}{10}$th of a grain of poison at 10-48 A.M.

NOON.—No symptoms of poisoning.

1-40 P.M.—Saliva dropping from the mouth, as if owing to increased secretion; vomited.

1-50 P.M.—Vomiting again.

4-15 P.M.—Quiet; has vomited once since 1-50 P.M.

6 P.M.—Is pretty well.

MIDNIGHT.—Appears to be all right; partook of food.

8 A.M.—Lying down in a comatose state; the body was cold and the heart was beating feebly; the animal could, however, be roused.

Injected 100 minims of the ammonia between 8 A.M. and 9-30 A.M.; the only effects of the injection were whining, spasm, and micturition, with slight, temporary acceleration of the heart's action.

9-45 P.M.—Dead, in 23 hours and 57 minutes.

The blood coagulated.

---

## No. 6.

*The Hypodermic Injection of ¼th of a grain of Snake-poison.*

10-7 A.M.—Hypodermically injected into a dog, weighing 9¾lbs, ¼th of a grain of poison.

10-24 A.M.—Appears to be drowsy.

10-30 A.M.—Vomited.

10-35 A.M.—Vomited.

10-38 A.M.—Is in pain; vomited.

12-4 P.M.—There has been no vomiting since 10-38 A.M.; is now slightly convulsed.

12-10 P.M.—Quite paralyzed; can neither stand nor raise its nose from the ground.

12-15 P.M.—Micturated freely; pupils dilated; tongue paralyzed.

12-24 P.M.—Slight spasms; cornea has lost sensation; heart beats 32 in a minute—very irregularly.

12-30 P.M.—Dead, in 2 hours and 23 minutes.

Blood in the heart partially coagulated.

---

## No. 7.

*The Hypodermic Injection of ⅕th of a grain of Snake-poison.*

11-27 A.M.—Hypodermically injected into a dog, weighing 12¼lbs, ⅕th of a grain of poison.

11-42 A.M.—Vomiting and defæcation.

11-48 A.M.—Vomiting.

11-56 A.M.—Vomiting.

12-10 P.M.—Constantly vomiting viscid mucus.

12-15 P.M.—Occasional convulsions; complete paralysis; heart's action regular; scarcely breathing.

12-18 P.M.—Dead, in 51 minutes.

Blood coagulated.

---

## No. 8.

*The Hypodermic Injection of ⅛th of a grain of Snake-poison, and the Intravenous Injection of 10 minims of Ammonia.*

11-29 A.M.—Hypodermically injected into a dog, weighing 14lbs, ⅛th of a grain of snake-poison.

11-44 A.M.—Vomiting.

11-48 A.M.—Injected 20 minims of the ammonia solution; violent spasms and vomiting were the result.

11-50 A.M.—Occasional convulsions.
11-54 A.M.—Respiration has ceased.
11-56 A.M.—Dead, in 27 minutes.
Blood coagulated.

---

## No. 9.

*The Hypodermic Injection of half the Poison, not quite ⅛th of a grain, extracted from a Snake.*

8-55 A.M.—Hypodermically injected into a dog, weighing 34lbs, half the poison taken from a snake.

12-12 P.M.—Appears to be restless, and the respiration is somewhat hurried; this is probably due to pain about the injected part.

1 P.M.—Is much easier.

4 P.M.—In the same state.

This animal became affected during the night, and was apparently dying at 11 A.M., but it did not die until 10 A.M. the day after, 49 hours and 5 minutes after the injection of the poison.

---

## No. 10.

*The Hypodermic Injection of the other half of the Poison of the Snake, used in Experiment 9, and the Injection of Ammonia, 40 minims.*

8-59 A.M.—Hypodermically injected the poison into a dog, weighing 30lbs.

9-49 A.M.—Had vomited three times, but appears otherwise unaffected.

10-54 A.M.—Injected 40 minims of the ammonia solution; spasm of the whole body, micturition, and pain followed; the heart at first began to beat quickly and then slowly.

12-42 P.M.—Is slightly uneasy.

4 P.M.—Injected 40 minims of the ammonia solution.

This animal died during the night.

---

## No. 11.

*The Hypodermic Injection of ⅛th grain of Snake-poison, and the Intravenous Injection of 140 minims of Ammonia.*

Hypodermically injected into a dog, weighing 35lbs, nearly ⅛th of a grain of snake-poison that had been kept in a dilute state for three days, at 9-1 A.M.

9-27 A.M.—Is somewhat restless, and the breathing appears hurried.

9-32 A.M.—Is now easy again.

9-45 A.M.—Vomited.

9-50 A.M.—Injected 50 minims of the ammonia solution.

12-32 P.M.—Vomited.

12-36 P.M.—Vomited.

12-43 P.M.—Vomiting.

12-45 P.M.—Injected 40 minims of the ammonia solution; pain, spasm, hurried respiration and acceleration of the heart's action followed the injection.

1 P.M.—Breathing labored ; is retching frequently.
1-26 P.M.—Vomiting ; is very restless.
1-35 P.M.—Vomited.
2-15 P.M.—Injected 80 minims of the ammonia solution ; the injection caused profuse micturition, general spasm, and slow and intermittent action of the heart.
3-55 P.M.—Is apparently dying ; injected 40 minims of the ammonia into a vein, and 20 into the heart.
4 P.M.—Dead, in 6 hours 59 minutes.

## No. 12.

*The Hypodermic Injection of ⅛th of a grain of Snake-poison, and the Injection of 30 minims of Ammonia.*

8-50 A.M.—Hypodermically injected into a dog, weighing 16lbs, ⅛th of a grain of snake-poison.
9-10 A.M.—Defœcation ; vomiting.
9-13 A.M.—Injected 20 minims of the solution into a vein; a spasm followed, the eyes became fixed, there was great whining and micturition, and some salivation.
9-15 A.M.—Vomited.
12-15 P.M.—Has now got complete paralysis ; pupils dilated ; heart beating regularly ; respiration rapid ; tongue paralyzed.
12-21 P.M.—Injected 20 minims more of the ammonia solution into a vein; heart's action at once became hurried, and after a minute became slow and intermittent ; spasm and micturition followed as usual.
12-52 P.M.—Convulsed ; injected 20 minims more of the solution into a vein ; it was followed by convulsions ; heart's action intermittent.
1-25 P.M.—Dead, in 4 hours 35 minutes.

## No. 13.

*The Hypodermic Injection of the Poison of one Snake.*

Noon, 12.—Hypodermically injected the poison taken from one snake into a dog, weighing 44lbs. This animal never became affected, or, at any rate, only very slightly so.

## No. 14.

*The Injection of 75 minims of Ammonia in Snake-bite.*

9-24 A.M.—A dog, weighing 38lbs, was bitten by a snake.
9-32 A.M.—Is apparently uneasy ; breathing rapidly.
9-57 A.M.—Drank some water greedily.
10-10 A.M.—Salivation ; vomited once ; paralyzed ; frothing at the mouth ; pupils dilated. Injected 80 minims of the solution ; temperature before the injection, 101° 6′ ; heart rapid and weak, after the injection of 60 minims.
10-15 A.M.—Heart's action stronger, but more rapid ; breathing hurried ; slight spasm of the lower jaw, followed by general convulsion and vomiting.

11-20 A.M.—Injected 120 minims of the solution; temperature rose to 101° 8' after the injection; tongue paralyzed; heart's action intermittent; vomited again at 11-28 A.M. Injected 40 minims of the solution into the left jugular vein; the first 20 minims were followed by strong spasms, second, by twitchings of the muscles, and then spasm of the extremities; eyes fixed.

11-34 A.M.—Dead, in 2 hours and 10 minutes.

---

### No. 15.

*The Injection of 30 minims of Ammonia in Snake-bite; unaffected.*

9-28 A.M.—A dog, weighing 18lbs, was bitten by a snake.

10 A.M.—No symptoms of poisoning; injected 60 minims of the ammonia solution; micturition; no expression of pain until the injection of the last 20 minims.

12-30 P.M.—No symptoms.

3-15 P.M.—No change.

This animal exhibited no signs of snake-poisoning.

---

### No. 16.

*The Injection of 60 minims of Ammonia in Snake-bite; unaffected.*

9-30 A.M.—A dog weighing 20lbs, was bitten by a snake.

9-54 A.M.—Injected 40 minims of the solution; pain extreme; expulsion of fœces and micturition; heart's action at first increased and then it became intermittent.

10 A.M.—Is uneasy on account of the ammonia; bowels moved.

11-15 A.M.—Sleeping quietly.

Noon.—Injected 20 minims more of the solution, caused pain and strong spasm; heart's action strong, but irregular.

12-30 P.M.—Seems slightly drowsy.

This animal never exhibited any symptoms of snake-poisoning.

---

### No. 17.

*The Injection of 40 minims of Ammonia in Snake-bite.*

9-40 A.M.—A dog, weight not recorded, was bitten by a snake.

9-47 A.M.—Injected 40 minims of the solution of ammonia into a vein; it caused pain, the heart's action was increased, fœces were expelled, there was micturition and general spasm, and after a few seconds the heart's action became intermittent and weak.

9-52 A.M.—Lying on its side; breathing very labored.

10-8 A.M.—Profuse salivation.

11-49 A.M.—Attempts to vomit; partially paralyzed.

11-55 A.M.—Injected 40 minims more of the ammonia solution; caused micturition and an expression of pain.

Noon.—Had one general spasm.

12-5 P.M.—Again convulsed.

12-30 P.M.—Dead, in 2 hours and 50 minutes.

## No. 18.

*The Injection of 30 minims of Ammonia in Snake-bite.*

11-38 A.M.—A dog, weighing 31lbs, was bitten by a snake.

NOON.—Vomited three times. Injected 60 minims of solution of ammonia into a vein; there were violent spasms after each injection, and the animal passed water spasmodically; it remained in a semi-comatose state, breathing hurriedly.

12-40 P.M.—In the same state; is unable to stand.

1-50 P.M.—Dead, in 2 hours and 17 minutes.

---

## No. 19.

*The Injection of 30 minims of Ammonia in Snake-bite.*

11-40 A.M.—A dog, weighing 35lbs, was bitten by a snake.

12-20 P.M.—Vomited, but in other respects appears well. Injected 60 minims of the solution into a vein; there were violent spasms after the injection, and the dog was unable to stand; it lapsed into a semi-comatose state, breathing hurriedly; it afterwards vomited, and was purged.

12-47 P.M.—When lifted up it staggered and fell down.

1-15 P.M.—Is standing up, but appears to be very weak.

3 P.M.—Appears to be slightly drowsy.

MIDNIGHT.—Dead, in 12 hours and 20 minutes.

---

## No. 20.

*The Injection of Ammonia in Snake-bite.*

11-47 A.M.—A dog, weighing 33lbs, was bitten by a snake.

12-5 A.M.—Vomited; injected 60 minims of the solution.

12-45 P.M.—Vomited bloody froth of a bright red colour.

12-55 P.M.—Again vomited; injected 40 minims more of the solution into a vein.

1-20 P.M.—When lifted up it goes staggering about.

2-30 P.M.—Dead, in 2 hours and 43 minutes.

---

## No. 21.

*The Injection of 10 minims of Ammonia in Snake-bite.*

11-42 A.M.—A dog, weighing 18lbs, was bitten by a snake.

12-15 P.M.—Vomited and defæcated; injected 20 minims of the solution into a vein.

12-50 P.M.—Can stand, but is unwilling to do so.

1-15 P.M.—Is apparently better.

Dead, in 2 hours and 23 minutes.

I

### No. 22.

*The Injection of 40 minims of Ammonia in Snake-bite.*

11-44 A.M.—A dog, weighing 39lbs, was bitten by a snake.

12-40 P.M.—Vomited.

12-45 P.M.—Again vomited.

12-49 P.M.—Again vomited.

1 P.M.—Injected 80 minims of the solution into a vein.

1-8 P.M.—Vomited, and appears much depressed.

1-12 P.M.—Vomited.

1-25 P.M.—Purged.

3 P.M.—Does not appear to be very much affected.

5 P.M.—Dead, in 5 hours and 16 minutes.

---

### No. 23.

*Snake-bite, without Ammonia.*

11-49 P.M.—A dog, weighing 34lbs, was bitten by a snake.

1-10 P.M.—Unaffected.

1-25 P.M.—Still unaffected.

2-45 P.M.—Dead, in 2 hours and 55 minutes.

---

### No. 24.

*The Injection of 80 minims of Ammonia in Snake-bite.*

SATURDAY, 9-4 A.M.—A dog, weighing 33lbs, was bitten by a snake.

9-41 A.M.—Vomited and defœcated.

9-50 A.M.—Had vomited three times since 9-41. Injected 100 minims of the solution into a vein; each time the injection was made there was considerable spasm, and the heart's action was ultimately considerably depressed.

SUNDAY.—Nothing particular to note.

MONDAY, 9 A.M.—Is lying down, breathing regularly; heart's action somewhat slow; the eyes are sensitive. Injected 60 minims of the solution. The only effects were spasms, groaning, hurried respiration, and micturition; the heart appears to be little affected.

8 P.M.—Dead, in 59 hours and 56 minutes.

This animal appears to have died from exhaustion.

---

*Cases of Snake-bite without Ammonia.*

---

### No. 25.

9-6 A.M.—A dog, weighing 26lbs, was bitten by a snake. Never affected.

---

### No. 26.

9-8 A.M.—A dog, weighing 16lbs, was bitten by a snake. Never affected.

### No. 27.

12-49 P.M.—A dog, weighing 41lbs, was bitten by a snake.
12-58 P.M.—Has been a great-deal salivated.
2-30 P.M.—Vomited.
Recovered.

### No. 28.

12-54 P.M.—A dog, weighing 18lbs, was bitten by a snake.
Never affected.

### No. 29.

12-57 P.M.—A dog, weighing 23lbs, was bitten by a snake.
Never affected.

### No. 30.

1 P.M.—A dog, weighing 42lbs, was bitten by a snake.
Never affected.

(Sd.)  JOSEPH EWART, M.D.,  *President.*
VINCENT RICHARDS,  } *Members.*
S. COULL MACKENZIE, }

# APPENDIX No. III.

---

## CORRESPONDENCE.

THE following letter, relative to the appointment of a Commission for the investigation of the subject, was addressed by Dr. Fayrer, to the Secretary of State for India, in November 1872. Dr. Anderson being about to proceed to England, Dr. S. Coull Mackenzie was appointed in his stead.

"Since my return to London, I have, in conjunction with Dr. Lauder Brunton, been making further investigations into the subject of snake-poisoning, especially with a view of ascertaining if there be any means of saving life, and though I cannot say that desirable object of research has been attained, I am satisfied that the results of certain experiments are interesting and important, as they point in that direction.

"I have recorded an opinion, derived from a long and elaborate series of experiments, that none of the so-called antidotes possess the virtues or powers attributed to them, but in the experiments recently made, it is ascertained beyond a doubt, that the life of an animal poisoned by cobra-virus may be prolonged for many hours by artificial respiration, and it is, therefore, possible that, if respiration be artificially continued for a sufficient length of time, life might be altogether preserved. In experiments performed upon the fowl and rabbit after the most complete development of the physiological action of the poison, amounting to total paralysis and convulsions, conditions which immediately precede death, the convulsions ceased, and in one case the heart was kept beating vigorously for about 9 hours (and probably then failed from imperfect respiration carried on in the cold)—a result never before attained by any means that I am aware of.

"There is apparently a strong analogy between the action of the cobra-virus, and that of the curara or wourali poison of South America. It has been ascertained that an animal poisoned by this agent, may, after apparent death for many hours, be restored if artificial respiration be carefully and continuously applied for a sufficient length of time, the temperature of the animal being at the same time sustained at blood heat by artificial warmth.

"Curara, it is believed, kills by paralyzing the peripheral distribution of motor nerves, thus inducing asphyxia by involving the muscles of respiration in the general paralysis.

"If, however, the heart's action can be sustained by artificial respiration, during a sufficient length of time to allow of elimination of the poison through the excreting organs (for whilst the heart acts, they continue to perform their functions), the paralyzed muscles regain their power, and life is slowly, but certainly, restored. I am not prepared to assert that cobra-poison kills in exactly the same way as curara;

I am inclined to the belief that it does not; but still analogy and the results of experiments support, or, perhaps rather suggest, the idea that, if artificial respiration be sustained in a case of cobra-poisoning, and life be thus artificially supported for a sufficient length of time, it might be for days, elimination of the poison may occur, and recovery may result. It is, however, I fear, only too probable that during its sojourn in the system, the poison may have, in the case of cobra-virus, done irreparable mischief to the nerve centres or peripheral distribution, which, after life, ceased to be artificially supported; but there is no proof as yet that such is the case, and, therefore, I am of opinion that further, and most careful, and often repeated and sustained experiments, should be made to test this very important subject.

"It is almost impossible to carry out completely the necessary investigations in this country for want of the snake-poison. The experiments referred to, were made with a small quantity of cobra-poison sent to England by myself, but which is almost expended. It will be necessary to have an apparatus, for conducting countinued artificial respiration, constructed for the purpose, and as it might have to be used for days continuously, it should be worked by power. This, however, would not necessarily involve much expense, as a very small engine would suffice. I have sent to India for more snake-poison, and when I succeed in obtaining it, I hope, with the assistance of Dr. Lauder Brunton, to continue the experiments; but as this is uncertain, I would strongly recommend that the Indian Government be requested, through the Medical Department of Bengal, to sanction the necessary investigation, and I would venture to suggest that the following gentlemen be invited to carry it out :—

"Dr. Ewart, Professor of Physiology    ···⎫ Calcutta.
"Dr. J. Anderson    ···⎬

"Mr. Richards, Civil Surgeon of Balasore, who has already done so much in snake-poisoning; subject, of course, to the approval of the head of the department, Dr. J. C. Brown, c.b.

" The investigations, I would propose, should be conducted in the manner hereafter detailed, and that this mode of treatment by artificial respiration and warmth be tried in any case of snake-poisoning in human beings that may come under observation in hospitals; in itself, it is absolutely unobjectionable, and can do no harm, whilst it may do good.

" I would distinctly be understood to say, that I do not recommend this as certain; it is tentative and experimental at present, but it is the only means that science, so far as I know at present, suggests of dealing with the matter in a rational way, and as such I would recommend it to careful trial. It may obviously be most satisfactorily tested in India, and, therefore, I venture to hope that the Indian Government will be pleased to accept of these suggestions, with a view to their being carried into effect, as I hope, by the gentlemen suggested, or if they be absent or unwilling, by others.

" Animals, such as dogs, goats, &c., &c., to be poisoned by the hypodermic injection of cobra-poison into the areolar tissue, avoiding

large veins,* and when the symptoms of poisoning make their
appearance, artificial respiration to be carefully kept up, in the case of
animals, through a canula in the trachea, in human beings, by Silvester's
method, or by the canula, the artificial respiration to be continued
uninterruptedly for hours, it may be days, and the temperature of the
individual to be carefully supported up to blood heat throughout.

" The urine or other secretions might be withdrawn during the
process, and tested by inoculation into other small and delicate animals,
such as pigeons, mice, so as to ascertain whether the poison was being
eliminated by that channel.

" The doses of cobra-poison inoculated should be of various degrees
of intensity, say, from a quarter of a drop diluted with water, to several
drops.

" Whatever the result, in cases where the dose of poison had been
overwhelming, there can be no doubt, I think now, that in smaller
quantities, such as would if left to themselves destroy life, the use of
artificial respiration by any of the most certain and approved methods
(the canula, if desirable) would be of use in the treatment of persons so
poisoned, and might save life.

" It is so simple in its application that it might be made generally
available; printed instructions, might, as in the case of the Humane
Society in England, be distributed throughout the country. Of course,
the canula could only be used by a surgeon, but happily any effective
artificial respiration can be practised without a surgical operation, and
may be done by any one.

" I would, therefore, recommend that in addition to the instructions
I have already suggested in my book on the poisonous snakes, and which
have been promulgated in some parts of India for the immediate
treatment of snake-bite, artifical respiration by Silvester's or other
methods, and the application of warmth, as well as the ligature, cautery,
and stimulants, alcoholic or ammoniacal, be had recourse to in all
cases of snake-bite, and that printed instructions to this effect, translated
into the vernacular, be distributed throughout the police thanas and
dispensaries in India."

---

No. 196, dated Calcutta, the 21st July 1873.

From—The President of the Commission for the investigation of Snake-
poisoning,

To—The Deputy Surgeon-General, Presidency Circle.

I HAVE the honor to solicit the favor of your moving the Surgeon-
General and His Honor the Lieutenant-Governor of Bengal, to obtain
for the Committee now investigating, under the orders of Government,
the influence of artificial respiration in saving life in cases of animals
poisoned by any of the *Thanatophidia* of India, at least a dozen of
the most poisonous snakes to be found in Australia.

2. As the Government are already aware, there is an important
difference between the results obtained by two distinguished *sarans*,

---

* When the poison enters a large vein in any quantity, death results almost instantaneously ; no
time is allowed for any treatment to offer hope of benefit. In some cases of snake-bite it is so. The
saphina vein may be harmed, and death is very rapid ; but in most instances the snake inoculates
his venom into the areolar tissue.

viz., Drs. Fayrer and Halford, in their respective experiments to test the powers of snake-poison, and the value of reported antidotes. Whilst Dr. Fayrer and his supporters declare that, no antidote has yet been discovered, Dr. Halford and his followers are equally positive that, in the intravenous injection of a strong solution of liquor ammoniæ he has discovered an antidote to the poison of the noxious snakes of Australia.

3. Dr. Halford tried the injection of ammonia on dogs, supposed and believed to be effectively brought under the influence of snake-poison. These dogs were restored after they were believed to have been mortally poisoned ; and he, therefore, arrived at the conclusion that, as the injection had proved so successful in dogs, it would probably prove equally advantageous in cases of snake-bite in the human subject.

4. I am of opinion that, if the Government will be pleased to ask the Governor of Melbourne to despatch to my address, by any of the ships chartered to bring horses for Messrs. Thomas Smith & Co., of this city, a good supply of the most poisonous snakes of Australia, such as the *Hoplocephalus curtus*, *Hoplocephalus superbus*, *Pseudechis porphyriacus*, and others, I shall, with the assistance of my colleagues, Dr. Richards and Dr. Mackenzie, be able to settle this vitally important question.

5. There is another point of great scientific importance requiring solution, viz., the exact mode of death in cases of snake-poisoning. I shall now, with the permission of Government, and by the help of my confrères on the Committee, institute a series of experiments, on dogs and the batrachia, with a view to determine this question finally. Its solution has a distinct bearing upon the treatment and the direction in which investigation should be taken, with a view to the discovery of an antidote.

6. The marvellous effects of chloroform, over the intellectual manifestation of the brain, no less than the wonderful restoration of animals by artificial respiration, when they have ceased to breathe after having been poisoned by the curara-poison, justify the hope that we should not despair in our attempts to discover an antidote to counteract the effects of snake-poison.

7. As an aid to the accomplishment of this object, it is in every way desirable to arrive at a correct conclusion, regarding the mode in which the poison causes death.

8. Dr. Fayrer believes that it proves mortal, first, by paralysing the great nerve centres, whilst its action on the peripheral portion of the nervous system is a secondary consequence, and immediately precedes the cessation of respiration. Dr. Halford, on the other hand, believes that the poison primarily acts upon the higher ganglia of the brain and the sentient portion of the organ, and that the symptoms which follow are mere expressions of this centric operation of the poison.

9. With a sufficient supply of the Australian snakes, I think the Committee will be able to finally settle this point of difference.

10. Mr. Dover, the principal member of Messrs. Smith & Co., Livery Stable Keepers, Calcutta, has promised to help in procuring snakes from Australia.

11. I understand they are only procurable in abundance during the Australian summer, from November to February.

12. To ensure a supply of these snakes being despatched without fail, I beg that His Honor the Lieutenant-Governor of Bengal be moved to address the Governor of Melbourne on the subject, in anticipation of the order of the Government of India. The expense entailed will not be great, consisting chiefly of the transport charge from Melbourne to Calcutta.

13. The snakes should be placed in separate boxes. The cost of the transport and of a dozen small boxes would probably not exceed Rs. 600, according to the advices received from Mr. Dover.

Memo. No. 7053A, dated Fort William, the 21st March 1874.

From—K. McLeod, Esq., M.D., Secretary to the Surgeon-General, Indian Medical Department,

To—Surgeon-Major, J. Ewart, M.D., President of the Snake-poisoning Committee.

Copy forwarded for information.

No. 294, dated Melbourne, the 28th January 1874.

From—J. G. Francis, Esq.,

To—The Honorable the Secretary to the Government of India.

Referring to previous correspondence, I have the honor to inform you that, by the present mail, Professor Halford has forwarded a case of black snakes, addressed to Dr. Ewart, of Calcutta. They go by steamer to Bombay, and thence by rail to Calcutta.

Professor Halford states that, he sent a cage of tiger snakes similarly addressed by the last mail, as you were advised.

### No. 108.

Copy forwarded to the Government of Bengal for information, in continuation of endorsement No. 64, dated the 9th ultimo.

T. J. C. Plowden,
*Offg. Under-Secretary to the*
*Government of India.*

Home Department,
  Medical ;
*The 9th March,* 1874.

### No. 1024.

Copy forwarded to the Surgeon-General, Indian Medical Department, for information and guidance, in continuation of this Office endorsement No. 605, dated 12th ultimo.

By order of the Lieutenant-Governor of Bengal,

J. Crawfurd,
*Offg. Under-Secretary to the*
*Government of Bengal.*

Calcutta, Medical ;
  *The 12th March,* 1874.

The following is a description of the two kinds of Australian snakes forwarded to us by Professor Halford:—

*First.*—Pseudechis porphyriacus—

Naja porphyriaca, Schleg.

Naja Australis, gray.

Scales in 17 rows.

Anal plates, 2.

Abdominals, 180 to 200.

Subcaudals variable from 50 to 60; sometimes all divided or all entire; generally the first 10 to 20 entire, and the remainder divided.

Total length of adult, 5 or 6 feet.

Head, 1 inch.

Tail, 6 inches.

Body elongate and rounded; tail moderate, not distinct from trunk; head rather small, quadrangular, with rounded muzzle; shields of crown regular; two nasals, no loreal; one anterior and two posterior oculars; scales smooth, imbricate in seven rows; anal bifid; first subcaudals entire, hinder ones two-rowed; in some individuals all the subcaudals are entire. Black above each scale of the outer series; red at the nose and black at the tip; ventral shields with black posterior margins; muzzle light brown.

The black snake is the most common of all our venomous snakes; it frequents low marshy places, is fond of water, swims and dives well, and subsists principally upon frogs, lizards, insects, and the smaller mammalia, in particular the young of the water-rat. (*Hydromyo leucogaster.*) On one occasion sixteen young of this rodent were taken out of a specimen, so that the reptile must have plundered from nests.

When irritated, the black snake raises about two feet of its body off the ground, flattens out the neck like a cobra, and then darts at its prey or enemy. The bite of this snake is highly venomous, killing good-sized dogs or goats within an hour.

"The number of young brought forth in March generally amounts to 15 or 20. During the winter the reptile retires into the ground."

KREFFT.

"*Brown-banded Snake; Tiger Snake (Hoplocephalus Curtus).*"

NAJA CURTA—SCHLEGEL.

Scales in 18 rows anteriorly, and 19 rows posteriorly.

Abdominal plates, 170 or more.

Anal plate, 1.

Subcaudals, in a single series, 40 to 50.

Total length, from 5 to 6 feet.

Head, 1½ inch.

Tail, 7 inches.

"Body moderately elongate, tail moderate, not distinct from trunk; head large and broad, crown flat, and muzzle rounded; the middle plate of the head (the vertical shield) is almost square, a distinguishing characteristic of this snake, and the *Hoplocephalus superbus.*

K

" The body scales are elongate, of equal size, and do not overlap each other ; there is a considerable piece of black skin between them, which shows very distinctly when stretched, or when the reptile, being angry, flattens its body. In this species the colour varies considerably from grey to almost black, with distinct or indistinct bands, and show yellow or bright orange abdominal plates. The younger the snakes, the clearer the bands are defined, and living subjects are generally copper-coloured. The posterior abdominal plates, and the subcaudals are darker and more clouded with grey or black than the anterior ones. Thirty or more young are produced every season, varying in colour quite as much as old individuals do. They retire into the ground in winter, and make their appearance, according to the temperature, in August, or the beginning of September; in southern districts much later. When attacked, and seeing no means of escape, this snake raises the forepart of the body off the ground, not unlike a cobra, to which it is closely allied, and flattens the neck, though not to such an extent as the Indian naja tripudians."

KREFFT.

No. 257, dated Calcutta, the 28th October 1873.

From—J. EWART, Esq., M.D., President of the Snake Commission,
To—The Deputy Surgeon-General, Presidency Circle.

I HAVE the honor to acknowledge the receipt of your Memorandum No. 3628, dated the 15th instant, forwarding extract from Government of Bengal's letter No. 4284, dated 18th September last.

2. I believe that no practical difficulty will be found in confining the rewards for killing snakes to the poisonous varieties met with in the jurisdiction of His Honor the Lieutenant-Governor of Bengal, because, by the observance of a few simple rules, these can be very easily identified. I cannot help thinking that the reward of 2 annas is inadequate. I do not know well how much should be given; but, perhaps, it will be found on enquiry that not less than 8 annas a head should be tendered by Government. If that is not sufficient, I would not hesitate to give a higher reward.

3. From the information I have received on the subject it is not improbable that the large expenditure in Bankoora of Rs. 20,000 per annum was incurred mainly for the destruction of harmless snakes. At any rate it is doubtful whether the means of distinguishing poisonous from non-poisonous snakes were employed.

4. I would encourage the destruction of poisonous snakes in all parts of the country, both in the cultivated and uncultivated parts. Because it is certain that they migrate to a great extent during the rainy season, and that many of the poisonous snakes found in inhabited and populous places have really migrated thither from neighbouring parts of neglected or jungle lands. This is annually exemplified in Calcutta where cobras have been found crossing the *maidan* towards the fort, or travelling along the drains and streets into the heart of the town. During the present year a man was killed by a cobra-bite in the middle of the city, and some years ago a native was mortally bitten under one of the large trees leading into the fort. I think further that it might be an object to procure men who would make it their business to hunt down and exterminate poisonous snakes. Mole-catching at home is a regular trade: the object there is the protection of meadow and grazing lands, &c., from the injuries inflicted by these moles. But in India the object in encouraging men to make it their business to catch and kill venomous snakes is, *first*, the preservation of human life, and, *secondly*, the preservation of the lives of such of the lower animals as are of essential utility to man.

5. The numerical amount of lives of human beings and lower animals annually sacrificed by venomous snakes has never been accurately ascertained; but it must be very considerable—quite large enough to justify the Government in organizing a system, even at a great cost, for their destruction. Most men, so far as I know, who have had much to do with poisonous reptiles, and who are experienced in the manners and customs of the natives, are of opinion that the figures given in Dr. Fayrer's valuable book rather underrate than overrate the annual sacrifice of human lives by the Thanatophidia of India.

6.   The thanatophidia, if, perhaps, we exclude the ophiophagus—and experience of the ophiophagus, in captivity at any rate, does not invalidate the rule—are, until provoked, perfectly inoffensive to all animals not required by them as food.  They seldom assume the aggressive until they are rudely and accidentally disturbed.  Thus, a native sleeping on the ground rolls over a venomous snake, or whilst walking in the jungle or long grass, or in the dark, treads upon some part of a snake's body.  In either case, the snake bites, if he can.  It is in this way that a large proportion of the snake accidents happen.

7.   A large number of lives would be saved annually, if the native population could be prevailed upon to sleep on charpoys, and if they got into the habit of never stepping from their beds at night without first seeing by means of a light that the ground below is clean and free from snakes.   Much of the immunity which Europeans and educated natives enjoy from snake-bite is due to their using these very necessary precautions, especially during the rainy season, and in the mofussil to their never walking abroad at night without a light.   There is scarcely a European of experience in the mofussil who cannot recount examples of lives (often their own) having been saved by means of these simple precautions.

8.   But though these means are doubtless invaluable in protecting the lives of the most intelligent and less bigoted class of the community there is a large class who, whether from prejudice or other causes, are not so protected.   To preserve these against the assaults of the thanatophidia of India it is absolutely necessary to institute a system for the widespread destruction of these reptiles.

9.   In the Civil Surgeons and the Sub-Assistant Surgeons and the more intelligent of the Native Doctors scattered over the country, the Government has the agency for identifying any of the poisonous snakes in the Bengal Presidency.

10.   In order to facilitate the recognition of the poisonous snakes met with in the provinces under the sway of His Honor the Lieutenant-Governor, I beg to submit a few simple rules :—

A.   Cobras (gókarrah, karris, &c.) are all hooded and, with but few exceptions, have spectacles or an ocellus upon the back part of the neck.   In the dead cobra the skin will be found to be hanging loose on each side of the neck, and if slight traction be made upon the loose skin simultaneously on each side, either the spectacles or the ocellus, as the case may be, will be brought into view.   Then on opening the mouth of a cobra or any other venomous snake, a prominent part will be found on the front portion of the upper jaw on each side immediately before the eyes.   If a piece of stick or a probe be pressed against these from behind forward, the fangs will be raised and brought into distinct relief.   Every venomous snake is possessed of these fangs, whilst all non-venomous snakes are destitute of them : these non-venomous reptiles have a row of teeth.   Cobras differ considerably in color.   Generally speaking, however, they are yellowish, grey, or black, the two first-mentioned kinds being found usually in old houses and rubbish, and the last variety in paddy-fields or the open country.

B.   Daboia Russelli.—Russell's Viper (úlú bora, chandra bora, shia chandra, &c.) is usually found about four feet long.   It has a triangular shaped head with a distinct neck. Superiorly, it is marked in black white-edged rings, the ground being either greyish or chocolate color. The markings somewhat resemble the pattern of a Cashmere shawl. The tail is short and thin. The fangs are very large—much larger than those of the cobra.

C. *Bungarus Ceruleus*—(*krait, dhomná chitti, chitti, &c.*) is generally about three feet long. It sometimes grows to the length of four feet. It is either steel-black or brown, striped with white. It will at once be recognized by the color and the single row of hexagonal scales running along the centre of the back. Its fangs are distinct. It is often confounded by the natives with the *Lycodon Aulicus** (an innocent snake).

D. *Bungarus Fasciatus*—(*réna*) is easily recognized by its triangular-shaped body and very prominent back. It is striped alternately blue and yellow, and like the krait has a dorsal row of hexagonal scales. Its fangs are also easily recognized.

E. *Ophiophagus*—(*háiráj* of Orissa) is of large size, hooded like the cobra, but not so much.

This hood can easily be made out after death by employing traction to the skin on each side of the neck. The fangs are easily made out. It ranges in length from nine to twelve feet.

---

* The *lycodon* is generally of a very much lighter color, and the bands of white stripes run vertically, instead of being single stripes running horizontally, as they are in the *krait*.